Opera at the Bandstand

A posthumous oil portrait of Sousa as leader of the U.S. Marine Band in the early 1880s. Painted, circa 1950, by John J. Capolino, a Philadelphia artist who served in the Marine Corps Reserves and did several projects for the corps. U.S. Marine Band.

Opera at the Bandstand

Then and Now

George W. Martin

THE SCARECROW PRESS, INC.
Lanham • Toronto • Plymouth, UK
2014

Published by Scarecrow Press, Inc.
A wholly owned subsidiary of The Rowman & Littlefield Publishing Group, Inc.
4501 Forbes Boulevard, Suite 200, Lanham, Maryland 20706
www.rowman.com

10 Thornbury Road, Plymouth PL6 7PP, United Kingdom

British Library Cataloguing in Publication Information Available

Library of Congress Cataloging-in-Publication Data

Martin, George Whitney.
Opera at the bandstand : then and now / George W. Martin.
pages cm
Includes bibliographical references and index.
ISBN 978-0-8108-8853-1 (cloth : alk. paper) — ISBN 978-0-8108-8854-8 (ebook)
1. Bands (Music)—United States—History. 2. Opera. I. Title.
ML1311.M19 2014
784.8'4—dc23 2013022167

∞™ The paper used in this publication meets the minimum requirements of American National Standard for Information Sciences—Permanence of Paper for Printed Library Materials, ANSI/NISO Z39.48-1992.

Printed in the United States of America.

Contents

Illustrations

Acknowledgments

The notes and appendixes will reveal that I cite as sources many books and unpublished theses on the period and personalities of the concert band era. Further, in research I have often turned to musicians, librarians, and archivists in various cities and universities for assistance—dates, places, programs, illustrations, news reports on audiences, and the impact of the music heard. Though I am grateful to all who helped me, many I cannot name for they answered my questions often without identifying themselves. But I do have seven to whom I would like to give a special word of thanks while describing briefly their extraordinary help.

First, Paul E. Bierley, an aeronautical engineer who found himself fascinated by Sousa, man and musician, but not finding much written about him, set out to write the book he felt was needed, thinking "I could easily produce such a book in my spare time, in about two years." Forty years later, in 2006 (and after publishing several shorter works on Sousa), he published *The Incredible Band of John Philip Sousa*, in which the detail is astonishing. He, not I, counted the band's concerts as a total of 15,623. Moreover, he offers a list of "what the band played" that is if not complete is at least nearly so. He also offers a fifty-page appendix, "Typical Sousa Band Programs," and other long lists: "Where the Band Played"; "All-Time Roster of Sousa's Band"; and "The Makeup of the Band" (its instrumentation). In sum, his book presents a host of facts, all preceded and accompanied by perceptive introductory texts and illustrations. As Sousa is the chief figure in the history of American concert bands, so is Bierley's book the bedrock for any discussion of him.

Similar in importance, because it is so comprehensive, is the unpublished doctoral thesis of James Thomas Madeja submitted to the University of Illinois in 1988 and titled "The Life and Work of Herbert L. Clarke (1867–1945)." Clarke, for many years considered the world's greatest cornetist, wrote many articles on band affairs and some about his youth; the latter material was gathered into a small book titled *How I Became a Cornetist.* But he never wrote much about his adult life, so, as with Bierley on Sousa, Madeja on Clarke is indispensable.

I thank also MGySgt D. Michael Ressler, historian of the U.S. Marine Band, in the Marine Band Library in Washington, D.C. Early in my research I sought to find some congressional or military act by which Sousa's march "Semper Fidelis" became the official march of the U.S. Marine Corps. Most everyone makes this assumption (including Sousa in his autobiography), yet I could not find a supporting act or date. So I wrote to the Marine Corps and soon had back from the band's historian, MGySgt Ressler, a clear answer to what turns out to be a curiosity (see chapter 4, note 6). Later, he shared with me his own survey of Sousa's Wagner performances, provided me with a copy of the band's 1885 catalogue, gave me much of the material that informs appendixes, 7, 8, and 9, and furnished me with many illustrations. He also read my drafts about the U.S. Marine Band, correcting my civilian slips. Though perhaps duty bound to answer my initial plea, he did much, much more.

Fourth, I thank the staff at the Goldman Collection, Library of the Performing Arts, University of Maryland—particularly Cassandra N. Berman, who most frequently answered my queries. Because there is considerably less published about the Goldman Band—nothing on the scale of Bierley on Sousa—facts here require a search. I asked such questions as: Did the Goldman Band play any ragtime numbers in the years 1971–1977? More specifically, any rags by Scott Joplin, "King of Ragtime"? And what excerpts of Verdi did Edwin Franko Goldman schedule in the years 1936–1946? The latter was a period in which I suspected he began to lessen the number of operatic excerpts in favor of original compositions for band. Always, the search was made and an answer found.

I also want to thank two musicians who had performed with bands about which, until I met with them, I knew little or nothing. The first of these was Victor DeRenzi, who in the years 1972–1976 had conducted the Staten Island Musicians Society and so was able to tell me much about its financing, performance schedule, and repertory. The other was Gustave Hoehn, an E-flat clarinetist who had played with a Community Band of America and also knew of the Windjammer Bands and the Dallas Wind Symphony. I had several meetings with each musician, which invariably were followed by material sent to confirm what had been said, and Hoehn, in addition, supplied several pictures. Thus, while revealing holes in my story, they filled them.

Lastly, I want to thank Byron Hanson, archivist at Interlochen Center for the Arts, which plays an important role in band history. He culled many facts for me, particularly on the career and personality of Frederick Fennell, under whom he had played and recorded, chiefly on the euphonium but also on bass and tenor over-the-shoulder horns for the Civil War centennial recordings, and on the trombone for a Gabrielli album. Moreover, he provided me with many illustrations, most of which we believe have never been used. He took the book in draft, read every word, including the notes and appendixes, and made suggestions. Most important, in a long series of e-mail exchanges, he often was able, as a veteran of a period I was trying to record, to add substance to my facts and nuance to my statements. I cannot exaggerate my gratitude to Mr. Hanson—we have never met—or my luck in finding such a friend to the book.

In closing, I would like to thank Dr. Mona Hersh-Cochran, professor emerita of the Texas Woman's University, who, in reading the book in draft, caught typing and grammatical inconsistencies, and the staff of the New York Public Library, where I did most of my research. And so, in view of help received, I fairly claim: mistakes are mine alone.

Introduction

Opera in the United States during much of the nineteenth century was a major part of popular entertainment. Starting in the 1830s, the tunes of opera, particularly of contemporary Italian opera, began to displace the older, musically simpler English, Scottish, and Irish ballads. Even those who, for whatever reason, never set foot in an opera house played and sang (often to new words) the favorite airs at home, danced and promenaded to them at balls, and heard them daily in the street from hurdy-gurdies. In this way, in the 1840s Bellini's aria-finale to *La sonnambula,* "Ah, non giunge," perhaps a bit simplified and disguised as "Ah, Don't Mingle," became a popular song. Similarly, "Una voce poco fa," from Rossini's *Il barbiere di Siviglia,* became "Once a King There Chanced to Be," or alternatively, "Tyrant, Soon I'll Burst Thy Chains."[1]

Bands of all kinds—large, small, amateur, professional, civic, industrial, scholastic, military—contributed greatly to this spread of operatic music. If Rossini's overture to *William Tell* soon became a favorite, which it surely did, most people heard it not in an opera house, for the opera was expensive to mount and rarely staged, but from bands. By 1850 there were about 3,000 bands nationally with 60,000 band members. By the century's end, when the country still had only some five or six major symphony orchestras, bands numbered upward of 10,000, with at least one estimate suggesting a total closer to 20,000. For most people living in these years, before the rise of symphony orchestras in the early 1900s and before the development of recordings and radio, the band concert, indoors or out, was the main source of live music. And though its signature work was always the military march, it usually offered a strong operatic repertory.[2]

Among bands of all kinds the most famous were the big, touring concert bands, typically employing forty or more musicians and led usually by a conductor with considerable flair. For the most part, in their peak years (roughly 1875–1930), these were civilian bands, though many in the nineteenth century kept some tie to a military regiment and the musicians wore uniforms in performance. But even in those years, they were typically hired by the regiment, not enlisting in it, and their scale of pay, particularly for the conductor and famous soloists, could be high. When not performing regimental duties, parades, funerals, concerts, and balls, these bands survived financially by frequent touring and performance. Not only did they crisscross the country and sometimes venture abroad, but in the larger cities, especially in parks and at expositions, they played as many as four concerts a day, some of which, it seems, must have been relatively brief sets. For the numbers are astonishing. In its busiest year, 1902, Sousa's Band played 730 concerts, and in 1914, after completing four European and one around-the-world tour, it was quite possibly the most active and best-known musical group in the world. Moreover Sousa, though most famous for his marches, liked opera and included many selections in his repertory, not only old favorites but also excerpts and overtures from operas seldom staged or from those only recently premiered.[3]

Yet a curiosity of operatic history in the United States is the scant attention paid by scholars and critics to the tie between opera and bands. Though that tie for many years, as will be shown, was close and mutually beneficial, by the 1920s it had begun to loosen, and fifty years later was all but undone. Reasons for this decline in operatic repertory and the loss entailed for opera are this book's chief theme.

Or, stated more positively, this book is a heartfelt plea for the bands of today to play more excerpts from the operas of today. A great deal of good theatrical music—opera, musical comedy, ballet, overtures—is too often ignored by bands and so not heard by the general public. A misfortune for opera (broadly defined).

To recount that misfortune, if all kinds of bands—municipal, industrial, military, and so on—were given equal space, several tomes would be required. And so to set some bounds on the subject for a single volume, I limit the history of the bands primarily to those which in their day were the best known: the big, civilian touring groups, of which the most famous was Sousa's, 1892–1932. But alas, by 1940 no civilian bands toured in the style of Sousa, and by 2006 only a few professional civilian concert bands survived. So, as well as the demise of the operatic repertory for bands, the decline of the big, touring civilian bands is also a theme of this book, but quite secondary to the first and described in less detail.

There were, of course, many nonmusical reasons for the decline of these big bands, among them the impact of technological developments, such as recordings, radio, and the arrival of the automobile. Another cause over which the bands had no control was the demographic changes in audience. And to these must be added the constantly increasing costs of travel, especially in the 1930s, and the increasing strength of the musicians' unions. I trust that these are sufficiently noted, for in themselves they had far more impact on the decline of the big touring bands than choice of repertory—though the latter, I will argue, had some small share in it.

In my discussion of the bands—which is, remember, not a history of all civilian touring bands but of only a representative few—I proceed chronologically, stressing the backgrounds and personalities of the musicians who led them, the men who chose the repertory. For my purpose these were, starting in 1853 with the Dodworth brothers and Mons. Jullien (in successive generations), chiefly Gilmore, Sousa, Clarke, the Goldmans (father and son), and Frederick Fennell. Thus the account of these outstanding leaders and their bands frames the less well-known history of the rise and decline of their operatic repertory.

First, however, a number of basic distinctions need to be made and definitions noted, for the customary language can be confusing. Many persons, for example, upon hearing or reading the word "band" think at once of a "marching" band, out-of-doors, coming down the street or parading on a football field, and in their minds they hear a march, likely by Sousa and likely "The Stars and Stripes Forever." A concert band, however, though it frequently plays that march (as well as others by Sousa!), is quite different from a marching band in several important respects. Like the latter it employs chiefly woodwinds, brass, and percussion, but because in concert it is seated, whether indoors or out, it frequently adds other instruments such as violins, cellos, string basses, harps, and, perhaps most strikingly, singers. And further, whereas marching bands often, for special occasions, turn themselves into concert bands, the latter almost never march. Sousa's Band, for example, in its forty-year span, 1892–1932, gave 15,623 concerts, yet marched only eight times.[4]

More basic still is the definition of a "band." Most dictionaries start with the concept merely of a group of persons gathered for a common purpose, then adding perhaps for the more musically minded something like "a group of players who perform as an ensemble." No definition, however, states what instruments the group plays, for bands of all kinds—military, civic, college, industrial, theater, jazz, swing, dance, or symphonic—recruit diverse instruments. Sousa, for example, frequently had a violin soloist for movements of Mendelssohn's Violin Concerto and for such lighter works as Fritz Kreisler's *Liebesfreude* as well as a cellist for "The Swan " from Saint-Saëns *Carnival of the Animals*; and the Goldmans (father and son) in addition to tubas usually had two string basses in their band, preferring the string sound to that of the bass tuba.[5]

Dictionary definitions of an "orchestra" are hardly more exact: "A large group of musicians who play together on various instruments, usually including strings, woodwinds, brass and percussion." That may describe a symphonic orchestra of fifty or more, but not, for example, the eleven-man dance band which in the 1920s achieved fame on radio as "Vincent Lopez and his Orchestra," or the twice as large concert and recording band "Paul Whiteman and his Orchestra."

Other definitions are equally slippery, such as the distinctions between military and civilian or between amateur and professional. For years, every kind of band, out of respect for its ancestral form, was called "military," even when composed entirely of students, factory workers, or townspeople. Thus, well into the twentieth century the term often included civilian bands of all kinds. The distinction between amateur and professional is still fuzzier. Usually, the amateur is thought to play for love of music and the professional, though loving music, for pay. But then what does one call an orchestra or band made up of students who receive no pay, yet the group, or its college, reaps income from recordings? Or a group, whose members receive no pay and which gives concerts free to the public, but whose expenses are defrayed by private or public subsidy? Or a group in which some are paid and others not, such as the paid professor-conductor of a college band composed of unpaid students? The variations of structure in paid and unpaid seem infinite.[6]

And another semantic confusion: whether to call some orchestral work, when re-orchestrated for band, an "arrangement" or a "transcription." Traditionally, a transcription merely substituted one set of instruments for another whose presence was lacking, such as clarinets for violins. The work's structure, its sequence of themes, keys, and climax, was not changed; whereas an arrangement often did more, by changing structure. Many critics, however, seem to use the words interchangeably. Virgil Thomson, trying to sharpen the distinction, once offered the following (with his emphasis): "I am not protesting against the *use* of *arrangements,* in so far as that term means free versions of familiar melodies. I protest against the *abuse* of *transcriptions,* by which I mean the translation to other instrumental media of works that are both satisfactory and easily available in the correct form." He approved of band arrangements of the sextet from *Lucia di Lammermoor* and the overture to *William Tell,* for these were not often heard in orchestral concerts. But he objected to transcriptions for band of such works as Sibelius's *Finlandia,* which orchestras in 1941 frequently offered. Whether Thomson's distinction is helpful, I leave to the reader, but in this book, to avoid confusion, I use only the term "arrangement."[7]

Lastly is the imprecision of what is meant by "serious," "art," or "classical" music as distinct from "popular," "folk," or "vernacular." Different authors favor different terms, and meanings often become blurred. One scholar, William Weber, has traced the shifts in meaning of "popular" and "serious" from roughly 1790 to 1914. Though most of his examples are from European cities, some are from Boston, and in his concluding chapter he quotes (though disapproving of the snobbery) general opinion as it was in English critical circles in 1909: "popular" was "something pleasant, graceful, elegant, and eminently musicianly; it was . . . empty of all that makes art valuable—the impetus to thought."[8]

Today, surely most music lovers would assert a difference between, say, a Beethoven symphony and a Gershwin song. The song to most ears is immediately accessible, the symphony somewhat less so, and many people feel, perhaps only because of a movement that Lawrence Levine in *Highbrow/Lowbrow* called the "sacralization" of musical culture, that the symphony is fundamentally different, that it not only entertains but also inspires and elevates. Not all agree, but in this book, focusing on the operatic repertory of bands, I will leave this aesthetic bramble aside and throughout use the terms "popular" and "serious" to mean what to the average person, only slightly schooled in music, is easily accessible and what is not; what, chiefly through rhythm and melody, is primarily for entertainment, and what through greater complication and diversity is meant for something more. Perhaps these many uncertainties of definition and the messiness they spread through the subject are reasons why scholars, critics, and opera historians tend to skim by concert bands.[9]

Another reason they are often passed over, however, is snobbery. In this, the later writers followed the lead of early critics who from the first tended not to review bands in any depth, merely stating which played and sometimes what pieces. One reason, no doubt, was the number of band concerts. When a band in New York in the 1850s was playing weekly in Central Park, where was the news? Whereas the New York Philharmonic then was giving only four to six concerts a year, and so was newsworthy. Moreover, the philharmonic drew a more limited and socially prominent audience than did the band, and on this count, too, was more newsworthy. But aside from news value there was snobbery. In 1851, for example, a critic reviewing a concert by the American Brass Band in Providence, Rhode Island, deplored a hostile attitude: "We would remark . . . that we do not acknowledge the validity of the objections made by some musical men to the reduction and arrangement, for brass instruments, of orchestral compositions. Such persons seem to us to be absurdly fastidious." And in 1899 a scholar writing in defense of bands declared: "Despite the humorous and sarcastic depreciation they have received from the press, the military bands [meaning also civilian bands] of the country are doing a great educational work among the people." Clearly he felt lonely in his view, and the more general critical prejudice, continually expressed, hung on to become popular belief: bands, somehow, were less worthy than symphony orchestras.[10]

For an example occurring 106 years later, move ahead to February 2005 when the College Band Directors National Association (often titling itself merely CBDNA) held its biennial conference in Carnegie Hall, presenting a series of programs that included original works for wind concert bands by such composers as Aaron Copland, David Del Tredici, Morton Gould, Mozart, Gunther Schuller, William Schuman, and Charles Wuorinen, as well as the premiere of works by John Corigliano, Richard Danielpour, Michael Daughterty, Donald Grantham, and Bright Sheng. All these works were played by distinguished groups, such as the Eastman Wind Ensemble or the Goldman Band. Though the critics of the *New York Times* were invited to come, not one reviewed the conference or the works, reportedly on the grounds that the *Times*—though daily boasting "All the News That's Fit to Print"—does not review school concerts. But inasmuch as the paper frequently reviews performances by the Juilliard, Manhattan, and Mannes schools of music, it seemed the decision was less against schools than against music composed or arranged for bands. And sadly, despite the new works of outstanding composers, none of the city's other major papers reviewed the concerts either.[11]

I return now to the book's main topic: the operatic repertory of the large concert bands. Because I like opera, I find that repertory interesting, and in recounting the history of professional (broadly defined) concert bands, I pay more heed to it than do most writers. As suggested, I believe it may have a part, though small, in the rise and decline of concert bands. Music from opera typically has certain qualities whose presence seems to please the public and whose absence is regretted. These qualities were well stated in the nineteenth century by the French novelist and playwright Victor Hugo, who had sixteen of his dramas turned into operas; and not only in the nineteenth century, for today one of musical theater's longest-running hits is based on his novel *Les Misérables*.

In Hugo's preface to his verse drama *Ruy Blas* (1838), he described the play-going public as being divided into three categories: women, thinkers, and the general crowd. The last wanted "action"; the women, "passion"; and the thinkers, "portrayals of human nature." One need not accept Hugo's partition of the audience by sex and character to grant that he has neatly stated the staples of opera: action, passion, and portrayals of human nature. And surely these staples strongly appeal to most audiences.[12]

One last point needs explanation. Why, in discussing the operatic repertory of the bands, and in the appendixes, I tend to focus more on Verdi than on other composers. Because with Verdi I can pose my thesis more clearly than with, say, Wagner, Puccini, or Meyerbeer. After World War I, Meyerbeer was dropped from the repertory both in opera houses and in arrangements for bands, and as yet has not been revived; whereas both Wagner and Puccini, once they entered the repertory, continued relatively stable with ten or so operas frequently staged and excerpted. In contrast, Verdi, except for the most popular five or six of his twenty-six operas, has a more uneven history in the opera repertory. He was in favor roughly 1850–1890, then fell out of favor during 1900–1940, and returned in 1950. His return was in part because of the so-called Verdi Renaissance, which arrived in this country in the 1940s. Hence, while Verdi was being disregarded in the world's opera houses, bands were playing excerpts of his works only rarely or even never staged, and thus were not only adventurous but influential.

For example, today the overture to Verdi's opera *Giovanna d'Arco* is considered one of his better, often ranked third after the overtures to *La forza del destino* and *I vespri siciliani.* But the opera had its U.S. premiere (in concert) only in 1966, and before then the Metropolitan Opera in its Sunday afternoon concerts (1883–1946) had played the overture only three times, in the years 1924–1931. Sousa, however, during the years 1894–1927 performed it multiple times in eleven seasons; and the Goldman Band, 1936–1962, in seven. Similarly, in the years 1895 through 1927, when Verdi's *Don Carlos,* at least in the United States, was generally pronounced a failure, the Sousa Band played selections from it for twenty-two of those thirty-two years. The Goldman Band, 1936 through 1946, played the aria "O Don fatale" from the opera in six of those eleven years. Then in 1950 the Metropolitan staged the opera, and in the current reappraisal of Verdi it was declared a masterpiece. But surely the two bands to some extent had tilled the soil.[13]

In sum, therefore, what follows is a survey of opera at the bandstand, suggesting its importance both to the spread of opera and the popularity of band concerts, with examples and background drawn from the history of the leading American professional concert bands of the nineteenth and twentieth centuries.

NOTES

At first mention each citation is given in full; thereafter the notes refer readers to the bibliography. Unless stated otherwise, sources were published in New York.

1. For this early history, see Katherine K. Preston, *Opera on the Road, Traveling Opera Troupes in the United States, 1825–60* (Urbana: University of Illinois Press, 1993), particularly 9, 42, 99, 113; Preston, "Art Music from 1800 to 1860, in *The Cambridge History of American Music,* ed. David Nicholls (Cambridge: Cambridge University Press, 1998), 189–90; Dale Cockrell, "Nineteenth-Century Popular Music,"

in *The Cambridge History of American Music*, 163; and *Complete Catalogue of Sheet Music and Musical Works, 1870* (repr. New York: Da Capo Press, 1973), entries under the individual operas.

2. Leon Mead, "Military Bands in the United States," *Harper's Weekly*, 28 September 1899, 785–88, declared: "Over ten thousand military bands." These were mostly adult amateur bands, and despite the term "military," many were town or industrial bands. Moreover, "in the smaller cities they average twenty-five men each. In small country towns they number from twelve to eighteen members." According to Dale Cockrell, 161: "[There were] more than 10,000 bands, only a bare handful professional, touring ensembles." H. W. Schwartz, *Bands of America* (Garden City, NY: Doubleday, 1957), 169, offers a higher estimate, approaching 20,000. For the surge in founding symphony orchestras, see the tables in Michael Broyles, "Art Music from 1860 to 1920," *Cambridge History of Music*, 225–26. And H. Wiley Hitchcock, *Music in the United States: A Historical Introduction* (Englewood Cliffs, N J: Prentice Hall, 1969), 222, quoting a survey by *Concert Music USA, 1968* (New York: Broadcast Music, Inc., 1968), estimated for 1967 about "1,436 symphony orchestras in the U.S.A. (more than half of the world's 2,000); 918 opera-producing groups"; and in American schools, "some 68,000 instrumental music organizations (of which 50,000 were wind bands)."

3. Sousa in 1902, Paul Edmund Bierley, *The Incredible Band of John Philip Sousa* (Urbana: University of Illinois Press, 2006), 4fn8, 143. Number of concerts per day: four in St. Louis in 1893, Patrick Warfield, "Making the Band: The Formation of John Philip Sousa's Ensemble," *American Music* 24, no. 1 (Spring 2006): 47; four in Willow Grove, Pennsylvania, in the 1920s, Bierley, *The Incredible Band,* 13. On the municipal band at Long Beach, California, "In addition to performances for local civic functions, the Municipal Band performed two concerts daily, six days a week, fifty weeks a year." See James T. Madeja, "Herbert L. Clarke and the Long Beach Municipal Band (1923–1943)," in *The Wind Band and Its Repertoire,* ed. Michael Votta, Jr. (Warner Bros. Publications, 2003), 195.

4. Total of Sousa concerts, Bierley, *The Incredible Band,* 143.

5. *The American Heritage Dictionary of the English Language,* 3rd ed. (Boston: Houghton Mifflin Co., 1992). Besides other dictionary definitions, see Richard Franko Goldman, *The Concert Band* (New York: Rinehart, 1946), 3, 62–63. On Sousa's use of strings, Bierley, *The Incredible Band,* Mendelssohn, 381; Kreisler, 370; Saint-Saëns, 396; and the tables of instrumentation by years, 251–52. On the pros and cons of using the string bass, quoting Sousa against, see Goldman, 105–07. For using strings in addition to tubas, for example, Goldman, 214.

6. Defining "military," Goldman, *The Concert Band,* 3–5.

7. Virgil Thomson, "Band Music," *Herald Tribune,* 22 June 1941, sec VI, 6. Republished in *The Etude,* July 1942, and in Thomson, *The Musical Scene* (New York: Knopf, 1947).

8. William Weber, *The Great Transformation of Musical Taste: Concert Programming from Haydn to Brahms* (Cambridge: Cambridge University Press, 208), 2, 35–36, 120, 301 (the quote), 303.

9. For others on these definitions, see *Cambridge History of American Music,* 158 (Cockrell quoting Richard Crawford); 201 (the Germania Society); 207 (Preston on J.

S. Dwight); 214–15 (Broyles); and 262 (William Brooks). Paul Charosh, "'Popular' and 'Classical' in the Mid-Nineteenth Century," *American Music* 10, no. 2 (Summer 1992): 117–135. Hitchcock, *Music in the United States,* 43–54. Charles Hamm, *Yesterdays: Popular Song in America* (New York: W. W. Norton, 1979), xvii–xviii, 76. And a comment on Levine, *Highbrow/Lowbrow,* Joseph Horowtiz, *Wagner Nights* (Berkeley: University of California Press, 1994), 324–26.

10. Howard Shanet, *Philharmonic: A History of New York's Orchestra* (Garden City, NY: Doubleday, 1975), 127, 135, 148, 160. Not until 1893 did the number of philharmonic concerts increase, and then only to eight, 179. Bierley, *The Incredible Band,* 4–6, points out that Sousa's Band in the years 1892–1900 probably played more concerts "than all six of the country's major symphony orchestras put together." For a 1851 critic, see Goldman, *The Concert Band,*168–170, quoting at length an article in a Rhode Island newspaper (10 March 1851) on bands, their repertory, and, despite criticism, the pleasure they give. In defense of bands, see Leon Mead, "Military Bands in the United States," *Harper's Weekly,* 28 September 1899, 785, col. 1.

11. For indignation over inaction by the *New York Times*, see Raoul Camus's review of *The Wind Band in and around New York ca. 1830–1950,* in *Journal of the Society for American Music* 3, special issue 1, (2009): 101–104.

12. On Hugo, see "Author's Preface" to *Ruy Blas* in *Three Plays by Victor Hugo,* translated by C. Crosland and F. L. Slous (New York: Howard Fertig, 1995), 213–20. *The New Grove Dictionary of Opera,* ed. Stanley Sadie (London: Macmillan, 1992), under the entry for Hugo lists eleven plays, four novels, and one epic used for operas, not including those projected but not completed; on the novel *Notre-Dame de Paris,* twenty-three attempts, not all completed; and on the verse drama *Ruy Blas,* twelve.

13. Bierley, *The Incredible Band*, 417. On the Goldman repertory, I thank Cassandra N. Berman at the Special Collections in Performing Arts Library, University of Maryland.

Chapter One

The Dodworth Bands and Jullien's Example

In the beginning, at least for the North American colonies of Great Britain, the only bands of more than three or four players heard in the late seventeenth and early eighteenth centuries were those attached to English regiments stationed in the larger cities. Even after the American Revolution, music in the United States and much else in life remained relatively simple. One old New Yorker in 1845 recalled the city as it was in 1795, when still a town of less than sixty thousand: "Certain it is that fifty years ago the people in New York lived much happier than they do now. They had no artificial wants—only two banks—rarely gave a note—but one small playhouse—no opera, no ottomans, few sofas or sideboards, and perhaps not six pianos in the city."[1]

By "no opera," however, he must have meant "no Italian opera," because, if sung and played as written, it did not arrive in the United States until 1825. But as early as 1750 the city had heard John Gay's *The Beggar's Opera* (1728), and soon thereafter such popular English operas as *The Contrivances*, *The Devil to Pay*, and *Love in a Village.* These English ballad operas mixed much spoken dialogue with songs, a duet or two, perhaps a trio, and for a finale a chorus of three or four actors to sing, likely in unison, the work's moral. And upon revival, which was frequent, they often interpolated the day's popular songs. But if New York's elderly gentleman was perhaps a bit misleading about "no opera," about "one small playhouse" he was quite correct. By then it was the John Street Theatre (1767–1798), which boasted two tiers of boxes, a pit and a gallery, and seated perhaps four hundred. For many years it had an orchestra of one, "Mr. Pelham and his harpsichord, or the single fiddle of Mr. Hewlett." On special occasions it might boast a few instruments more, but mostly it offered spoken plays, usually followed by a farce, with each introduced and sometimes accompanied by a bit of music.[2]

The plays and English ballad operas were performed with much ad-libbing and frequent calls from pit to stage, for audiences then were loud in remarks, whether for or against, frequently ribald, and, if not promptly appeased, aggressive. And in the revolutionary years and for some time thereafter, audiences frequently, and often seemingly on whim, demanded a patriotic song. "Yankee Doodle" was a favorite, and one night in 1796 when two drunken sea captains seated in a stage box demanded it, the audience "hissed them; they threw missiles in the orchestra, and defied the audience, some of whom pressed on the stage and attacked the rioters in conjunction with the peace-officers; one of the latter was injured by a blow from a club." And the performance resumed.[3]

Even on the theater's opera nights, the pit band or orchestra might number no more than four or five players. During the revolution, however, when the British occupied New York (1776–1783) and the house was titled "Theatre Royal," the English officers sometimes lent or leased their regimental bands to the theater, and the orchestra then might swell to a magnificent fourteen and include such rarities as trumpet, horn, flute, oboe, clarinet, or bassoon.[4]

Less admired were the officers' assaults on Shakespeare, tackling Macbeth, Othello, the two King Richards—"All," according to a contemporary American historian, "far above their reach." To his relief, "none attempted the philosophic, university-bred Prince of Denmark." The first attempt of *Hamlet* in this country, which in his view was "the bow of Ulysses to the actor," took place in the John Street Theatre, or so he claims, on the night of 16 January 1786. Lewis Hallam, the younger, was the actor.[5]

Throughout the revolutionary years, English regimental bands usually had two groups: one of fife and drum, twenty or so men, for "field" music, with wages paid by the army; and one for entertainment, indoors or out, hired and paid by the officers. The latter typically were a smaller, more polished group of ten or twelve, consisting usually of "pairs of wind instruments (oboes, horns, bassoons, possibly clarinets)." Strings generally were not included because when played outdoors, especially in humid weather, they lose much of their tone and resonance—a reason for some the term "band" connotes out of doors and without strings.[6]

After Yorktown and the British withdrawal, the American regiments and militias which succeeded the English started in much the same way, with a fife and drum corps and a smaller band primarily of wind instruments. But as these bands began to play more frequently for nonmilitary occasions, they increased in size, and by the 1830s typically numbered fifteen to twenty. Their instrumentation, however, had begun to change, dropping woodwinds and adding brass, in part because of technical improvements in the latter (especially the introduction of valved instruments). Consequently, when playing on nonmilitary occasions (though always in colorful uniforms), they often were called "brass bands." Twenty years later, as they began again to include woodwinds, seeking to increase the smoothness and variety of sound, they became "brass bands with winds," till finally, circa 1900, as the wind instruments (especially clarinets which often replaced an orchestra's strings) began to outnumber the brass by three to two or even two to one, they became "wind bands with brass," or simply "wind bands," or even "wind symphonies." But these changes did not come in lockstep; growth was very uneven. Bands of all kinds continued to play, and still do; hence terms and definitions are uncertain.[7]

Moreover, in early years some bands were remarkably flexible in their number and use of personnel. For example, in New York City in 1836 a family of musicians named Dodworth had a band, one with only occasional military ties and yet one of the country's best and largest (at most perhaps thirty players). Much admired, it had been invited to Washington in the years 1837–1841 to play for the inauguration of Presidents Van Buren, Harrison, and Tyler. By the 1850s this band could field at least sixty players, all, as a legacy of their regimental origin, in splendid uniform. But Dodworth's sixty, at full strength called simply the Dodworth Band, seemingly could increase their number or subdivide into Dodworth's Cornet Band (primarily for concerts or outdoor promenades), Dodworth's Quadrille Band (usually with strings and playing for balls), and sometimes (often at public occasions) Dodworth's Brass Band. According to historian John Graziano, on one Fourth of July "no fewer than three Dodworth bands were playing in various parts of the city." But, as he notes, whether additional players were recruited for the occasion and how players and instruments were apportioned is not recorded.[8]

Such gaps in knowledge may have discouraged critics and scholars from pursuing the subject, but as suggested in the introduction, another reason is snobbery, and its rise may be seen in a memory penned by the Boston critic, scholar, and historian John Sullivan Dwight. In 1881, he recalled a scene from childhood where he distinguished between "a real band" and a "mere band of brass":

> Among other incitements and sweet opportunities, the music-loving school-boy of the period (about 1825) must not refuse the debt of gratitude to the military band which, under the name of the Brigade Band, would tempt his feet to follow through the streets beyond the city's bounds, though he might find the homeward journey tiresome without the music. Many a Boston boy caught the tuneful fever from those dulcet and inspiring strains. And that was a real band; it had clarinets and flutes and oboes, bugles and French horns (some famous players too!), and was not the mere band of brass now used to penetrate the Babel of street noises.[9]

Along with his childhood memory, however, Dwight recorded his mature scholar's lament over yet another gap in knowledge: "Much might be learned of the musical tastes of that period from a list of the publications which were in demand; but no chronological lists are possible so long as music publishers refuse to date their issues."

Figure 1.1. Allen Dodworth. The New York Public Library.

Yet amid these uncertainties of early history, a foothold on the development of brass bands may be found in a short book published in 1853 by Allen Dodworth, then the Dodworth Band's conductor. He was not only a much admired cornet player, but a violinist for the New York Philharmonic as well as a composer whose Duetto for Two Clarinets the philharmonic played in 1846. He was also known, however, as an arranger of pieces for band, and he titled his book *Dodworth's Brass Band School: Containing Instructions in the First Principles of Music: Together with a Number of Pieces of Music Arranged for a Full Brass Band.*[10]

His preface offers some context of history—"The increasing demand for such a work, caused by the rapid advancement of the brass bands of our country, made it necessary that some one should furnish that which is so much needed." And he hoped the book might "be the means of assisting brass music to rise to that point it deserves, and must eventually attain." Allen Dodworth, who in 1834 had created what may have been the first all-brass band in the country, plainly heard something unique and attractive in its wind band sound, and apparently by 1853 so, too, did many others.[11]

He offered one simple bit of advice to those interested in bands concerning the shape of the brass instruments' bells: "In selecting the instruments, attention should be paid to the use intended; if for military purposes only, those with bells behind, over the shoulder, are preferable, as they throw all the tone to those who are marching to it, but for any other purpose are not so good. These were first introduced by the Dodworth family in the year 1838. For general purposes, those with bells upward, like the Sax Horn, are most convenient, and should be adopted by all whose business is not exclusively military; care should be taken to have all the bells one way."[12]

In his "List of Instruments for Bands of Different Numbers," he started with a band of only four brass, a soprano, an alto (a fourth below the soprano), a tenor (an octave below the soprano), and a bass (an octave below the alto). Then adding one instrument at a time he enlarged the band to twenty-one (with some percussion, usually bass drum, snare drum, and possibly cymbals), and for each new player he suggested the instrument to be added, thus keeping some balance in sound. Evidently, despite the size and versatility of his own band, he expected most bands in the 1850s to number twenty-four players or less. Hence the arrangements of tunes that he offered in his book, including "The Star Spangled Banner," are for twelve instruments. And if more could be added and parts doubled, he advised on the part and instrument. A typical band of the day may be seen in a drawing of the admired Boston Brass Band as constituted in 1851, and it shows a band of seventeen: four soprano saxhorns (chromatic valved bugles, an advance in bugle design), four alto (or tenor) saxhorns, three trombones, and three bass saxhorns, with cymbals, snare and bass drum.[13]

Figure 1.2. Boston Brass Band, 1851. *Gleason's Pictorial*, 20 September 1851.

In his book, however, Dodworth also anticipated Dwight's later complaint that brass bands all too often simply sought to penetrate "the Babel" of the streets.

> The author would take occasion to say here that the addition of trombones and trumpets is more in accordance with the public taste than with his own, for these fine instruments are so constantly abused, by those who mistake noise for music, that the appearance of one of them in a band, is an object of very considerable annoyance. For what reason, almost all who use these instruments think it necessary to blow them until they crack or snarl, is difficult to understand. . . . This is a most unfortunate error, and is an error that has had a very mischievous effect upon the public mind, with regard to brass instruments and bands.[14]

So Dwight's censure of the "mere band of brass," though perhaps too inclusive, was not without reason. Yet in a sense Dodworth wrote prophetically, for by the late 1890s one of the most astonishing and powerful effects of Sousa's Band was its ability, even in purely brass passages, to play softly—yet with a lush tone that reached the farthest row of a large audience. But in much of the mid-nineteenth century, many persons, and not only critics and scholars, complained that "the trumpet and trombone occupy, in our concerts, the *posts of honor.*" Still worse to some ears was how the place of "the more manly trumpet" had been usurped by "the cornet," whose "soap-opera" tone, said some, was "vulgar."[15]

Starting in the 1830s, as bands enlarged and increasingly played for the civilian public, the portion of their repertory that was operatic in origin also expanded, usually following the fashion of the moment. Thus until the 1870s when Wagner began to be heard more frequently, the operatic composers whose overtures, arias, and ensembles were most often arranged for band were Auber, Flotow, Meyerbeer, Weber, and among the Italians, Rossini, Donizetti, and, after 1850, Verdi.

Consider, for example, the programs offered by the Dodworth Band in the summer of 1859, during a series of eight free band concerts in New York's Central Park. This series, underwritten by "private subscription," started a tradition that a century later would come to extraordinary flower with the Goldman Band's fifty-concert series funded by the Guggenheim Foundation (see chapter 9). But in 1859 for the opening series in the park's "Ramble," the band, now led by Allen Dodworth's younger brother Harvey, for at least the first seven of the Saturday afternoons scheduled some arrangement of Verdi (see appendix 1 and photospread). The program for the final concert is lacking. In order of concert, however, the first six offered a potpourri from *Traviata*; a sextet from *Ernani*; the sextet repeated; selections from *Trovatore* and the quartet from *Rigoletto*; a cavatina from *Nabucco*; and a quartet, "Fra mortali, " from *Luisa Miller* and the Anvil Chorus from *Trovatore*; with the seventh program repeating the sixth. And though at the time *Ernani, Rigoletto, Trovatore,* and *Traviata* were often staged, *Nabucco* and *Luisa Miller* were not.[16]

The following year the *New York Times* ran an editorial on the concerts: "Who the audience are and How they deport themselves." Among other matters it revealed: "There is no reservations of front seats, and no distinction of pit and parquette, gallery and dress-circle. . . . Seats are provided for a few, standing-places for the many, and either are the property of the first comer. . . . The queerest contrasts in dress and manners are visible." It listed some hazards: the occasional spitter, the over-perfumed lady, the stink of beer and scattered clouds of "a villainously flavored cigar." And yet, at the seventh concert, "arias from *Poliuto* and *Traviata* fell upon unaccustomed ears, and were appreciated by souls to whom the names of VERDI and DONIZETTI are unknown."[17]

Similar, at least in variety of program, was a New York 7th Regiment Band concert in December 1863, which scheduled "gems" from *Ballo in maschera,* an opera currently popular, and, more surprising, from *I Lombardi,* which had not had a performance in the city in ten years and would not again until 1886. And at a regimental ball at the city's Academy of Music in January 1874, the same band alternated the quadrilles, polkas, waltzes, and galops with promenades, in which the ladies (usually escorted by gentlemen), by walking in a large circle (usually counterclockwise), could display their gowns, men in the family, and unmarried daughters, while greeting friends and nodding to acquaintances who might be sitting on the side and admiring. For the twenty promenades—to limit discussion for the moment to one composer—of Verdi, the band programmed selections not only from *Ernani* and *Trovatore* but also from the less often staged *Nabucco, Attila,* and *Luisa Miller.*[18]

Returning now to the development of the bands, the year 1853 was chiefly important, not for the publication of Dodworth's book, but for the August arrival in New York of a musician well known in London and Paris, Mons. Louis Antoine Jullien. A violinist, conductor, and composer of marches, quadrilles, and polkas, he was also known for his flamboyance. In Britain, where he had been performing for the last fifteen years, he had become famous for the size of his orchestra, which often reached a hundred, a number that usually included at least one military band, and when on tour to provincial cities he splattered their walls with announcements of his coming and then staged performances in a style more sumptuous than ever before seen or heard. For the United States he planned the same.[19]

Figure 1.3. Mons. Louis Jullien. The New York Public Library.

He was not the first to come. At least four chamber ensembles preceded him, all from Germany. The first to arrive were nineteen Styrians, who came in 1846 calling themselves the Steyermarkische Company. They opened in Boston, played a season in New York, and then went on a tour. Their programs included waltzes, polkas, a Hungarian march by Liszt, the *William Tell* overture, an excerpt from *Linda di Chamounix,* and, their most sensational number, a "Railroad Galop," which portrayed a steam engine train starting up, rolling along, and pulling in to a station. "Not exactly music," remarked the New York *Tribune,* but immensely popular.[20]

The Styrians were followed by a larger group of thirty-two, led by the then famous Hungarian composer of marches and dances, Josef Gungl. The group had several outstanding soloists, whom Gungl featured in special arrangements, and was much admired for its performances of Weber's overture to *Oberon.* Among the most popular of his numbers was an arrangement of Stephen Foster's "Oh! Susanna," set as a polka. And even as Gungl and his men were in New York, there arrived in the city the Saxonia Band, a group of twenty-four from Dresden. Besides light dance music, they also played the overtures to Auber's *La muette de Portici* and to Mendelssohn's *A Midsummer Night's Dream,* and an arrangement of the finale to Bellini's *I Capuletti ed I Montecchi.*[21]

The group with the most lasting influence, however, was the Germania Musical Society, variously numbered at twenty-one to twenty-five, which came in September 1848 and stayed until it dissolved in 1854, by which time it had given some nine hundred concerts in Canada and the United States. Longevity, however, was only one source of its influence; it was also generally judged the most accomplished of the four German bands, and upon dissolution its members stayed in the country to teach and play in other groups. Besides the dance music of Gungl and Strauss, it played the usual operatic overtures, including the *Stradella* by Flotow and *Zanetta* by Auber, to which it added, however, the Finale from Beethoven's Fifth Symphony. Perhaps its most admired work, however, was the overture to *A Midsummer Night's Dream,* which appeared on almost every program and reportedly was always encored.[22]

The scale of Mons. Jullien's venture, however, was considerably more ambitious. He contemplated an orchestra of one hundred for the larger East Coast cities and sixty for touring. He brought with him twenty-five soloists, all virtuosi, of which the most famous were cornetist Adolph Koenig, soprano vocalist Anna Zerr, and double bass player Giovanni Bottesini. The balance of the band he hired locally; although, as appendix 2 shows, for special occasions he often recruited existing musical groups as entities, such as Dodworth's Cornet Band and the Germania Musical Society, allowing them to retain their identity and even at times to play alone. But even without a special occasion, Jullien's hundred-man orchestra for larger cities and sixty men when on tour were stunning events for audiences.[23]

Opening in New York on 29 August, he played forty-one concerts in fifty-four days, all at Castle Garden, which, according to the *Mirror,* his wife, a professional florist, had transformed "into a second Aladdin's palace." The night's first piece was an operatic number, Weber's overture to *Der Freischütz,* which Jullien later followed with Mozart's "Queen of the Night" aria, sung by Anna Zerr; a fantasy on themes from Bellini's *La sonnambula,* played by Giovanni Bottesini; and an arrangement of themes from Meyerbeer's *Les Huguenots.* In between he offered movements of symphonies by Beethoven and Mendelssohn interspersed with many waltzes, polkas, and quadrilles. He did not hesitate, however, to improve on Beethoven. Reportedly, for the storm in the "Pastoral" Symphony he added the sound of falling

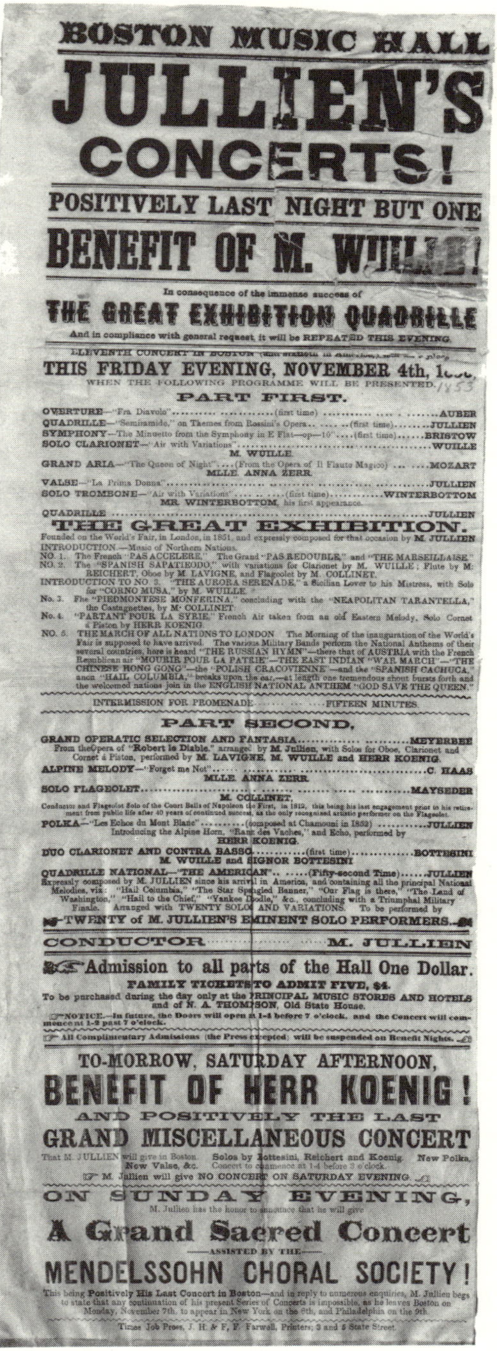

BOSTON MUSIC HALL

JULLIEN'S CONCERTS!

POSITIVELY LAST NIGHT BUT ONE

BENEFIT OF M. W[illegible]!

In consequence of the immense success of

THE GREAT EXHIBITION QUADRILLE

And in compliance with general request, it will be REPEATED THIS EVENING.

ELEVENTH CONCERT IN BOSTON [illegible]

THIS FRIDAY EVENING, NOVEMBER 4th, 1[illegible],

WHEN THE FOLLOWING PROGRAMME WILL BE PRESENTED. 1853

PART FIRST.

OVERTURE—"Fra Diavolo".......................(first time)......................AUBER

QUADRILLE—"Semiramide," on Themes from Rossini's Opera.........(first time)........JULLIEN

SYMPHONY—The Minuetto from the Symphony in E Flat—op—10"....(first time)......BRISTOW

SOLO CLARIONET—"Air with Variations"..WUILLE

M. WUILLE.

GRAND ARIA—"The Queen of Night"....(From the Opera of Il Flauto Magico).........MOZART

MLLE. ANNA ZERR.

VALSE—"La Prima Donna"..JULLIEN

SOLO TROMBONE—"Air with Variations"..........(first time)............WINTERBOTTOM

MR. WINTERBOTTOM, his first appearance.

QUADRILLE..JULLIEN

THE GREAT EXHIBITION.

Founded on the World's Fair, in London, in 1851, and expressly composed for that occasion by M. JULLIEN

INTRODUCTION.—Music of Northern Nations.

NO. 1. The French "PAS ACCELERE," The Grand "PAS REDOUBLE," and "THE MARSEILLAISE."

NO. 2. The "SPANISH SAPATIEODO," with variations for Clarionet by M. WUILLE; Flute by M. REICHERT, Oboe by M. LAVIGNE, and Flageolet by M. COLLINET.

INTRODUCTION TO NO. 3. "THE AURORA SERENADE," a Sicilian Lover to his Mistress, with Solo for "CORNO MUSA," by M. WUILLE.

No. 3. The "PIEDMONTESE MONFERINA," concluding with the "NEAPOLITAN TARANTELLA," the Castagnettes, by M. COLLINET.

No. 4. "PARTANT POUR LA SYRIE," French Air taken from an old Eastern Melody, Solo Cornet á Piston by HERR KOENIG.

NO. 5. THE MARCH OF ALL NATIONS TO LONDON. The Morning of the inauguration of the World's Fair is supposed to have arrived. The various Military Bands perform the National Anthems of their several countries, here is heard "THE RUSSIAN HYMN"—there that of AUSTRIA with the French Republican air "MOURIR POUR LA PATRIE"—THE EAST INDIAN "WAR MARCH"—"THE CHINESE HONG GONG"—the "POLISH CRACOVIENNE"—and the "SPANISH CACHUCA," anon "HAIL COLUMBIA," breaks upon the ear,—at length one tremendous shout bursts forth and the welcomed nations join in the ENGLISH NATIONAL ANTHEM "GOD SAVE THE QUEEN."

INTERMISSION FOR PROMENADE..........FIFTEEN MINUTES.

PART SECOND,

GRAND OPERATIC SELECTION AND FANTASIA..........................MEYERBEER

From the Opera of "Robert le Diable," arranged by M. Jullien, with Solos for Oboe, Clarionet and Cornet á Piston, performed by M. LAVIGNE, M. WUILLE and HERR KOENIG.

ALPINE MELODY—"Forget me Not"..C. HAAS

MLLE. ANNA ZERR.

SOLO FLAGEOLET..MAYSEDER

M. COLLINET,

Conductor and Flageolet Solo of the Court Balls of Napoleon the First, in 1812, this being his last engagement prior to his retirement from public life after 40 years of continued success, as the only recognised artistic performer on the Flageolet.

POLKA—"Les Echos du Mont Blanc"..........(composed at Chamouni in 1852)...........JULLIEN

Introducing the Alpine Horn, "Ranz des Vaches," and Echo, performed by HERR KOENIG.

DUO CLARIONET AND CONTRA BASSO...........(first time)..............BOTTESINI

M. WUILLE and SIGNOR BOTTESINI

QUADRILLE NATIONAL—"THE AMERICAN"........(Fifty-second Time)......JULLIEN

Expressly composed by M. JULLIEN since his arrival in America, and containing all the principal National Melodies, viz: "Hail Columbia," "The Star Spangled Banner," "Our Flag is there," "The Land of Washington," "Hail to the Chief," "Yankee Doodle," &c., concluding with a Triumphal Military Finale. Arranged with TWENTY SOLOS AND VARIATIONS. To be performed by

TWENTY of M. JULLIEN'S EMINENT SOLO PERFORMERS.

CONDUCTOR..........M. JULLIEN

Admission to all parts of the Hall One Dollar.

FAMILY TICKETS TO ADMIT FIVE, $4.

To be purchased during the day only at the PRINCIPAL MUSIC STORES AND HOTELS and of N. A. THOMPSON, Old State House.

NOTICE.—In future, the Doors will open at 1-4 before 7 o'clock, and the Concert will commence 1-2 past 7 o'clock.

All Complimentary Admissions (the Press excepted) will be suspended on Benefit Nights.

TO-MORROW, SATURDAY AFTERNOON,

BENEFIT OF HERR KOENIG!

AND POSITIVELY THE LAST

GRAND MISCELLANEOUS CONCERT

That M. JULLIEN will give in Boston. Solos by Bottesini, Reichert and Koenig. New Polka, New Valse, &c. Concert to commence at 1-4 before 3 o'clock.

M. Jullien will give NO CONCERT ON SATURDAY EVENING.

ON SUNDAY EVENING,

M. Jullien has the honor to announce that he will give

A Grand Sacred Concert

—ASSISTED BY THE—

MENDELSSOHN CHORAL SOCIETY!

This being Positively His Last Concert in Boston—and in reply to numerous enquiries, M. Jullien begs to state that any continuation of his present Series of Concerts is impossible, as he leaves Boston on Monday, November 7th, to appear in New York on the 8th, and Philadelphia on the 9th.

Times Job Press, J. H. & F. F. Farwall, Printers; 3 and 5 State Street.

Figure 1.4. Interlochen Center for the Arts.

hail by rattling dried peas in a tin container. And for the Fifth Symphony he is said to have added four ophicleides (bass brass), saxophone and side drums.[24]

After the "farewell" concert, on 21 October, he toured through the northeast, chiefly to Boston; came back to New York for another month before revisiting Boston for two weeks; returned to New York for a grand dress ball before departing on a tour to cities in the South, among them Baltimore, Charleston, Cincinnati, and New Orleans; and lastly, returned to New York for a series of eleven farewell performances. In his ten-month tour of the country he presented 214 concerts, with 105 of them in New York.[25]

All were staged with panache, announced by posters luridly colored "infernal scarlet and black," accompanied by myriad portraits of himself and his soloists, and for the opening concert in New York "a vast and ponderous card of admission printed in scarlet and gold in the folio form, upon brilliantly enameled board, and bound in crimson morocco." Onstage his podium, placed in the middle of the orchestra, was red, tinged with gold, and from it rose "a fantastic gilt figure supporting a desk, and behind the stand, a carved arm-chair decorated in white and gold, and tapestried with crimson velvet." In conducting, he favored broad, ecstatic gestures, and at the conclusion of a long piece, with an air of grand emotion, he would step from the podium to the chair, and collapse.[26]

Richard Grant White, reviewing the opening night concert for the *Courier and Enquirer,* began: "Monsieur Jullien is a humbug . . . not a pitiful humbug, or a timorous humbug; or, worse than all, an unsuccessful humbug; he is a splendid, bold, and dazzlingly successful humbug, one who merits his great success almost as much as if he had not employed the means by which he has achieved it." Among the means, whenever about to conduct a work by Beethoven, he would don white gloves and use a jeweled baton delivered on a silver tray.[27]

For his final series in New York, playing in the Crystal Palace (capacity 40,000), built in 1853 (in today's Bryant Park) to house the country's first World's Fair, Jullien titled the run "A Grand Musical Congress." The city's *Albion,* a weekly dedicated to arts and literature, called it "the first truly grand Musical Festival in this country." Enlarging the orchestra to five hundred, he recruited a chorus of a thousand (drawn from several northeastern cities), and on opening night, 15 June 1854 (see appendix 2), among other gems offered the "Hallelujah Chorus," the *William Tell* overture, and the as yet little-known overture to *Tannhäuser,* the last conducted by Carl Bergman and performed by the Germania Society, which Jullien had recruited into his forces. The *Albion* remarked: "Wagner's Overture to *Tannhäuser* was played by the Germania Musical Society. It is another proof of the sleepiness and old fogeyism of our Philharmonic Society that this should have been the *first* time of the performance of this great work in New York." The Germania group, devoted to spreading music as a "fine art," had already introduced it to Boston, Philadelphia, Pittsburgh, St. Louis, and Chicago.[28]

Also, at the sixth concert, on 21 June, "Herr Bergmann" and the Germania Society played an arrangement, the "Finale" from *Tannhäuser,* which like the overture they had played in other cities but apparently not yet in New York. The opera, however, would not have its American stage premiere until 4 April 1859, at New York's German Stadt Theater, that performance being the first of any Wagner opera, as so far discovered, in the Western Hemisphere. The rest of the operatic part of the program was more usual: Hérold's overture to *Zampa,* an arrangement of themes from Auber's *Masaniello,* and three selections from Rossini's *Stabat Mater,* a theatrical work which, except for its words, seems more operatic than sacred.[29]

The chief work of the Grand Musical Congress, however, repeated at every performance, was wholly new, composed for the occasion by Jullien. It was titled *The Fireman's Quadrille* and dedicated to the city's firemen. According to the program, the first four parts of the quadrille depicted the Firemen's Annual Parade. The fifth opened with the city at night:

> Perfect silence reigns. When "The Fire-Fiend," sweeping onward through the night, breathes destruction around, while the unsuspecting slumber. Suddenly a shower of sparks glitter in the air, and awake the vigilance of the night-watch; while, in the distance the deep-toned tocsin sounds the alarm of fire! That dreadful word is echoed from mouth to mouth, and a few instants only elapse ere the rattle of engines and hose carriages break upon the ear—now approaching rapidly, now fading slowly away. The alarm-bell continues to toll, and is responded to from tower and turret, far and near, o'er the wide expanse of the City. They come! They come! Engine after engine is rushing onwards toward the conflagration—the leader of each gallant troop, trumpet in hand, urging on his eager followers. The scene is reached. The devouring element is raging furiously. A dull, red glare illumines the horizon, while the thousand forked tongues of the fire-fiend shoot hither and thither, bent on destroying all within their reach. Now begins the elemental war. The firemen at once commence the attack on the gigantic enemy. Dauntless, they scale the surrounding walls and roof trees, pipe in hand, bent on conquering; and cutting off all retreat, they compel the demon of fire to stay his course. Streams of rushing water pour from all direction. Baffled, he obeys; and as the crashing walls fall on the expiring embers, he acknowledges their sway, while the mingled cheers of the brave firemen and the assembled multitude proclaim the victory.[30]

For certain musical effects in the quadrille, the distant calls, the responses, the galloping horses and nearing engines, Jullien added the Dodworth Band and the Bloomfield U.S. Military Band, and for the spectacle he ignited real

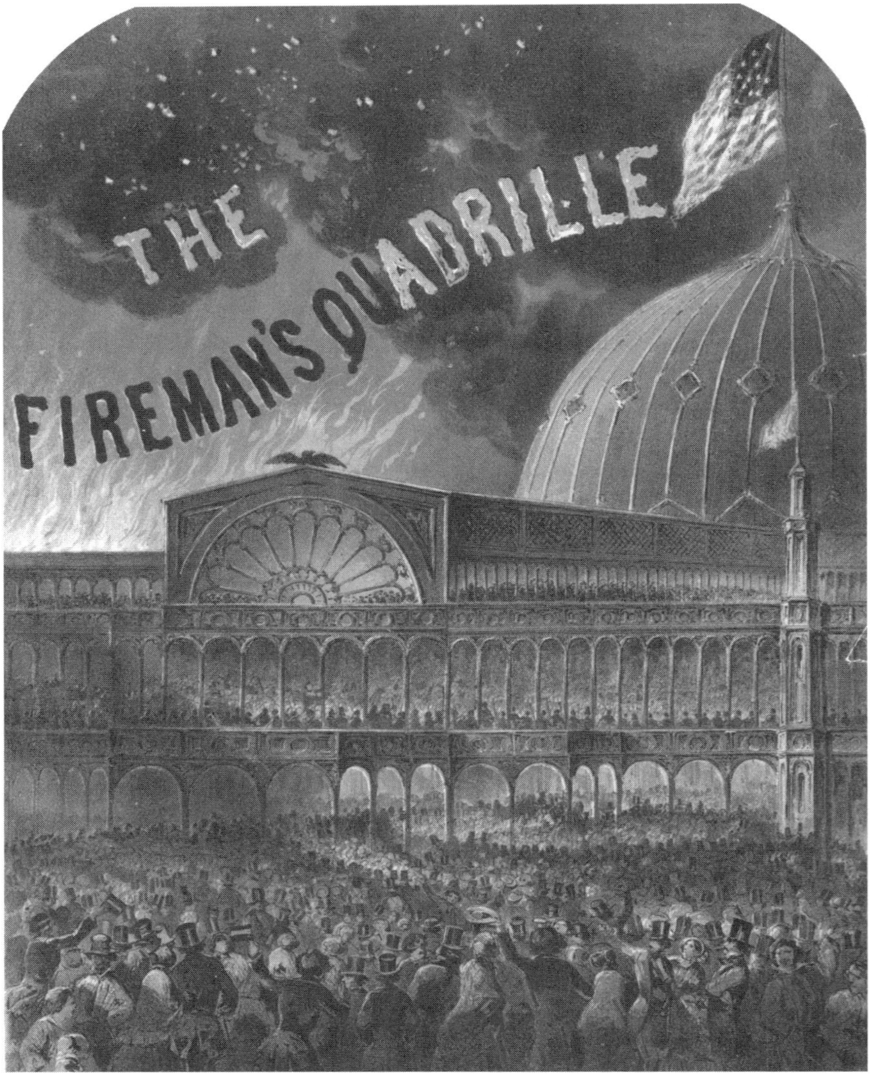

Figure 1.5. Cover for the sheet music for *The Fireman's Quadrille*. The New York Public Library.

and fake fires (with much use of sparkling strontium) in and around the building. The program promised the audience that despite the real and apparent flames it had nothing to fear, and immediately before the quadrille Jullien had his business partner for the Congress, P. T. Barnum, repeat the message from the stage. According to the *Times,* "Mr. Barnum addressed the audience, like *Snug,* the Joiner, to desire that they would not be alarmed at the frightful effects which would be introduced."[31]

In performance the music proved less memorable than the accompanying action. At appropriate moments, as real and artificial flames colored the ceiling, three companies of firemen, shouting commands, rushed into the hall, their hoses spouting real water, their axes smashing fake wooden doors and shattering glass. In the audience some screamed, others fainted—who could trust what Barnum said!—and some laughed, as ushers in the aisles asserted it was all a show. And at the end calm was restored as the audience joined the orchestral forces in singing "Old Hundred" (the Doxology). The next morning the *Times* reported: "The Quadrille was certainly not heard to advantage last night, for the enthusiasm was frequently so great that whole passages were lost," and the *Tribune* recommended that some of the fire effects, especially the burning of strontium, "could well be omitted." And among the news journals, at least, a pall of silence fell over the quadrille, though it apparently was repeated on each of the ten remaining nights, and always with success. Then, two days after the close of the Grand Musical Congress, having been honored with a memorial golden wreath, Jullien steamed back to England. And four years later the Crystal Palace, built of glass and iron and supposedly fireproof, burned and "was completely consumed" in "thirty minutes." Happily, despite some panic, the two thousand or so persons viewing the current exhibit (which included forty pianos valued at $20,000) all got out.[32]

What Jullien left behind for American band leaders to ponder, besides stress on the role of a conductor, were chiefly three new ideas, no doubt previously considered by some but until his active demonstration of them seldom practiced. He had shown that he and his large band, which included all kinds of instruments, could prosper without any military connection. He had shown that a huge audience, if carefully prepared, was ready to support such a band; and on a scale never before attempted he had introduced the general public to the classical composers and for many, with his jeweled baton for Beethoven, started the "sacralization" of some of them. Life in New York was no longer as simple as in 1795 when the city had only 60,000 people, "perhaps not six pianos," and when by definition all music, except sacred music, was popular. By 1860 the country's population would top 31 million; Manhattan alone had more than 800,000 people, and combined with Brooklyn, more than a million. The Steinway family was making and selling almost a thousand pianos each year; and among the nonsacred, so-called popular composers, the distinctions between popular and serious music were beginning to be drawn.[33]

Moreover, Jullien had shown how to avoid a surfeit of exposure and to fill slack seasons by frequent touring, which happily also increased the number of lucrative "farewell" and "opening night" concerts. The ideas reinforced each

Figure 1.6. Cover for the sheet music for *The Farewell Valse*. The New York Public Library.

other. Not having to be on hand for military reviews, honor guards, funerals, and regimental balls gave a band more freedom to plan tours. And touring in these years was becoming easier as more railroads connected more cities: New York to Boston in 1848; New York to Buffalo in 1853; New York to Chicago and westward to St. Joseph, Missouri, in 1860; and New York to San Francisco in 1869.

Lastly, in his extensive tours and programs, Jullien had confirmed (though few then doubted) the strength and popularity of the operatic repertory—action, passion, portrayals of human character—which since the 1840s had been steadily growing. But soon, the advent of the country's Civil War halted for a time any imitation of his example as bands in both the North and the South patriotically hastened to serve again as regimental units and adopted a repertory more dominated by martial music.

NOTES

1. Grant Thorburn, *Fifty Years' Reminiscences of New York* (New York: Fanshaw, 1845), 208.

2. *The Beggar's Opera,* U.S. premiere at Nassau Street Theatre, New York City, 3 December 1750; see Julius Mattfeld, *A Handbook of American Opera Premieres, 1731–1962* (Detroit Studies in Music Bibliography, no. 5, 1963). One-man orchestra, William Dunlap, *History of the American Theatre and Anecdotes of the Principal Actors*, 2nd ed. (1797; repr. 3 vols. in one, New York: Burt Franklin, 1963), vol. 1, 391.

3. Dunlap, ibid., 302.

4. Dunlap, ibid., 101.

5. Shakespeare, Dunlap, ibid., 114. According to Lawrence Levine, *Highbrow/Lowbrow, The Emergence of Cultural Hierarchy in America* (Cambridge, MA: Harvard University Press, 1988), 16, the first documented performance of a Shakespeare play in the United States took place in 1750.

6. Typical English regimental band, see Richard Crawford, *An Introduction to America's Music* (New York: W.W. Norton, 2001), 56–58.

7. For a general history, see entry for "Brass band" in the *New Grove Dictionary of Music and Musicians,* ed. Stanley Sadie (London: Macmillan, 1983); and in greater detail, R. F. Goldman, *The Concert Band*, ch. 2, 18–61, and 62–63. On improvements in brass instruments, see Jon Newsom, "The American Brass Band Movement in the Mid-Nineteenth Century," *The Wind Ensemble and Its Repertoire,* eds. Frank J. Cipolla and Donald Hunsberger (Rochester, NY: University of Rochester Press, 1994), 83–84. Newsom, 8 and 83, starts the era of pure brass bands in 1835, and notes the beginning of its slow decline as early as 1852. Schwartz, *Bands of America,* 105–07, has figures on the increase in wind instruments. And according to Bierley, *The Incredible Band*, 1: Sousa's "group was called a band but could more accurately be termed a wind symphony."

8. On the Dodworth family, their band's prestige, and playing at presidential inaugurations, see Shanet, *Philharmonic,* 8. The U.S. Marine Band, which later dominated public events at the White House, was in these years still a small band and not of first rank. When its first exceptional leader, Francis Scala, joined in 1842, it had only ten or twelve members. See David M. Ingalls, "Francis Scala: Leader of the Marine Band from 1855 to 1871" (master's thesis, Catholic University of America, June 1957), 9. According to Schwartz, *Bands of America*, 169, at President Cleveland's inaugural parade in 1893 seventy-one bands marched. For a brief history of the Dodworth

band as recalled by Harvey B. Dodworth, see *New York Times*, "Band Music Then and Now," 29 June 1879, 10. For some of the band's brief associations with New York's 7th Regiment, see Raoul F. Camus, "Grafulla and Cappa: Bandmasters of New York's Famous Seventh Regiment," in *European Music and Musicians in New York City, 1840–1900,* ed. John Graziano (Rochester, NY: University of Rochester Press, 2006), 198, 205, 208. Groups within the Dodworth Band, John Graziano, "New York Bands in the Nineteenth Century," *The Wind Band in and around New York ca. 1830–1950*, 39–40. For a picture of Harvey B. Dodworth and two of the band's programs, see Graziano, ibid., 44–45.

9. John Sullivan Dwight, "History of Music in Boston," chap. 7 in vol. 4 of *The Memorial History of Boston, including Suffolk County Massachusetts, 1630–1880,* ed. Justin Winsor (Boston: J.R. Osgood and Co., 1880–1881), 422.

10. Allen Dodworth, *Dodworth's Brass Band School: Containing Instructions in the First Principles of Music: Together with a Number of Pieces of Music Arranged for a Full Brass Band* (New York: H. B. Dodworth, 1853). His was not the only such book published. In 1844 Elias Howe issued his *First Part of the Musician's Companion*, which included arrangements of "new and popular pieces" for brass bands of six or eight players. And in 1846 E. K. Eaton published *Twelve Pieces of Harmony for Military Brass Bands*, for brass bands of fifteen plus side drums. Reportedly the earliest such book, with most of its arrangements in three parts, is *The Bellamy Band Book*, in manuscript dated 1799. See Frederick Fennell, *The Civil War, Its Music and Its Sounds*, Mercury Recording 432 591–2, 16.

11. "All-Brass Band," Schwartz, *Bands of America,* 41. See also, Newsom, "American Brass Band Movement in the Mid-Nineteenth Century," 83.

12. Dodworth, *Dodworth's Brass Band School*, 12, 36, 37. For a recording of "The Star-Spangled Banner" arranged by Allen Dodworth for an all-brass band (and also his "Gift Polka" and arrangement of "Home Sweet Home"), see *19th Century American Ballroom Music, Waltzes, Marches, Polkas & Other Dances* (Nonesuch Records H-71313), played by the Smithsonian Social Orchestra & Quadrille Band, James Weaver, director, and using "historical instruments."

13. This drawing, often republished, can be seen in Schwartz, *Bands of America,* 42; in *European Music and Musicians in New York City, 1840–1900,* ed. John Graziano, 200; in John Graziano, "New York Bands in the Nineteenth Century," 43; and in the *New Grove Dictionary of Music and Musicians* at the entry for "brass band." Valveless bugles can sound only the natural harmonics of the instrument's basic note; for example, a typical military B-flat bugle can sound the low B-flat, F, B-flat, D, and upper F. Thus in military calls, pitch being limited, rhythmic variation is important.

14. Dodworth, *Dodworth's Brass Band School*, 33.

15. Bierley, *The Incredible Band*, 8, describes the Sousa's Band characteristic sound as "smooth," and attributes it to Sousa's wish for a uniform clarinet tone to dominate the brass. On playing softly, see Bierley, *John Philip Sousa, American Phenomenon* (Englewood Cliffs, NJ: Prentice-Hall, 1973), 138–39, citing the *Columbus* (Ohio) *Dispatch,* 21 September 1901. "Posts of honor," Frédéric Louis Ritter, *Music in America*, 2nd ed. (New York: Scribner's, 1890), 219, quoting an unidentified critic. For six contrasting views (including "vulgar") on the merits of the cornet

versus the trumpet, see Percy Scholes, *The Oxford Companion to Music* (London: Oxford, 1955), 253; for views uniformly disparaging, see Arthur A. Clappé, *The Wind-Band and Its Instruments* (New York: Holt, 1911), 120–24; for a more positive view, Edwin Franko Goldman, *Band Betterment: Suggestions and Advice to Bands, Bandmasters, and Band-players* (New York: Carl Fischer, 1934), 115–123; and for its "soap-opera" tone, R. F. Goldman, *The Concert Band,* 14–15. For Dwight on the trumpet and improvements in brass instruments, see Jon Newsom, "The American Brass Band Movement," 85–86.

16. Private subscription, *Albion,* 16 July 1859, 343. For the operatic repertory, see appendix 1. Harvey B. Dodworth, "Band Music Then and Now," states that these concerts began the practice of summer concerts in New York's Central Park.

17. *Times,* 9 October 1860, 8.

18. Gems from *Ballo* and *Lombardi,* see Graziano, *European Music and Musicians in New York City,* 4, citing the *Evening Post*, 26 December 1863. Ibid., 212, reprinting a report on the ball from the *Times, 7* January 1874, 5.

19. On Jullien, see Vera Brodsky Lawrence, *Strong on Music*, vol. 2: *Reverberations, 1850–1856, The New York Music Scene in the Days of George Templeton Strong* (Chicago: University of Chicago Press, 1995), 356–79, with illustrations. Also George C. Foreman, "The Remarkable Monsieur Jullien and His Grand American Tour," *The Wind Band in and around New York,* 2–29, with illustrations. And Richard Grant White, *Courier and Enquirer*, 30 August 1853, 3. Lawrence quotes White's review at length.

20. New York *Tribune,* 1 January 1848, quoted in Lawrence, *Strong on Music*, vol. 1: *Resonances, 1836–1850* (New York: Oxford University Press, 1988), 546. For a general account of the four German groups, see Lawrence, ibid., 544–49. For a briefer account, see Katherine K. Preston, "Art Music from 1800 to 1860," *The Cambridge History of American Music,* 201.

21. Gungl and the Saxon band, see Lawrence, ibid., 548–49.

22. The Germania Musical Society, Lawrence, ibid., 546–48, and Preston, "Art Music from 1800 to 1860," 201. There is uncertainty about the number of men in the group. A photo in Lawrence (facing 546) shows twenty-one men, but in text (546) she states twenty-four, and Preston (201) mentions twenty-five. For the group's program in Worcester, Massachusetts, on 5 June 1849, see illustration 18 in Weber's *The Great Transformation of Musical Taste*; on other programs, see page 218.

23. Authorities disagree on the number of Jullien's core players. The *Mirror*, which had interviewed Jullien, states "over twenty solo players," 9 August 1853, 3. Lawrence, *Strong on Music*, vol. 2: *Reverberations*, 359, and Foreman, "The Remarkable Monsieur Jullien," 8, both state twenty-five, and Preston, "Art Music from 1800 to 1860," 205, twenty-seven. Conversely, Schwartz, *Bands of America,* 21, and White, *Courier and Enquirer*, 30 August 1853, 3 (and quoted by Lawrence, 361), state forty. Giovanni Bottesini, the double bass player, had previously toured in the United States with the Italian Opera Company from Havana, and in 1871 in Cairo would conduct the world premiere of *Aida.* On his thirteen operas, see Thomas G. Kaufman, *Verdi and His Major Contemporaries: A Selected Chronology of Performances with Casts* (New York: Garland Press, 1990), 27–30.

24. "Aladdin," *Mirror,* 9 August 1853, 2; "the public may expect something dazzling," *Mirror,* 12 August, 2; "illusion of a fairy scene," 30 August, 2. For the additions to Beethoven's "Pastoral" Symphony, see Lawrence, *Strong on Music,* vol. 2, 359, and to the Fifth Symphony, see *The New Grove Dictionary of Music and Musicians,* entry under "Jullien."

25. Number of concerts, Foreman, "The Remarkable Monsieur Jullien," 13.

26. White, *Courier and Enquirer,* 30 August 1853, 3. Quoted at greater length in John Tasker Howard, *Our American Music: Three Hundred Years of It,* 3rd ed. (New York: Crowell, 1946), 222. For half-column announcements of the season, unprecedented for their day, see the 24 and 27 August 1853 editions of the New York *Tribune,* 1; the *Herald*, 7; and the *Times*, 5. On Jullien's baton, White: "He does everything with that unhappy bit of wood but put it to its legitimate purpose of beating time." The jeweled baton, Schwartz, *Bands of America*, 28–29; and Foreman, "The Remarkable Monsieur Jullien," 7.

27. White, *Courier and Enquirer,* 30 August 1853, 3.

28. The Crystal Palace described, George C. D. Odell, *Annals of the New York Stage*, vol. 6: *1850–1857* (New York: Columbia University Press, 1931), 260–61. The 15 June 1854 concert reviewed, *Albion*, 17 June 1854, 284: [The audience numbered] "20 to 35,000 persons. . . . [The program contained] twenty-four, mostly long, musical pieces. . . . [The building] is not a good Music Hall and not favorable to the conveyance of sound. Add to this the constant swaying to and fro, and the agitation and massive murmurings (unavoidable) of the immense audience, and it will readily be understood why the vocal and instrumental solos met with comparatively little success." The *Tannhäuser* overture, *Albion,* ibid., H. Earle Johnson, *First Performances in America to 1900: Works with Orchestra* (The College Music Society, 1979), 377–78. The Germania Society, Preston, "Art Music from 1800 to 1860," 203.

29. *Tribune,* 21 June 1854, 1.

30. *The Fireman's Quadrille* described in the program, White, *Courier and Enquirer,* 30 August 1853, 3.

31. Barnum, Snug the joiner, *Times,* 16 June 1854, 1. Also, Foreman, "The Remarkable Monsieur Jullien,"12.

32. Reviews, *Times,* 16 June 1854, 1; *Tribune,*16 June 1854, 5. Schwartz, *Bands of America,* 27–28, gives a more lurid account of the quadrille's performance, but without citation. On those who laughed and the singing of the Doxology, see Ezra Schabas, *Theodore Thomas: America's Conductor and Builder of Orchestras, 1835–1905* (Urbana: Illinois University Press, 1988), 10, quoting an apparent eyewitness. Review of the final concert on June 26, *Tribune,* 27 June 1854, 4. For the strange silence, e.g., *Albion,* 17 June 1854, 284, and 1 July 1854, 308. The palace burned on Tuesday, 5 October 1858, the fire starting at 5 p.m. See Foreman, "The Remarkable Monsieur Jullien," 28n41, 28n42. Also, *Herald,* 6 October 1858, 4, and 7 October 1858, 1.

33. In 1854 all music was either sacred or popular, see Weber, *The Great Transformation,* 190.

Chapter Two

Patrick S. Gilmore, His Jubilees, and the "Anvil Chorus"

The United States' Civil War began early on the morning of 12 April 1861 when the state forces of South Carolina fired on those of the federal government stationed at Fort Sumter in Charleston harbor. Those within the fort, though almost out of food and supplies, replied as best they could, and then on the afternoon of the next day surrendered. Within three weeks of the assault, the federal government's War Department in Washington issued its General Order No. 15, authorizing state regiments entering its Union Army to enlist bands in their ranks, but, by Order No. 49, limited the number of players to twenty-four. The department hoped the bands, with parades and concerts, would encourage recruitment—the government had asked for seventy-five thousand volunteers—and, as the regiments doubled in size, become the cores for larger bands, manned in part by players drawn from the ranks. In New York, the Dodworth Band, or part of it, led by Harvey B. Dodworth, joined the state's 71st Regiment and was present at the battle of Bull Run.[1]

In Boston an independent band responding to the call was led by Patrick Sarsfield Gilmore, whose band, though recently founded, was already well known in the Boston area. A talented cornetist, he had come to the city from Ireland in October 1849, and after a variety of jobs in musical groups had joined the Suffolk (Massachusetts) Brass Band. He left it in 1853 to lead the Boston Brigade Band, one of the city's best and oldest, and the one followed in 1825 by the "music-loving boy" who grew up to be the critic and scholar John S. Dwight. But Gilmore, still restless, resigned in 1856 to take over the Salem (Massachusetts) Brass Band, on which he could have a more personal impact. He led the band to the top rank of New England bands, not only musically but as a manager, organizing the popular Fourth of July concerts on Boston Common, which the city later underwrote, and taking the band

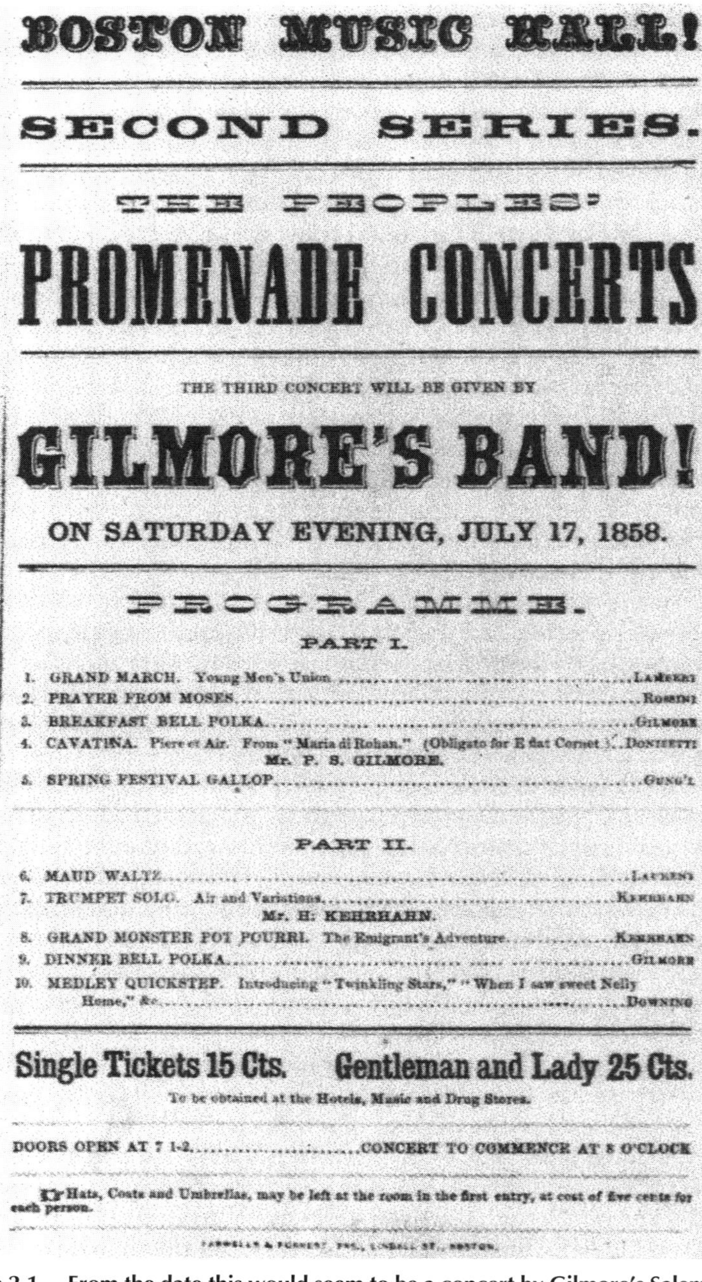

BOSTON MUSIC HALL!

SECOND SERIES.

THE PEOPLES'

PROMENADE CONCERTS

THE THIRD CONCERT WILL BE GIVEN BY

GILMORE'S BAND!

ON SATURDAY EVENING, JULY 17, 1858.

PROGRAMME.

PART I.

1. GRAND MARCH. Young Men's Union .... LAMBERT
2. PRAYER FROM MOSES .... ROSSINI
3. BREAKFAST BELL POLKA .... GILMORE
4. CAVATINA. Piere et Air. From "Maria di Rohan." (Obligato for E flat Cornet.) .. DONIZETTI
Mr. P. S. GILMORE.
5. SPRING FESTIVAL GALLOP .... GUNG'L

PART II.

6. MAUD WALTZ .... LAURENS
7. TRUMPET SOLO. Air and Variations .... KEHRHAHN
Mr. H. KEHRHAHN.
8. GRAND MONSTER POT POURRI. The Emigrant's Adventure .... KEHRHAHN
9. DINNER BELL POLKA .... GILMORE
10. MEDLEY QUICKSTEP. Introducing "Twinkling Stars," "When I saw sweet Nelly Home," &c .... DOWNING

Single Tickets 15 Cts. Gentleman and Lady 25 Cts.

To be obtained at the Hotels, Music and Drug Stores.

DOORS OPEN AT 7 1-2 .... CONCERT TO COMMENCE AT 8 O'CLOCK

☞ Hats, Coats and Umbrellas, may be left at the room in the first entry, at cost of five cents for each person.

Figure 2.1. From the date this would seem to be a concert by Gilmore's Salem Band.

to Washington in 1857 to march in the inaugural parade of President James Buchanan.[2]

Early in 1859, however, Gilmore, with Jullien perhaps in mind, left Salem to organize his own band, which he had well started when the Civil War broke out; whereupon he and twenty-three men, enlisting as a band, joined the Massachusetts 24th Volunteer Regiment.

Such regimental concert bands played for reviews, parades, balls, banquets, and burials, and in battle often served as hospital corpsmen. Their repertory, particularly at the start of the war, was mostly patriotic songs and marches, and less often than before, arrangements from operas. Gilmore's regimental programs apparently are lost, but the part books of another federalized band (twenty-six men stationed at Port Royal, South Carolina, a post held by the Union forces throughout the war) show a repertory of fifty-two works, of which five were operatic in origin, excerpts from Flotow (*Martha*), Verdi (*Ballo*), Weber (*Freischütz*), Wallace (*Maritana*), and Donizetti (*Belisario*). All were arranged as "quicksteps" (instead of 75 steps per minute, 108), a tempo tending to preclude any opera's more soulful numbers. Other popular arrangements of the day played by other bands included, along with some lesser known operatic pieces, selections from *Faust,* airs from *The Magic Flute, Trovatore,* and *Rigoletto,* and the "Anvil Chorus" from *Trovatore*.[3]

In August of 1862, with the war going badly for the Union, Congress discharged all these special bands from their regiments, to the regret of many in the services, for the smaller bands that could be recruited directly from the ranks were less able and inspiring. Thus Gilmore and his twenty-two men (for one had died of typhoid fever) suddenly found themselves back in Boston, where they began again to give concerts with a mixed repertory of popular, serious, and sacred, but with an emphasis on patriotism.[4]

By now, however, Gilmore's talents as an organizer were recognized, and the governor of Massachusetts put him in charge of a program to improve all bands playing for the state's regiments. In this capacity, Gilmore, in 1863, accompanied two bands to Louisiana, then mostly occupied by Union forces and where the Union general Nathaniel S. Banks, also from Massachusetts, was attempting to "reconstruct" the state so that it could resume its place in the federal Congress and Union. Faced with a sullen, hostile population, Banks saw in music a tool to soothe in some small way the people's anger, and saw in Gilmore the man to do it. So Gilmore remained in New Orleans.

While there he accomplished two things, of which the less important and more controversial was perhaps the longer lasting. He composed "When Johnny Comes Marching Home Again," fitting his words, in all likelihood, to an Irish melody and publishing the song under the name Louis Lambert. Or did he? Perhaps the most that can be said is, "Gilmore always claimed the air as his, and no one rose to deny it." Sung in both the North and the South, in popularity it ranked third perhaps only to "Dixie" and "The Battle Hymn of the Republic," and, like them, is still sung.[5]

His other project, an outcome of a series of promenade concerts, was to celebrate the election of the state's first "reconstruction" governor, Michael Hahn, who as a German immigrant to Louisiana, Banks hoped, might be less biased against the North and its forces than most of the state's citizens. For the occasion, a concert in New Orleans's Lafayette Square, Gilmore, consciously or not, imitated Jullien's "Grand Musical Congress." He merged several of his bands into one of five hundred men, assembled a chorus of more than five thousand, recruited chiefly from the city's public schools, and offered a program of patriotic songs, including "America," "The Union Forever," and "The Star-Spangled Banner." The most astonishing and popular number, however, was "Hail, Columbia," the program's spectacular, adorned by the city's church bells and a battery of thirty-six cannon. It was the first of several mass concerts associated with his name.[6]

Shortly thereafter, still only thirty-six, he returned to Boston, started again to create his own band, and soon had a vision (he favored such terms) of how he might organize a national celebration in music to mark the close of the war and the country's return to peace. And it was this Peace Jubilee, ultimately held in Boston in June 1869, that made him a national figure. To fund it, publicize it, and recruit his forces he had to persuade a host of businessmen and musicians, both in and beyond Boston, to back him. Initially he proposed three concerts, for which he would build a temporary hall to seat an audience of 50,000; he would have an orchestra of 1,000 and joint choirs totaling 20,000. And he would invite President Grant and his cabinet to attend. The number of choristers would seem to proclaim the jubilee a choral festival, but then the size of the orchestra and number of bands, with their emphasis on the brass and wind instruments, would seem to imply something else. The mixture of the three was not unusual at the time, when orchestras and bands shared much the same repertory. But the jubilee in spirit was essentially a band concert, in part because Gilmore, the leader, was a bandmaster, in part because the programming was less austere than what, say, the Germania Musical Society typically had scheduled, and in part because of the air of razzle-dazzle in which it clothed itself, projecting its image "with mysterious stories in the Boston papers, framed at first so as to arouse without gratifying curiosity."[7]

In seeking support, Gilmore (see photospread) at first had an easier time with musicians than businessmen, for the musicians saw in the project a chance to educate thousands in the charms of music. His most important recruit in this respect was Eben Tourjee, founder and director of the New

Figure 2.2. Patrick S. Gilmore, circa 1856.

England Conservatory of Music, who agreed to select and supervise a chorus of from ten to twenty thousand persons. Ultimately Tourjee collected some 10,300 choristers from nine states, with 8,500 from Massachusetts, most of the rest from nearby states, and a few hundred from Ohio and Illinois. And because the stage, as built, had seats for only 10,000, extra seats for some thousand choristers had to be added, apparently somewhat apart, at "the promenade in the southern end of the building."[8]

Gilmore, however, according to the Boston *Daily Advertiser,* had far more trouble with the business community: "In one day he called upon seventy business firms and obtained seventy refusals to subscribe." Yet gradually he gathered pledges of "forty thousand dollars—about one quarter of the amount originally estimated as likely to be required." Then at a meeting in mid-March with businessmen, he managed to ignite one with his enthusiasm, Eben D. Jordan, of the Jordan-Marsh Company. Known as a benevolent patron of musical ventures, Jordan agreed to serve as treasurer of a National Peace Jubilee Association, ensuring that his staff of clerks and accountants would oversee the finances—whereupon his example encouraged and shamed others into subscribing. The Erie Railroad, for example, was the first of several to promise half-price fares to attend the concerts, and so, according to Dwight, now editor and publisher of *Dwight's Journal of Music*, a Boston-based biweekly: "The application of Dry Goods and Railroad methods saved the whole. The work was well laid out among responsible committees. The word went forth."[9]

Meanwhile, even though Boston then was considered a leader in the country's musical affairs, Gilmore was shrinking the size of the project. Not only would the chorus be smaller than his original estimate, but also the hall itself. Instead of accommodating 50,000, it would seat only 30,000 (not including the roughly 11,300 chorus members and musicians); and instead of being built on Boston Common, an idea that had roused opposition, it would rise in St. James Park, on Dartmouth Street. On the other hand, to please musicians and educators, he agreed to enlist a second chorus of 7,000 school children and present them in a program of their own, and also to present a number of symphonies on "classical" days. Hence, the number of concerts rose from three to five.

Promptly in March, "The Coliseum," as the hall was named, began to rise, employing over two hundred workmen and requiring huge deliveries of lumber driven daily through the city. Newspapers and journals, in and out of state, reported constantly on the building's progress, on the recruiting for the orchestra and choruses, and on the likely programs. That is, all newspapers except *Dwight's Journal of Music,* which, though it may never had had more than fifteen hundred subscribers, was perhaps the country's most prestigious musical publication. Conspicuously, throughout the period of preparation, it remained silent.[10]

Nevertheless, Dwight followed the preparations closely, and when the concerts began, attended most of them, and ultimately devoted an entire issue to his report. In its eight pages, each with three columns in small type, he quoted at length comments of the Boston *Daily Advertiser,* the *Springfield Republican,* the *New York Sun,* the *New York Tribune,* and included also his own appraisal of the concerts he had written for the *Tribune.* In sum, a review of the jubilee in all aspects.[11]

In his account for the *Tribune*, Dwight, whose biographer described him as a "small man, short, slender, with a most genial face, kindly and benevolent," but "very positive in his opinions"—his idols in music were Beethoven, Bach, and Mozart—imagined the sort of questions anyone might have put to Gilmore in the early stages of the project: "Why have 20,000 voices, when even the grandest of Handelian Choruses are better sung by 1,000?" As he pointed out, in Dusseldorf, Germany, even with Mendelssohn as conductor, such a festival limited itself to seven or eight hundred performers and the programs were presented in "a spirit of sincere, true art and poetry and piety"—whereas, Gilmore's publicity promised "the greatest feast of Sublime and Inspiring Harmony ever heard in any part of the World!" Anyone, or so Dwight suggested, would have concluded that what Gilmore was proposing was a lot of crowd-pleasing "clap-trap."[12] (See photospread.)

Yet Gilmore proved more in step with the public than Dwight. Where the latter sought an audience eager to learn, quiet to listen, and seeking a moral uplift in the music—say, Beethoven's *Eroica* symphony—the American public in 1869 was more earthbound. By its patronage and excitement over Jullien's mass concerts, over Gilmore's festival in New Orleans, and by its interest in every detail of the planned jubilee, it declared that it wanted something huge, like the country and the democracy it was creating; something memorable, a milestone planted in history; and, no less important, something entertaining. It still predominantly thought of music as being either sacred (oratorios, masses, motets,) or popular, with the latter for pleasure, not moral uplift. In this way the jubilee was conceived, and finally the Coliseum (Boston's largest building and raised at a cost of $132,000) was roofed, the orchestra and choruses recruited and rehearsed, and the opening concert set for the afternoon of 15 June.

The program on that first day played to an audience of only 12,000 (seats cost two to five dollars), and it opened with the full chorus, orchestra, and an organ specially built for power blasting forth in Martin Luther's hymn "Ein' feste Burg" (A Mighty Fortress Is Our God). The effect was stunning, the applause tremendous, whereupon an orchestra of six hundred players launched into Wagner's overture to *Tannhäuser*. Then came the Gloria from Mozart's *Twelfth Mass,* sung by the full chorus, with orchestra and organ, which was followed by the Bach-Gounod "Ave Maria," sung by Madame Parepa-Rosa with the violin *obbligato* played by not one but two hundred violinists. Her voice, Dwight later wrote, "penetrated the whole space, although it sounded far off and in miniature, as if heard through the wrong end of an opera glass." To close the concert's first half, "The Star-Spangled Banner" was sung and played by the entire force with the addition of bells and cannon.[13]

According to reviewers, two facts immediately became apparent. First, in a hall of such size the huge chorus sounded no louder than an ordinary full chorus in an ordinary hall. And next, as a critic for the *Springfield Republican* put it, "The adage that large bodies move slowly was proved anew." Because of the swollen chorus, the Mozart Gloria "moved . . . at least one-third too slow." Moreover, the chorus "constantly tended to drag. . . . There is a limit in numbers beyond which the best-drilled chorus becomes unwieldy. . . . Whether that limit is one thousand singers or five thousand is by no means plain, but the chorus at the Boston Jubilee over-reached it."[14]

To open the concert's second half, Gilmore offered "A Hymn of Peace," written by Boston's distinguished Dr. Oliver Wendell Holmes and fitted to the music of Matthias Keller's "American Hymn," sung by the full chorus and backed by the orchestra, organ, and a military band. Then followed Rossini's *William Tell* overture, which the program promised would be played by a "select orchestra of five hundred." Unhappily, according to Dwight, the opening for five solo cellos, though played by sixty, was quite lost in the hall, but the finale, the most familiar of the four sections, fared better. Next, also by Rossini, was the "Inflammatus" from his *Stabat Mater,* sung by Parepa-Rosa, whose voice managed to soar appropriately above the full chorus, organ, and orchestra. Ninth in the program of eleven pieces was the "Coronation March" from Meyerbeer's *Le Prophète,* played by the full orchestra of one thousand—in Dwight's phrase, "business enough for all their throats of brass." And tenth, from Verdi's *Il trovatore,* the "Anvil Chorus," with full chorus, orchestra, band, organ, one hundred anvils, and cannon. To stage the Chorus, Gilmore had a hundred firemen in scarlet uniforms march into the building, then split into files of fifty going to opposite sides of the orchestra, where each man, with a hammer held musket-style to his shoulder, came to a halt behind an anvil. On the conductor's signal, they crashed their hammers down, the anvils clattered, and as the organ thundered and the full orchestra, band, and chorus let forth, the city's bells rang, and Gilmore at appropriate moments pushed buttons which electrically fired canons stationed outside the hall. After which, to close the concert, Gilmore offered "My Country, 'Tis of Thee," played and sung by all the forces with the audience joining on the final stanza.[15]

Though Rossini's "Inflammatus" from the *Stabat Mater* is not from an opera, it is an intense, dramatic aria—sacred chiefly in its words—and so five of the eleven numbers were operatic in nature, two by Rossini, and one each by Wagner, Meyerbeer, and Verdi, with the last's "Anvil Chorus," according to Dwight, causing the concert's "wildest excitement." In contrast, for the second day, with President Grant and many government dignitaries present and the audience now doubled in size, Gilmore scheduled a "Grand Classical Programme," featuring before the intermission choruses from Handel oratorios, a bit of Mozart and of Mendelssohn, and after, as the afternoon's main work, Schubert's Symphony in C. Except that, reportedly at the request of President Grant, before the symphony and without any announcement, "The Star-Spangled Banner" and the "Anvil Chorus" (with all its firemen, bells, anvils, and cannon) were performed. According to Dwight, who was present, "the building shook with thunder of applause; all mood for finer music was destroyed, all fine conditions broken up . . . . the Symphony was killed; knocked on the head by anvils! . . . But it had grown late; people were weary, restless, moving about, or starting homeward, talking aloud, in no mood to listen or let others hear; so the first movement and the Scherzo were omitted."[16]

Quite aside from Gilmore the popularity of the "Anvil Chorus" was countrywide, but his arrangement of it, with bells and cannon, however pleasing to many, stirred some harsh criticism, much of which has stuck to the chorus and perhaps unfairly. It is not just a happy tune but an imaginative work, carefully constructed and orchestrated. It opens with an orchestral introduction in E minor, followed by a downward phrase for the chorus in G major that steadily mounts the scale only to fall back and end with a strong offbeat. Then the main tune enters, surprisingly not in the expected A major but in C major, a sudden shift described by one Verdi enthusiast as "electric in the theatre." The scholar Julian Budden stresses the "abruptness of the motifs themselves," "the wandering key scheme," and "the frequent shifts of the principal accent from first to third beat of the bar . . . where the men strike their anvils in alternation, tenors on the weak beats, basses on the strong." Seemingly, despite the criticism by Dwight and others, the tunes in their simplicity have strength and are well presented.[17]

The jubilee's third concert, titled "The People's Day," again scheduled the "Anvil Chorus," which—despite Dwight's complaint that the anvils, for all their number, had a "toy-like sound, jingle of sleigh-bells rather than the honest Vulcan *ring*"—was proving to be the jubilee's most memorable work. And on the fourth day, though not scheduled, it was the cause of a considerable interruption. The program announced as the featured work Beethoven's Fifth Symphony, but in performance, like Schubert's symphony, it was shorn of its first and third movements. There then remained on the program only Handel's "Hallelujah Chorus," but before it could begin—as Dwight later reported—"Think not that *all* those 20,000 people came there without some inward assurance that the Anvil Chorus would appear and take its throne as matter of course, by divine right of its own, divine right of disorder! Loud was the clamor for it. Fortunately, the means and men for it were absent." But the uproar and confusion, the uncertainty and delay, upset the singers and damped the spirit of their "Hallelujahs."[18]

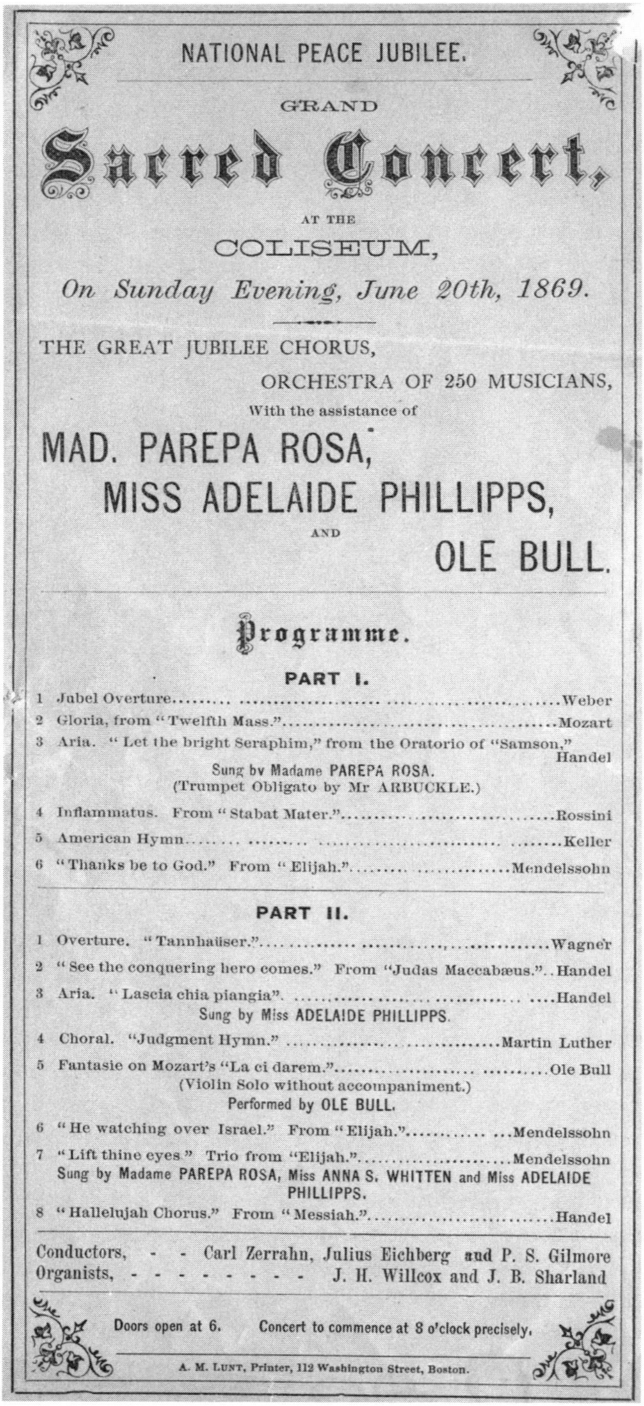

NATIONAL PEACE JUBILEE.

GRAND

Sacred Concert,

AT THE

COLISEUM,

On Sunday Evening, June 20th, 1869.

THE GREAT JUBILEE CHORUS,

ORCHESTRA OF 250 MUSICIANS,

With the assistance of

MAD. PAREPA ROSA,

MISS ADELAIDE PHILLIPPS,

AND

OLE BULL.

Programme.

PART I.

1 Jubel Overture.......................Weber
2 Gloria, from "Twelfth Mass."......................Mozart
3 Aria. "Let the bright Seraphim," from the Oratorio of "Samson," Handel
Sung by Madame PAREPA ROSA.
(Trumpet Obligato by Mr ARBUCKLE.)
4 Inflammatus. From "Stabat Mater."......................Rossini
5 American Hymn......................Keller
6 "Thanks be to God." From "Elijah."......................Mendelssohn

PART II.

1 Overture. "Tannhaüser."......................Wagner
2 "See the conquering hero comes." From "Judas Maccabæus."..Handel
3 Aria. "Lascia chia piangia"......................Handel
Sung by Miss ADELAIDE PHILLIPPS.
4 Choral. "Judgment Hymn."......................Martin Luther
5 Fantasie on Mozart's "La ci darem."......................Ole Bull
(Violin Solo without accompaniment.)
Performed by OLE BULL.
6 "He watching over Israel." From "Elijah."......................Mendelssohn
7 "Lift thine eyes." Trio from "Elijah."......................Mendelssohn
Sung by Madame PAREPA ROSA, Miss ANNA S. WHITTEN and Miss ADELAIDE PHILLIPPS.
8 "Hallelujah Chorus." From "Messiah."......................Handel

Conductors, - - - Carl Zerrahn, Julius Eichberg and P. S. Gilmore
Organists, - - - - - - - - J. H. Willcox and J. B. Sharland

Doors open at 6. Concert to commence at 8 o'clock precisely.

A. M. LUNT, Printer, 112 Washington Street, Boston.

Figure 2.3. Sacred Concert, 20 June 1869. University of Maryland Libraries.

In his comprehensive appraisal of the jubilee, Dwight's chief complaint was the "incongruity" of the programming. "Musically, the Jubilee had its chief triumphs in precisely those selections which were the least purely musical, of no account as Art, no interest to earnest music lovers." Moreover, the size of the forces combined with the size of the hall were detrimental. "Music," he declared, "has its limits," and the symphonies and overtures in particular failed to achieve "their effect." Yet, in the execution of the music, there was "much to praise. In the great chorus there was far more unity, precision, light and shade in rendering than almost any one of musical experience could have believed possible. . . . Generally, the grave, slow Chorals sounded best." He concluded:

> Whether the Festival considered musically were very good or not, it musically *did* good. At any rate to all those singers and performers. It was a great experience for them. It has given them a new impulse, a new consciousness of strength, a new taste of the joy of unity of effort, a new love of cooperation, and a deeper sense of the divine significance and power of music than they ever had. It has caused hundreds of choral societies to spring into existence for the time being, many of which will certainly prove permanent. . . . Finally, in a still wider way it has done good. It has given to tens of thousand of all classes (save, unfortunately, the poorest), who were there to hear, and, through them, to thousands more, to whole communities, a new belief in Music; a new conviction of its social worth; above all, of its importance as a pervading, educational and fusing element in our whole democratic life. . . . It has done incalculable good.[19]

And in that opinion, critics, scholars, and historians all seem to agree. As Michael Broyles recently concluded: "Whatever their musical value, and that was hotly debated in the nineteenth century, monster festivals built audiences for art music." And not long after the last note was sounded, Mother Nature, as if to put her seal on the affair, blew a gale, and the coliseum collapsed, destroying the unique organ. Yet even so, the jubilee as a whole, no doubt to the surprise of many, returned a profit of $7,000—even after, reportedly, Gilmore received for services almost $40,000.[20]

Excited perhaps by the figures, he already was planning a similar jubilee in New York to celebrate the centennial of Beethoven's birth, 1770. Instead of building a coliseum, he hired one known familiarly as the Third Avenue Rink, which could seat perhaps as many as twenty thousand, announced an orchestra of "550 virtuosi" in addition to his band and a chorus from at least nineteen societies and opera companies for a total of "3,165 voices." In the opening concert, however, though the full orchestra performed Weber's overture to *Der Freischütz,* only 350 "selected instrumentalists" played the chief work, Beethoven's Fifth Symphony, and the full chorus seems to have sung only in the two closing numbers, Handel's "Hallelujah Chorus" and "The Star-Spangled Banner."

In six days, 13–18 June 1870, he gave ten concerts, during which the programs, with admission lowered on the third day, veered steadily toward a more operatic repertory. By the centennial's end, because he had played of Beethoven only the Fifth Symphony twice and the *Fidelio* overture once, the critic for the *Tribune* referred to the event merely as a festival. In all, Wagner, not yet popular, was represented only by the overture to *Rienzi* and Weber by the overtures to *Der Freischütz* and *Oberon* (twice), but even combined they were outnumbered by selections from Flotow's *Martha* and *Stradella.* The two most frequently heard composers were Rossini and Verdi, the former with his "Inflammatus" and the overture and a trio from *William Tell,* and Verdi with selections from *Ernani, Attila, Rigoletto, Trovatore,* and *I vespri siciliani.* From *Trovatore,* in addition to the final act's miserere and "slumber duet," the "Anvil Chorus," with fifty anvils, organ, cannon, and full chorus, appeared on at least seven of the programs, and once, when the audience began to cheer and wave handkerchiefs in its midst, received an encore. According to a critic present, on the repeat the cannon were in better tempo.[21]

Undaunted, Gilmore planned an even larger festival for 1872, again in Boston, a World Peace Jubilee, to celebrate "a union of all nations in harmony," and more particularly the close of the Franco-Prussian War in 1870, which had been waged "with all the improved machinery of death." This time he would build a larger hall, double his forces, have an orchestra of 1,000 as well as a band of 1,000, a chorus of 20,000, charge five dollars a ticket, and schedule fifteen days of concerts instead of five. To provide the international flavor, he would recruit the best bands of Europe and its most distinguished soloists, and remarkably, at the opening afternoon concert, 17 June 1872, he had on hand, besides a distinguished roster of soloists, twenty-nine American bands, the English Grenadier Guard Band (fifty-eight members), the French Garde Républicaine (fifty-three), the Prussian Grenadier Regiment Band (forty-eight), and from Vienna, in person, the "Waltz King," Johann Strauss Jr. As events proved, the three foreign military bands and Strauss gave the jubilee its greatest success, for otherwise, in the opinion of Dwight, most critics, and even members of the chorus, the affair was a musical hodgepodge and for the most part an artistic failure.[22]

In its programming, Gilmore attempted less. This time there were no "classical days" with symphonic excerpts; indeed no symphonic excerpts at all. Operatic excerpts, however, were again plentiful, generally comprising between a third and a half of each program. (For details of these and the Strauss waltz repertory, see appendix 3.) This timse the Handelian choruses did less well, for the doubled chorus proved twice as hard to keep together, and while singing "All We Like Sheep Have Gone Astray," proved the text, provoking audience laughter. And on "God Save the Queen," another disaster: The conductor, according to several members of the chorus, ignored the printed directions for when the chorus should rise and begin to sing. Summoning them to stand sooner than expected, they straggled up, as a chorister reported, "in mortified confusion," and upon entering "at the marked place," he treated them "like children," bid them to "be silent," causing the New York critics to "sneer at the failure," and "the rest of the performance goes into history a wretched fiasco."[23]

Many chorus members, disappointed in the festival, departed before its end. One, when interviewed, echoed the critics: "We think the incessant performance of the Anvil Chorus [sung at almost every concert, including the 'English,' 'French,' and 'German' Days] a blunder. The best of music becomes tiresome, and if it is poor—Heaven help us!" Another added: "The opera music we object to altogether. It may be very fine to have the chorus read it at sight, but we don't care to do it often. . . . Choral and concerted sacred music is our only forte." After the first week, the number of choristers turning up for performance, by Dwight's estimate, had halved, dropping from eighteen to nine thousand. And adding financial injury to artistic failure, though Gilmore this time received $50,000 for his work, the jubilee's deficit ultimately totaled "$150,000, to be paid out of the Guarantee Fund."[24]

The foreign military bands, however, all proved exceptional, as did Strauss, conducting a small part of the huge orchestra in such favorites as *The Blue Danube*, *Tales from the Vienna Woods*, *The Pizzicato Polka*, and *Wine, Women and Song*. The New York *Weekly Review*, commented: "We have learned something from Herr Johann Strauss. . . . It has been our practice to play waltzes too fast." Moreover, the "dizzy pace" of American bands and orchestras failed to allow the waltz "that variety of expression without which the performance is mere mechanism." Thus Strauss, as a conductor, proved his waltzes more musical and significant than most Americans had believed.

He also became the celebrity of the jubilee; thin, elegant, dynamic, with moustache, whiskers, and a full head of jet-black hair, he stirred feminine interest. Offstage he and his wife, according to the Chicago critic George Upton, were charming, a couple who divided their household duties. He "spent most of his time smoking, card-playing, and receiving visitors," while she answered the many notes he received from ladies asking for his autograph or a lock of his hair. And in reply, she would sign his name and snip a wisp of black hair from her poodle.[25]

Of the three foreign bands, which each day in splendid uniform marched into the coliseum to take their places, the most popular and critically approved was the French Garde Républicaine. (For its typical repertory, see "French"

Day in appendix 3.) Besides its superb soloists, it was the most praised, in part, because it achieved the greatest variety of expression, and because of its balance of woodwinds to brass, twenty-seven (of which nine were clarinets) to twenty-five, and also one bass drum, cymbals, and two side drums. The sound, while just as full and deep as American bands where the brass at this time usually outnumbered the woodwinds by three to one, was smoother, more lush and beautiful. Moreover, nothing was considered beyond the scope of the Garde Républicaine. Its purpose, according to an article in *Dwight's Journal,* was to reproduce "in military music all the dispositions of ordinary music, increased considerably in sonority, inasmuch as military music is so often called upon to be played in the open air, and its warlike qualities are its first requisite."[26]

Yet many left the jubilee disappointed. Some regretted the lack of symphonic music, some the misperformance of the choral music, and some the operatic emphasis. By 1872, it seems, the general public's desires in music were changing from a delight in hearing a mixture of all kinds to a desire to hear the different kinds in their best settings. But what many took away with pleasure was the conviction that the European bands, in their size, skills, soloists, balance of woodwinds and brass, and even in their repertory, were simply better than the American bands. And one of those most impressed was Gilmore, who, for the next twenty years, would devote himself almost entirely to creating such a band in the United States.

But before then he had a commitment to honor, a commitment made while he was still recruiting forces for the International Peace Jubilee and before its partial artistic failure. The new stage would be Chicago, and the occasion would mark the city's return to life and leadership after its fire of 1871—a fire in a city built of wood which had killed several hundred people, rendered some 90,000 homeless, and destroyed some 200 million dollars' worth of property. Nevertheless, within a year Chicago, "the city of GO," was rebuilding in stone and steel, ready to celebrate, and its committees had planned a three-day festival, 5–7 June 1873. Commented *Brainard's Musical World,* published in Cleveland, "Chicago, as usual, is trying to do the *unusual* thing. She is always inclined to be somewhat sensational. Even the great fire was by some looked upon as a capital advertisement for the city, expensive though it was." And for its great occasion, the city's festival committee planned to use as an auditorium the new passenger station of the Lake Shore Railroad, a narrow hall, nearly two city blocks long, which could accommodate some 40,000 people. Moreover, they had recruited in advance an orchestra of some 300, a chorus of 1,000, as well as a chorus of 1,000 schoolchildren, all of which would be added to the band led by the man himself, the now nationally famous Patrick S. Gilmore.[27]

He, or so his actions suggest, was no longer stirred by such festivals. He brought to Chicago only about half his band, some thirty men, and did not arrive in the city until the evening of 3 June. His band came even later, on the evening of the next day, less than twenty-four hours before the first performance and with little or no time for joint rehearsal.

The program, however, was simpler even than in Boston in 1872. No piano or vocal soloists, only the massed singing and playing of the more successful numbers of previous festivals: from Handel's *Messiah,* the "Hallelujah Chorus"; from Haydn's *The Creation,* "The Heavens Are Telling"; "The Star-Spangled Banner"; "The American Hymn"; and the Gloria from Mozart's *Twelfth Mass*. Initially, Gilmore and the committee disagreed about the "Anvil Chorus." The committee in charge wanted it just as in Boston, with anvils, cannon, and bells. According to one historian, however, Gilmore "tried to beg out of it," but finally compromised on a performance with anvils, but no cannon or bells.

The Chicago jubilee's first night opened with a commissioned work, "New Chicago Hymn of Praise," included the "Anvil Chorus," with "all the anvils Gilmore could beg or borrow on the South side," and closed with the audience joining in the hymn "Nearer My God to Thee." The acoustics, as feared, proved dreadful. With the orchestra and chorus massed at one end of the long, narrow hall, with stone and concrete floor, walls, and ceiling, the sound bounced from side to side, producing a jumble of echoes. For the second concert, Gilmore moved his forces to the middle of the hall, but its narrowness required him to stretch his band and chorus along the side wall, too far from him to hear or control. For the third concert, when the additional children's choir of a thousand was added, so, too, in an effort to reduce the hall's reverberations, were many more flags and bunting in the ceiling. But the difficulties were not cured. Throughout, Gilmore smiled, audiences cheered, and at the festival's end the local citizens declared it a great success. Yet the local historian, George P. Upton, comparing it to the two Boston jubilees, called it "an insignificant affair," and even Gilmore's enthusiastic biographer, Marwood Darlington, declared it artistically "of no consequence."

The jubilee closed, however, with a ball, held in the city's new Chamber of Commerce and advertised as "the most magnificent and select social affair ever given in the country." For the evening Gilmore provided three orchestras, one for the dance, one for the promenades, and one for "the collation." As Upton observed, "It was worth while living here then. . . . All citizens were 'distinguished' in Chicago's early days, all balls were '*recherché,*' all suppers were 'collations,' and all the ladies were 'the fairest daughters of our city.'"[28]

Gilmore, seemingly relieved to have the venture over, hurried back to Boston, and contrary to expectations, never staged another jubilee. Rather, he set about creating, in imitation of the Garde Républicaine, the best military band in the United States.

NOTES

1. General Orders No. 15 and No. 49, 4 May 1861 and 3 August 1861; Fennell, *The Civil War: Its Music and Its Sounds,* 8–9. Dodworth Band, interview with Harvey B. Dodworth, "Band Music Then and Now, *Times,* 29 June 1879, 10.

2. Gilmore's early career, Frank J. Cipolla, "Patrick S. Gilmore: The Boston Years," *American Music* 6, no. 3 (Fall 1998): 281–92. His war service, Marwood Darlington, *Irish Orpheus: The Life of Patrick S. Gilmore, Bandmaster Extraordinary* (Philadelphia: Olivier Maney Klein, Co., 1950), 23–36. For general history of Gilmore, see Leon Mead, "The Military Bands of the United States," *Harper's Weekly,* 28 September 1899, 786.

3. The ephemerality of band arrangements, Jon Newsom, "The American Brass Band Movement in the Mid-Nineteenth Century," 86. Also, Hitchcock, *Music in the United States: A Historical Introduction,* 114: "Band music was seldom published as such; because of the lack of a standard band instrumentation each band usually made its own arrangements." The Port Royal band books, Library of Congress, Music Division, under Band Music for the Civil War Era, the Port Royal band books, at http://memory.loc.gov/ammem/cwmhtml/cwmhome.htnl. The band had seven woodwinds, seventeen brasses, and two drums, large and small. Other band arrangements, same source.

4. Darlington, *Irish Orpheus,* 30–31.

5. Darlington, ibid., 35. Also, George P. Upton, *Musical Memories: My Recollections of Celebrities of the Half Century 1850–1900* (Chicago: McClurg, 1908), 195–96. Stating that Gilmore received royalties on the song, Schwartz, *Bands of America,* 52. Also Cipolla, "Patrick S. Gilmore: The Boston Years," 286–87, and 292n18.

6. New Orleans concert, Darlington, *Irish Orpheus,* 33–35; Upton, *Musical Memoirs,* 195; Cipolla, "Patrick S. Gilmore: The Boston Years," 284–86; and thirty-six cannon, Broyles, "Art Music from 1860–1920," 233, citing Ronald L. Davis, *A History of Music in American Life,* vol. 2, 1.

7. Original plan for the jubilee and its style of publicity, *Dwight's Journal,* 3 July 1869, 8, 57, republishing an article from the Boston *Daily Advertiser,* 15 June 1869. Also, Dwight's similar comment, ibid., 61. And Darlington, *Irish Orpheus,* 40.

8. *Dwight's Journal,* ibid.; Cipolla, "Patrick S. Gilmore: The Boston Years," 287.

9. *Dwight's Journal,* ibid., 57; and Dwight, ibid., 61.

10. Boston as the country's musical leader, Michael Broyles, "*Music of the Highest Class": Elitism and Populism in Antebellum Boston* (New Haven: Yale University Press, 1992), 8, 13. Darlington, *Irish Orpheus,* 44. Dwight's "small circle of subscribers," Irving Sablosky, *What They Heard: Music in America, 1843–1881, from the*

Pages of Dwight's Journal of Music (Baton Rouge: Louisiana State University Press, 1986), 6. Also, Preston, "Art Music from 1800 to 1860," 207, and Broyles, ibid., 306: "The precise circulation of the journal has never been ascertained."

11. *Dwight's Journal,* 3 July 1869, 57–64.

12. George Willis Cooke, *John Sullivan Dwight: Brook-Farmer, Editor, and Critic of Music* (1899; repr. New York: Da Capo Press, 1969), 265. And Sablosky, *What They Heard,* introduction, 6. Dwight republishing his own report to the *New York Tribune, Dwight's Journal*, 3 July 1869, 60.

13. Luther's chorale and Parepa-Rosa, Dwight, ibid., 61–62.

14. The choruses, the *Springfield Republican,* quoted in *Dwight's Journal,* 3 July 1869, 57–58, and Darlington, *Irish Orpheus,* 42–43.

15. Darlington, ibid., 52–53 prints the program. The cellos, Dwight in his report to the *Tribune, Dwight's Journal*, ibid., 62. Meyerbeer, Dwight, ibid.

16. "Wildest excitement," Dwight, ibid., 62. President Grant and the "Anvil Chorus," Dwight, ibid., 62; Upton, *Musical Memories,* 199.

17. "Electric," Spike Hughes, *Famous Verdi Opera: An Analytical Guide for the Opera-Goer and Armchair Listener* (London: Robert Hale, 1968), 140. Julian Budden, *The Operas of Verdi*, vol. 2: *From* Il Trovatore *to* La Forza del destino (London: Cassell, 1978), 81–82.

18. Clamor for the anvils, Dwight, *Dwight's Journal,* 3 July 1869, 62.

19. Dwight, ibid., 57–64; and on the programs, performance numbers, and the chorales, 63.

20. Broyles, "Art Music from 1860 to 1920," 235. Profit of $7,000, Mead, "The Military Bands of the United States," 786, and Schwartz, *Bands of America,* 69; Gilmore's pay and the gale, Darlington, *Irish Orpheus,* 57.

21. Reviews from the *Times* and the *Tribune,* 13–18 June, 1870. See also Mark Curtis McKnight, "Music Criticism in the *New York Times* and the *New York Tribune*, 1851–1876" (PhD diss., Louisiana State University, 1980; University Microfilms International, 8103641), 349–51. Cannon in tempo, *Times,* 18 June 1870, 5.

22. Dedication of the World Peace Jubilee, Darlington, *Irish Orpheus,* 59, quoting Gilmore's announcement to the press. On Strauss and his orchestra, there is disagreement. Schwartz, *Bands of America,* 70, Darlington, ibid., and Cipolla, "Patrick S. Gilmore: The Boston Years," 289, all state he brought his own orchestra. But Dwight, *Dwight's Journal,* 27 July 1872, 278, reports that he used what "he found before him," and the *Times,* 17 June 1872, 2, prints as a "Correction," following an interview with Strauss, that he did not bring his own orchestra and cannot understand how the rumor started.

23. "Gone astray," Schwartz, *Bands of America,* 71; Darlington, *Irish Orpheus,* 72; and Upton, *Musical Memories,* 202. Another fiasco on "The Star Spangled Banner," see Darlington, ibid., 72, and Upton, ibid., 199. "God Save the Queen," *Dwight's Journal,* 29 June 1872, 261, republishing "What the Chorus Thinks of Itself," first published in the Boston *Daily Advertiser,* 21 June 1870.

24. "What the Chorus Thinks," *Dwight's Journal,* ibid. On the "Anvil Chorus," Boston *Daily Evening Transcript,* 21 June 1872, 2, "given now *ad nauseam.*" Chorus halved, Dwight, *Dwight's Journal,* 13 July 1872, 271. Also, ibid., 27 July 1872,

278. Gilmore's fee, Schwartz, *Bands of America,* 71. The deficit, *Brainard's Musical World* vol. 9, no. 104 (August 1872), 118. One reason for the deficit was a storm that knocked down the planned larger hall when only partially built, requiring debris to be cleared and work to begin again, this time on a simpler hall. The unexpected expense was estimated at $30,000 to $40,000. See *Times* report, 29 April 1872, 8, "From the *Boston Advertiser*, April 27."

25. *Weekly Review,* 18 July 1872, republished as "The True Waltz Tempo—Strauss in New York," *Dwight's Journal,* 27 July 1872, 76. Also, the Boston *Daily Advertiser,* "The Jubilee—A Retrospect," republished in *Dwight's Journal*, ibid., 275. For an account of Strauss conducting, violin in hand, see Upton, *Musical Memories,* 203. Also, *Brainard's Musical World*, vol. 9, no. 104 (August 1872), 117, and vol. 10, no. 116 (August 1873), 118. The poodle, Upton, *Musical Memories,* 204.

26. The French band, Dwight, *Dwight's Journal,* 29 June 1872, 264; its purpose, 277. Also, ibid., 263, republishing a comment by the weekly Worcester *Palladium.* And *Brainard's Musical World* vol. 10, no. 112 (April 1873), 52–53.

27. Chicago and other Midwestern cities eager to have jubilees, *Brainard's Musical World* vol. 10, no. 109 (January 1873), 3.

28. Schwartz, *Bands of America,* 73. "Insignificant," Upton, *Musical Memories,* 197, and Darlington, *Irish Orpheus,* 76. Chicago in early days, Upton, ibid.

Chapter Three

Mr. Gilmore and His 22nd Regiment Band

The jubilees had made Gilmore famous or, depending on opinion, notorious, but everyone, on hearing he was back in Boston, began to speculate on what he might do next. Boston, after two jubilees seemed unlikely to stage a third, but there were other cities and occasions that might want one, and Philadelphia, which was planning to celebrate the country's centennial in the summer of 1876, seemed the most likely.

Gilmore, however, started negotiations in another direction, and in April 1873 *Brainard's Musical World,* a monthly published in Cleveland, reported to its readers:

> When Gilmore invited the foreign bands to come over and play for our entertainment at the Boston hubbub, we believed he had simply the Jubilee in view. Events prove this, however, to have been different. While yet deeply engaged in the managing of the Jubilee, he had already an eye to future operations. First, he gives us an opportunity to hear these foreign bands, and then he proposed to our Government the establishment of just such a band, which is to represent us abroad, whenever they get up a Jubilee in Europe. The Marine Band is but a miserable failure when compared with these red-coated, red-panted, spiked-headed fellows. We suppose the new band was to be called the "Washington-Gilmore-Columbia Band." Thus Gilmore would be the chief musician of all the land, and might beat time with a stick ornamented with the U.S. eagle, while he could flourish in uniform, and would be addressed as the "Captain of the Musical Guards of all these United States."[1]

The journal's anonymous critic plainly viewed the prospect with distaste, warning of a day when all musical manuscripts, before being published, might need Gilmore's approval and a censor might be put on every music journal to ensure no comment "against His Excellency." So his conclusion

ACADEMY OF MUSIC!

Tuesday Ev'g, November 18, 1873.

FIRST APPEARANCE OF

GILMORE'S

22d REGIMENT BAND!

SIXTY-FIVE PERFORMERS,

UNDER THE DIRECTION OF

P. S. GILMORE,

Projector and General Director of the Great Musical Jubilees held in Boston in 1869 and 1872.

SOLOISTS AND PRINCIPAL INSTRUMENTALISTS

M. ARBUCKLE, Cornet,

H. A. LEFEBRE, Saxophone. E. LETSCH, Baritone.

P. DIEZ, Trumpet; C. SIEDLER, Flute; H. GOORTELMEYER, Oboe; J. KOCHKELLER, E flat Clarinet; C. KEGEL and F. WENDELSCHAEFER, B flat Clarinets; W. E. BULESCHA, Soprano Cornet; F. GEWALT, Horn; WILLIAM SAUL, Trombone; LOUIS FRIEDRICH, Fagotti; CONRAD LISTMANN, Tuba; SIGISMUND BERNSTEIN, Tympani.

PROGRAMME.

PART I.

1.—MARCH, "Salute to New York," (first time.) - P. S. GILMORE.
Respectfully Dedicated to the citizens of New York.
GILMORE'S 22D REG'T BAND, 65 PERFORMERS.

2.—OVERTURE, "Semiramide," - - - - - ROSSINI.
BAND.

3.—SOLO FOR CORNET, "7th aire et varie," - - - DE BERIOT.
M. ARBUCKLE, with full Band accompaniment.

4.—REMINISCENCES OF VARIOUS OPERAS, - - - BELLINI.
Introducing variation on "Non-piu Mesta," for Clarinet. Played by the twelve principal Clarinetists of the Band in unison; the closing cadenza, by Mr. Carl Kegel; also an aria for Baritone, from Robert Bruce, played by W. F. Letsch.
BAND.

5.—CONCERT POLKA, for Cornets, in unison, - - - ARBAN.
Messrs. ARBUCKLE, DIETZ, LEHMANN, KALTENBORN, DAVIS, LEIBOLDT, BURMEISTER, and GILMORE.

INTERMISSION 15 MINUTES.

PART II.

1.—MARCH, "22d Regiment," (first time.) - - P. S. GILMORE.
Respectfully Dedicated to the officers and members of the 22d Regiment.
FULL BAND AND DRUM CORPS.

2.—OVERTURE, "Der Freischutz," - - - - - - WEBER.
BAND.

3.—SOLO FOR SAXOPHONE, "Fantasie air Suisse," - SINGELEE.
EDWARD A. LEFEBRE.

4.—GRAND SELECTIONS FROM MARTHA, - - - FLOTOW.
Introducing the Last Rose of Summer, and the principal gems of the Opera.
BAND.

5.—INTERNATIONAL POT POURRI, introducing the "Star Spangled Banner," "Hail Columbia," "German Fatherland," "Russian Hymn," "The Marseillaise," "God save the Queen," "The Harp that once through Tara's Halls," and "Yankee Doodle," with brilliant variations.
BAND.

ADMISSION, ONE DOLLAR.

Reserved Seats 50 cents extra. Doors open at 7, Concert at 8.

Figure 3.1. Gilmore's inaugural concert with his 22nd Regiment Band. *The Guidon* no. 1, 18 November 1873.

was joyful: "But then Gilmore didn't get the place." And he closed with the common query, "What next?"

By midsummer of 1873, Gilmore had signed a contract with New York's 22nd Regiment, stationed in New York, with an armory on Fourteenth Street near Sixth Avenue. Of the regiments based in the city for social and military prestige it perhaps was second only to the 7th, which already had an excellent band. To match it, the 22nd agreed to clothe in colorful uniforms a band of sixty-five musicians of Gilmore's choosing, to pay him and the band for certain services, mostly to be performed in the armory or on parade, and otherwise to leave him free to support himself and the band with whatever engagements or tours he could arrange. In three months he had recruited a band, hired several distinguished soloists, and set his inaugural concert for 16 November at the Academy of Music.[2]

Though the announcement gave its largest type to "22d Regiment Band!," Gilmore's name directly above, set in heavy bold type, was no less prominent. Four of the ten works scheduled were operatic in origin: Rossini's overture to *Semiramide,* "Reminiscences of Various Operas" by Bellini, Weber's overture to *Freischütz*, and "Grand Selections" from Flotow's *Martha.* The balance of the program offered a solo for cornet and one for saxophone, a polka for eight cornetists (including Gilmore), a medley of national anthems, and two new marches by Gilmore, one of which he dedicated to "the officers and members of the 22d regiment" and the other, to open the concert, a "Salute to New York."[3]

The reviews next morning were favorable. The *Herald,* for one, proclaimed Gilmore's "experiment . . . deserves success. It was the inauguration of a new military band, selected from the best materials that this country can supply, and designed in time . . . to approach near to or reach the standard of the best European bands, a favorable example of which we have had here in the band of the Garde Républicaine, of Paris."

The reviewer continued, writing mostly of the operatic numbers, which he seemed to consider the most important:

> The band distinguished themselves in the overture to *Semiramide,* and the brilliant music of Rossini in their hands lost none of its lustre. The opening bars of the overture of *Der Freischütz* were marred to some extent by the want of promptness *en attaque,* but the syncopated measures of the second part were given with precision and *esprit.* The band warmed up as they penetrated further into the intricacies and golden regions of this immortal overture, and the *finale* was interpreted in the most eloquent manner. . . . The band made a very pretty appearance in their fanciful uniforms and opportunities were given to show their proficiency in military drill.[4]

Building on success, Gilmore promptly announced for 22 November, "the first of the series of GRAND PROMENADE CONCERTS" on Saturday evening at the regiment's armory, repeating on request the inaugural concert's program. And for the next week, the program offered selections from Meyerbeer's opera *Il crociato in Egitto,* Strauss's *Blue Danube* waltz, and Weber's *Jubel* overture.

Meanwhile, of course, other bands were competing for attention, and one of the most notable events of the winter of 1874 was a charity ball, hosted by the 7th Regiment at the Academy of Music on Twelfth Night, 6 January. The band, led by Claudio S. Grafulla, was smaller than Gilmore's, numbering only fifty, but thought by many to be equally good, and throughout the city Grafulla was a well-known, popular figure. Like Gilmore, he conducted a series of weekly promenade concerts at his regiment's armory, at the time still on Third Avenue between Sixth and Seventh Streets. The charity ball at the Academy of Music, however, was something special, and its program, besides Suppé's overture to *Banditenstreiche* and selections from Rossini's *La donna del lago,* included among its promenades, scheduled between the twenty dances, selections from Verdi's *Nabucco, Attila, Trovatore, Luisa Miller,* and *Ernani.* In all, opera provided seven of the twenty-three works announced, or, as seemed usual in the early 1870s, about a third of the program.[5]

Gilmore, however, outpaced all competitors in enterprise. For the summer of 1875 he rented P. T. Barnum's Hippodrome, an arena for horse shows of various kinds, and transformed it into a summer garden, modeled to some extent on Vienna's Volksgarten, where Johann Strauss presided. In New York's Hippodrome, as the *Times* reported: "Where the horses were accustomed to career round the arena will be a splendid promenade, grottos, arbors, and rustic bowers will take the place of stables and dressing-rooms, and the late abodes of Mr. Barnum's collection of wild beasts will be given over to bars and restaurants." At one end of the garden would be a huge cascade, water pouring from a cave and falling over rocks to a pool surrounded by palm trees. In addition to the promenade around the garden's rim, in the center Gilmore planned seating for an audience of 2,500, to face an octagonal bandstand in the garden's center. The whole would be brilliantly lit at night by "2000 lights of the most variegated colors," all reinforced by "twenty-four large reflectors on the outer space of the ellipse, and fourteen in the inner."[6]

For the season Gilmore increased the band from 65 to a 101, "which exceeds the number in any other band of the kind," and in imitation of the Garde Républicaine increased the proportion of woodwinds. Seeking to soften the band's tone and increase its ability to imitate the sound of strings, he even hired some clarinetists direct from the French band. Ultimately he had 60 woodwinds, 37 brass, and 4 percussion, and his aim, reported the *Times*, was "to furnish the most popular music, rather than the severely classical, and people are to be supplied with music which they can understand, or at least appreciate." And yet on 4 June, in his varied style, besides a familiar fantasia on Meyerbeer's *Le Prophète* he played two less well known operatic selections, an overture by Suppé based on Schubert songs and gems from Verdi's *Macbeth.*[7]

Opening officially on 29 May and performing almost nightly and Saturday afternoons to 28 October, the band played 150 consecutive concerts, reaping a notable success, both artistic and financial. Though the band's uniforms still were military and Gilmore always appeared with his chest laden with medals, and though the band still was technically and in announcements a unit of New York's 22nd Regiment, the newspapers and most people now referred to it simply as "Gilmore's Band" and the Hippodrome, even if only temporarily, as "Gilmore's Garden." Thus his success, "with the music of the finest brass band in the country," was as much personal as regimental.[8]

In his programming, which did not include symphonies, Gilmore scheduled arrangements of all the usual operatic works, overtures by Auber, Rossini, and Weber and music of Donizetti, Meyerbeer, and Flotow, including among them some pieces less well known, such as the overtures to Spohr's *Jessonda,* Verdi's *Giovanna d'Arco,* and Weber's *Peter Schmoll,* and two vocal pieces, "Infelice! e tu credevi" from Verdi's *Ernani,* and "Let All Obey" from Balfe's *Enchantress.* So popular was the garden season that Gilmore repeated it in 1876 and 1877.[9]

Meanwhile, in the spring of 1876, he took a band of "fifty eminent musicians," his core group, and five distinguished soloists across the country to San Francisco, the first such transcontinental tour by rail of professional musicians. Along the way he gave concerts in Buffalo, Detroit, Chicago, Omaha, and Salt Lake City, and then settled into the Mechanics' Pavilion in San Francisco for a two-week stand, during which the newspapers and likely most people referred to the band simply as "Gilmore's," not the regiment's.[10]

He decorated the pavilion in his usual style, with plants and flowers, a bandstand in the center with chairs for an audience, a promenade around the outer rim, and assured those who bought reserved seats (at no extra charge) that these would be held for them while they strolled. And at the first half-price matinee, when the audience perhaps was thought to be less experienced, the promise of seats held was repeated and the audience was urged to promenade, in particular during the playing of Meyerbeer's "Schiller Festival March." In all, in the thirteen days between April 17 and 29, the band played seventeen concerts, fifteen in the pavilion, of which three were matinees, as well as a Friday matinee in Oakland and a Sunday evening concert of "Sacred and Select Music" in Woodward's Garden, which, in Gilmore's estimate, drew an audience of "nearly 20,000."[11]

On their arrival in San Francisco, the visiting bandsmen, as members of New York's 22nd Regiment, had been met by San Francisco's First Infantry Regiment, 2nd Brigade (led by Colonel G. W. Grannis), accorded military honors, and escorted to their hotel. In return, Gilmore invited the colonel and his men as honored guests to a "Grand Military Night!," which would feature a "National, Patriotic, and Centennial Programme."[12]

Another special occasion occurred when the emperor of Brazil, His Imperial Majesty Dom Pedro d'Alcantara, who was visiting the city, attended a performance in his first public appearance. As he entered the pavilion the band struck up the Brazilian national anthem while an audience of 2,500 stood till he was seated. The next day the *Chronicle* reported, "The Emperor seemed to enter into the enjoyment of the music with his whole being, keeping time often with his head and hands. . . . In the Grand Centennial Quadrille, into which are introduced the airs of all nations, when the Brazilian air was reached Dom Pedro and his suite stood up, the audience following their example, and when the 'Star Spangled Banner' was introduced and the whole audience as if electrified rose up, the Emperor was not behindhand, but remained standing during its performance." And like many of the city's citizens, the emperor soon returned for a second night.[13]

The programs, so far as discovered (see appendix 4), were much the same as Gilmore had offered in New York, though tilted more strongly to opera, with Meyerbeer the favored composer. And of more "serious" music, though not including any symphonies, he offered arrangements of Beethoven's *Egmont* and *Prometheus* overtures, the concert waltz "Immortellen" by Josef Gungl, composed in 1849 in memory of Johann Strauss Sr., and Liszt's Hungarian Rhapsody No. 2, the most frequently played selection. And for a choral night, such as 28 April, when joined by the San Francisco Handel and Haydn Society and the Oakland Harmonic Society, he scheduled the "Hallelujah Chorus" from Handel's *Messiah* and from Haydn's *The Creation* "The Heavens Are Telling" and "The Marvelous Work."

Featured soloists for the tour were the soprano Emma C. Thursby, baritone Adolph Sohst, alto saxophonist Edward A. Lefebre, the cornetist Jules Levy, whom he described as "The Greatest Cornet Player living," and a second well-known cornetist, Matthew Arbuckle, whom he advertised as "the best Cornet Player in America (excepting the great Levy)." Among these greatest and best, as might be expected, egos were large, and Gilmore took care to balance opportunities for showing off. Most frequently, the instrumentalists played some work composed primarily to display their instrument, or on occasion some well-known air with variations on it—whether operatic, such as Rossini's "Una voce poco fa" from his *Il barbiere,* or popular, such as "Willie, We Have Missed You," that the local critic condemned it as "trivial." Clearly, one of Gilmore's assets as a leader, in addition to his business competence and his Barnum-like flare for publicity, was his manner in private: by all reports, honest and genial. A bandsman once reported of him that though "musicians are proverbial cranks," and though "there is hardly a time when there is not some one of the band mad at the director," the man's anger seldom lasted longer "than a day or two, and then he becomes a firmer friend to Gilmore than ever."[14]

Whether on tour or at home, the band played almost daily, and perhaps in part out of necessity. By the early 1870s, all Gilmore's men were members of the Musical Protective Union, receiving relatively high pay for performances, and to hold them he needed to keep them employed or they would hire out to other bands. And so besides fulfilling the occasional regimental duties and armory concerts, he kept the band busy with summer seasons in New York, short tours up and down the East Coast, and an occasional tour to the West.[15]

At the close of his 1876 summer season at the Hippodrome, he introduced a new vocalist, an example of his ear for new talent and swift recognition of it. The singer was a young soprano, Lillian B. Norton, born in Maine and trained at the New England Conservatory in Boston. The *Herald* described her debut as "the pleasantest feature of the evening. . . . This lady has a pure soprano voice of charmingly bright, fresh quality, and plenty of range." Unhappily, she was introduced toward the end of the program, "when the building was full of tobacco smoke, which interfered with her singing."[16]

The "lady," accompanied always by her mother, for she was barely twenty years old, sang occasional engagements with Gilmore for another year, including a lengthy tour starting in November 1877, which throughout the winter held concerts in a hundred cities from Maine to California. Then in May 1878, she started with him on a tour to Europe, apparently the first such tour to visit more than England. For the event, the 22nd Regiment gave their bandsmen new uniforms, relatively simple in cut and color, but stylish, of blue cloth with braided collar and cuffs, and a simple officer's hat bearing on it a "22" and "Gilmore's Band."[17]

Norton was the only vocal soloist Gilmore took with the band, which numbered sixty, all men, twenty-eight of them Germans, seven Americans, with five other nationalities represented. Only some two generations later, in the mid-1920s, could Sousa achieve a band in which all the musicians were born in America. Meanwhile, Gilmore's multinational group landed at Liverpool on 14 May at eleven a.m., and at noon gave a concert in Royal St. George's Hall. At that pace the trip proceeded, and in the first six weeks they gave sixty-five concerts. After one in London's Crystal Palace, in which they were joined by five English bands and a choir of three thousand, the *Monthly Musical Record* reported: "The chief interest of course centered in the American Band, who certainly as a band play extremely well, with almost orchestral effects, greater prominence being given to the clarinets, flutes and bassoons than to the brass tone as in our own military bands. They were most enthusiastically received." The reviews for Norton, who as a young singer perhaps was not at her best in the huge Crystal Palace, were more mixed: one suggested, "Before she attempts *Ernani* again she should take a few lessons in Italian pronunciation, avoid the necessity of singing some passages an octave higher than written, and cultivate style."[18]

In Paris, in thirteen concerts the band had a great success, both onstage and off. Gilmore required the men to wear their uniforms throughout the day, and in the street the more handsome of them were reportedly sometimes mobbed by women. In Paris, however, Norton and her mother, rather than continuing to Germany, stayed behind, so that Lillian could perfect her French and take lessons in acting. Three months later, they went to Milan, where she studied Italian and singing and made a successful debut in opera, first as Elvira in *Don Giovanni* and then, quite sensationally, as Violetta in *Traviata*. During this period, on the advice of her Italian singing teacher, she adopted the name Nordica (Norton not being easily pronounced in Italian), and as Lillian Nordica she soon became one of the world's great singers, with a career that lasted from 1878 to 1913 and in which she sang almost every sort of role, from Violetta to Isolde. Yet her career began with Gilmore, and in her later comments on it she always spoke kindly of him.[19]

And so, without their vocalist, Gilmore and his men continued on, returning home at the end of September, only days before their furlough from the 22nd Regiment expired. In the four and a half months they had given more than 150 concerts, chiefly in England, Scotland, France, Belgium, and Germany. In reply to reports that the tour had not been a financial success, he told a reporter from the *Times,* "Money, was not our object; we did not cross the ocean to make our fortunes, but to compare our skill with that of foreign organizations, and to show, if possible, that America has the best musicians in the world. While we were abroad we played with 15 or 16 of the best bands in Europe, and public opinion, as expressed through the newspapers, was that not one of them could compete with us." If he exaggerated, it was not by much, and he added: "We have not come home with a ship-load of money, but we have earned some fame, I flatter myself, that will add to our success at home in the future." And it surely did, for Americans then loved any homegrown artist who could match the best in Europe.[20]

Gilmore, however, was not the first bandleader to take a group to Europe. That distinction is usually awarded to Frank Johnson (1792–1844), a Black artist from Philadelphia who in late 1837 took four of his band to London, where they played for six months. The repertory, according to the scholar Eileen Southern, included operatic arias, instrumental works, comic songs, and arrangements of American and English patriotic songs. But five talented men are not Gilmore's sixty, and Johnson visited only England, whereas Gilmore went to England, Scotland, France, the Netherlands, Belgium, and Germany. Though the tours may not be comparable, their difference in size, expense, and format well suggests how far music in America had developed in the years between 1837 and 1878.[21]

After his European tour Gilmore's schedule fell into a pattern that continued for fourteen years, until 1892: In the winter, concerts, balls, parades, and other regimental engagements in New York; in the summer, an independent three-month summer season, with at least two concerts a day, at the Manhattan Beach Hotel at Coney Island; and in the slack months of the spring, his tours. In those months in 1889, for the twentieth anniversary of his first Boston jubilee, he went on tour to San Francisco and took with him anvils and six cannon, and again scheduled the "Anvil Chorus." And though these tours, according to one band member, only "just about paid expenses," they did hold the band together and kept them well rehearsed.[22]

Again, the unnamed bandsman, asked by the reporter to describe "Gilmore's peculiarities as a conductor," replied:

> The nicest equilibrium. He never loses his head, although, in his actions, he appears to be nervous. Take it when we're playing the polka caprice by Strauss. He marks the stops, the shadings, and the gradations of time and the changes with the snap and jerk of a fox's jaw. Really, he looks as he faces us as though he was biting and breaking off delicious morsels of something good to eat.[23]

Moreover, on the podium Gilmore, unlike Jullien, did not indulge in antics for effect, and in performance of the music he discouraged any impromptu flights by his instrumentalists. Even the featured soloists were directed to play their airs and variations as written, or, if in some way different from the score, then only as approved by Gilmore. Each soloist thus could make up his own score, fitted to his particular skills, but then had to stick to it until a change was sanctioned. The result, not surprisingly, was a highly polished performance with well-honed nuances.[24]

Always he had competitors, and of these one of the best was a close neighbor, the 7th Regiment Band, led first by Claudio Grafulla, and after his death in 1880 by the band's solo trombonist, Carlo Alberto Cappa. This band, usually numbering fifty to fifty-five, was smaller than Gilmore's, and its roster, quite different: thirty-five brass, sixteen woodwinds, and four percussion, the brass outnumbering the winds by almost two to one, whereas Gilmore at the very least reversed the ratio. Thus each band had a distinctive sound, the 7th Regiment's being the more martial and brassy. Its annual schedule was much like Gilmore's, with the winters, after 1880, in its splendid new armory between Park and Lexington Avenues at 66th and 67th Streets, and summers at the Brighton Beach Hotel at Coney Island. For the slack season Cappa toured like Gilmore, but not so vigorously, and also from time to time, like Gilmore, engaged visiting celebrities to perform, but not so frequently.[25]

Moreover Cappa, like both Gilmore and Jullien, on occasion composed special numbers for his band, and one of these was titled "Reminiscences of Veteran Firemen." According to a historian of bands in America: "It started out with conversation in the engine-house, then came the fire alarm, the commotion to get started, the thrilling run to the fire, the battling of the flames, the collapse of a wall, the eventual triumph over the conflagration, and the grand finale." At park concerts it was a favorite.[26]

One setting in which the 7th Regiment Band made a unique name for itself was New York's Central Park, where every summer, on Saturday and Sunday afternoons, continuing the tradition started by the Dodworth Band, it gave a series of free concerts in the mall, attended usually by a crowd estimated at twenty to forty thousand people. Following the first twelve of these in 1892 a reviewer for the *Musical Courier* noted that the band had played, "One hundred and eighteen different pieces . . . in only twelve concerts and in only forty-five days," and he noted further that the feat could have been accomplished only "by a corporation of true professors—born artists—and in perfect accordance with the artistic sentiments of their chief."[27]

As was typical of the decade, Cappa's programs offered a mixture of serious and popular music, with many operatic numbers in both categories, and at least once he offered an important operatic premiere. In the first week of March 1887, only a month after Verdi's *Otello* had its first performance in Milan, Cappa, the band, and a soprano, Isidora Martinez, offered the American premiere of the opera's "Ave Maria" in New York's Steinway Hall. As the full opera did not have its American premiere till five weeks later, Cappa's effort may have been the first public performance in the country of any of the opera's music. The *Times,* while disparaging the performers, said of the work: "It might be unwise, on a first hearing to pronounce this better music than Gounod's 'Ave Maria,' but it certainly is written in a higher style. It made an instantaneous impression upon last night's audience and had to be repeated."[28]

Cappa's concert repertory, however, was slowly changing. The band played more "serious" music, chiefly movements from six of Beethoven's symphonies and Mendelssohn's Third (Scotch) Symphony complete (see appendix 5). And in its operatic repertory it tended to follow current fashion, no longer limiting Wagner to *Rienzi* and *Tannhäuser.* Among operatic works by Frenchmen, for example, the lighthearted, lightly scored overtures by

Auber, even to his seemingly immortal *Fra Diavolo,* had been replaced by heavier-hued works of later generations. These, influenced by Wagner, often gave greater prominence to woodwinds and brass, and so were well suited to bands. And this new, "Romantic" sound, carried round the world by the immense success of *Carmen* (1875), led to a surge in scheduling the works of Bizet, Massenet, and Berlioz—of Bizet, fantasies from *The Pearl Fishers* and *L'Arlésienne*; of Massenet, the ballet music from *Le Cid*; and of Berlioz, the *Roman Carnival* overture. For a time, too, in the early 1880s, there was much Offenbach, following his tour of the United States in 1876–1877.

Similarly, change unsettled the balance of German and Italian operatic selections. Whereas in the 1850s Rossini might be represented by any of five or six overtures, by the 1880s the number of choices had dwindled commonly to three, to *Barbiere, Semiramide,* and *William Tell.* Bellini almost totally disappeared and Donizetti, too, except for arrangements of the sextet to *Lucia*, and even Verdi, in the mid-1870s, declined, while Wagner's preludes, marches, and overtures steadily rose. A historian of Wagner in the United States, Joseph Horowitz, puts the peak of his popularity here, with New York its chief source, in the years 1880–1900.[29]

And among English composers, with the enormous popularity of *H.M.S. Pinafore* (1878) and its successors, Sullivan swiftly displaced such oldsters as Balfe, Wallace, or Bishop—the shift assisted in part by the country's lack of copyright protection for works which had premiered abroad. One of the best of the many pirated arrangements of *Pinafore*, one widely played in this country and later taken to Australia, was made for the Church Choir Company of Philadelphia by a young violinist in its orchestra, John Philip Sousa, who many years later in his autobiography would happily report that Sullivan, on hearing a performance in New York, had been overheard to pronounce the orchestration "excellent."[30]

Sousa, also in his autobiography, ascribed to *Pinafore* a large role in a shift taking place in the 1870s and 1880s in the United States among theaters and audiences. The "innocence, purity, and cleanliness" of the operetta and the eight that quickly followed—a total of nine in twelve years, 1878–1889—swept away much of the lingering Puritan and Quaker prejudice against the theater, and even in England they had much the same effect, a conscious purpose of their authors and producer, Richard D'Oyly Carte. Moreover, in the United States, more than in England, another reason for the expanding audience was the continual influx of immigrant Germans, French, and Italians who arrived without a bias against theater, music, or opera.[31]

Yet even before the purge of Gilbert and Sullivan, the audience for musical theater had begun to expand as the American public began to regard operas, especially those with allegedly immoral plots, such as *Rigoletto* and

La traviata, in a slightly different fashion. The scholar Karen Ahlquist, using *Traviata* as her prime example, has described how the public came to view the fate of Violetta less as a death deserved for a sinful life than as a cause for sympathy, taking the work less as a theatrical than a musical experience. Or, as another scholar, Michael Broyles, phrased the shift: "*La traviata* became acceptable not because the plot was palatable but because the music transcended it. Audiences came to hear music, not drama." And perhaps, too, after years of hearing the arias sung to innocuous words, they wanted to hear them sung in context.[32]

The operettas, however, and their many imitations, encouraged a division among theaters and audiences. Certain theaters became associated with the operettas, generally charging lower prices, and an audience grew for what ultimately would develop into American musical comedy; whereas opera, needing a larger orchestra, more skilled singers, and increasingly sung in foreign languages, became limited to certain houses which generally charged higher prices. Before the Civil War everyone had gone to the same theater, which on successive nights had presented every sort of entertainment, operas, plays, farces, and even horse shows. As one New Yorker, after a performance of *La sonnambula* at Castle Garden in 1851 had noted in his diary: "Everybody goes, and nob and snob, Fifth Avenue and Chatham Street [poor German Jewish immigrants], sit side by side fraternally on the hard benches."[33]

By 1865, however, as the population soared, the theaters and audiences had begun to specialize, a slow process some came to regret. It decreased the sense of community, and to some even seemed antidemocratic. In 1883, with the opening of the Metropolitan Opera House, New York's social elite finally succeeded in establishing a house exclusively for opera, one with three tiers of boxes and for those buying cheaper seats a separate entrance on a side street. The change injured opera, gradually turning it in the eyes of many into merely a toy and playpen of the upper class. But all this occurred slowly and was never complete; opera houses in the next century, even the Metropolitan, often filled their cheaper seats first, and some who sought high culture in Wagner's *Ring* cycle continued to enjoy *The Pirates of Penzance*.[34]

Meanwhile, the great event in the United States scheduled for 1893 was the World's Columbian Exposition, commemorating Columbus's discovery of the New World and to be held in Chicago, May through November. Some three years before then, Gilmore, seeing an opportunity for something like a jubilee, began to plan. He would have a hundred-piece band, the largest with which he had ever toured, and start with an extended tour in the United States, ending with several months in Chicago, and soon thereafter, for a second time, take the band to Europe. Though he still had to fulfill engagements for the regiment—his relationship with New York's 22nd would continue until his death—the band was now known everywhere as "Gilmore's," and in the spring, summer, and early fall he had time and need for touring. (See photospread.)

With that enlarged band in mind, he began a search in 1891 for the additional men needed, one of whom was to be a cornet soloist. Though he had several in hand, he wanted another, for the cornet was in some respects the voice of the band. In expressing pathos, for example, it has been said that it "comes closer to the human voice than the other instruments."[35]

Now it happened that a trombone soloist in Gilmore's band, Ernest Clarke, had a younger brother, Herbert, who was at the time the cornet soloist for a band in Toronto, and in view of Gilmore's plans for Chicago and Europe, Ernest thought his brother should be part of them. Herbert, however, though greatly admired in Toronto and with a repertoire of three hundred solo arrangements, was only twenty-four, and shy, and Ernest had to write repeatedly, urging him to hurry to New York for an audition. Finally in February 1891 Herbert came, and after several nervous hours alone in Central Park went with his cornet to an appointment with "Mr. Gilmore," who lived on the park's west side.[36]

The audition perhaps is typical of what Gilmore sought in his players, not only in technique but in range of repertory, for he evidently expected Clarke to know the works by heart. He asked Clarke, for example, to play five pieces, allowing the first three to be of Clarke's choosing, a polka and two cornet arias; then, on request, a popular song which required sustained, legato phrasing, "The Last Rose of Summer," and finally, an operatic aria in which the cornet had to substitute for a soprano pleading for mercy from her lover, "Robert, toi que j'aime," from Meyerbeer's *Robert le Diable.* This last, if the cornet is to make anything of it, requires extraordinary breath control and also a good understanding of the meaning behind the now unheard words.

As Clarke later described the audition, he was ushered by a maid into the library, asked to wait, and after "about half an hour," Mr. Gilmore appeared:

> And greeted me so affably, a characteristic that made him such a lovable man to all, that I really forgot my excitement for the moment. He talked quite a while about conditions in Canada . . . and then requested me to take out my cornet and play something for him. Before starting he advised me to "warm up a bit," but I could not think of a single piece to play. He noticed my hesitation and began to encourage me, saying that he realized just how I felt. His manner was so delightful that I forgot my self-consciousness and commenced playing one of my most difficult solos; I think it was Levy's *Whirlwind Polka.*
>
> When I had finished this number in a creditable manner, Mr. Gilmore simply nodded his head and said, "Go on." I then played a difficult "air varie," finishing on a very high note, top F, that was not in the music. His exclaiming "Bravo!" en-

> couraged me to play another solo with more execution, or technique. I was then told to rest, during which time he asked me some question regarding what experience I had had in the band field, also what music I had been used to playing.

Clarke recounted his teachers, all of whom were well known to Gilmore, and said that he had been "well drilled in all the standard oratorios, symphonies and operatic selections." Gilmore then asked him to play a simple ballad, suggesting "The Last Rose of Summer," which Clarke knew and was able to play well. But after four numbers he was beginning to feel "a bit exhausted," and with fatigue always came a dry mouth, stiff lips, and an inability to make a good tone, or even a tone at all. Clarke was hoping "he would let me go, telling me whether or not I was capable of becoming a member of his band." Instead, Gilmore chatted for a few moments, and

> then he suddenly asked me if I knew the popular soprano aria from *Robert the Devil,* by Meyerbeer, I answered "yes." "All right, play it," he said. So I carefully blew all the water out of my cornet, and at the same time braced myself for this number, for I knew it required more endurance than any polka to interpret properly. Taking a little time in starting, I felt my confidence return, as I had been coached many times in this aria by my old bandmaster, who had explained its words and sentiment as well as its dramatic meaning in the opera.
>
> After I had finished, Mr. Gilmore came over to me, patted me on the back, and told me that he had been looking for a great cornet player who could play musically, with the endurance I had displayed this afternoon, and that he had found one! [See photospread.]

So Herbert L. Clarke, who in time would become one of the world's great cornetists and an important leader in the history of American bands, was hired by Gilmore. But first he was asked about his contract in Toronto: Could he be "released honorably," for "Mr. Gilmore was too square a man to take away any player from an organization, unless it could be done ethically." Assured on that point, Gilmore offered the post of cornet soloist, and Clarke was told to report for rehearsals in April, to join the New York Musical Mutual Protective Union (which all the band's members had to do), to outfit himself with the current uniform and all necessities for travel, and to provide copies of all his solos with band arrangements.[37]

That spring he and the smaller band, for the larger one was not yet fully recruited, toured through New England, played a month in New York at Madison Garden, then throughout the summer at Coney Island, and finally in September went to the St. Louis Exposition. In the winter it was back in New York, and then in the spring, one hundred strong, it started on much the same schedule, but one that would continue on to its pre-Columbian tour, then to Chicago, and finally, to Europe. But long before Europe, or even Chicago, in St. Louis on 24 September 1892, Gilmore died of a heart attack during the night. Without him the planned tour dwindled and before long Chicago was cancelled.

Gilmore's influence on others was great. His repertory, for example, his particular mixture of serious and popular music, with excerpts from opera apparently fitting comfortably into either category, did not change, and was much copied. More important, he worked continually to improve his band's sound, trying to match its tonal colors to what he heard in his head. As one scholar summarized his changes: He substituted "a flageolet to counter the more brilliant sound of the piccolo, flutes pitched in both F and C, a full range of saxophones, a large clarinet section, and four sarrusophones, which were keyed brass instruments blown with a double reed. Other brasses included flugelhorns, tenor horns, and low-pitched E-flat trumpets to soften the more brilliant sound of the cornets, trumpets, and trombones." Ultimately, he had a band in which clarinets, other woodwinds, and the brass each formed a third, so that the woodwinds dominated the brass two to one.[38]

As the balance suggests, his aim was to soften the brassiness of his band, and bring within its scope the softness, smoothness, and flexibility of a symphony orchestra. Though many bandleaders followed his lead, it seems fair to say that even the best among them, such as Grafulla and Cappa with the 7th Regiment Band, lagged considerably behind.

From the mid-1870s until his death in 1892, Gilmore was the country's outstanding bandleader, and throughout his career he kept the balance between operatic and other numbers in his programs to roughly one in three, and by the extraordinary number of his performances introduced many operatic gems to many, many people. As the scholar Raoul F. Camus observed of this period in American music, "More Americans heard serious art music in band transcriptions than in their original form."[39]

Gilmore viewed his work in part as educational, and especially so in concert performances, for in these he could include an overture by Wagner or Rossini. But he approached his work less as an educator than as an entertainer. The audience should have music that it "could understand or at least appreciate." And for that purpose he believed in his mind, in his ear, in his heart, in the superiority of a wind band. Late in life and perhaps thinking of the martial sound of brass and woodwinds, he once declared:

> Figuratively speaking, the stringed orchestra is feminine; the military band masculine. The stringed orchestra may be as coarse as a very coarse woman, or made as refined as the most accomplished lady. So, too, the military band may remain like a rough street tramp, or he may undergo a polishing that will make a perfect gentleman, equally fit, from a critical stand-point to occupy the concert room with his more sensitive sister. This is what I have tried to make of my

band. Someone may bring the stringed orchestra to such a degree of perfection as to make it a very queen among its kind, but my military band shall be king.[40] (See photospread.)

NOTES

1. *Brainard's Musical World*, vol. 10, no. 112 (April 1873), 52–53.

2. Frank J. Cipolla, "Patrick S. Gilmore: The New York Years," in *European Music and Musicians in New York City, 1840–1900*, ed. John Graziano (Rochester, NY: University of Rochester Press, 2006), 182.

3. Program reprinted in Cipolla, ibid., 185. For a detailed announcement, see *Times*, 18 November 1873, 7.

4. Concert reviewed, *Herald,* 19 November 1873, 7; *Times,* ibid., 4.

5. *Times*, 7 January 1874, 5, reprinted in Raoul F. Camus, "Grafulla and Cappa: Bandmasters of New York's Famous Seventh Regiment," *European Music and Musicians in New York City, 1840–1900,* 212–16.

6. For a report on Strauss's style of conducting in the Volksgarten, see *Brainard's Musical World,* vol. 10, no. 116 (August 1873), 118. Conversion of the Hippodrome, *Times*, 20 May, 1875, 10. Change in design of the cascade, *Herald*, 5 June 1875, 7.

7. Clarinetists from the Garde Républicaine, *Herald,* ibid. His aim, *Times*, 20 May 1875, 10. Program, *Herald*, 5 June 1875, 7.

8. Number of concerts, Schwartz, *Bands of America,* 90. Finest brass band, *Times*, 10 June 1875, 6.

9. *Times*, 19 August 1875, 4.

10. First transcontinental tour, Cipolla, "Patrick S. Gilmore: The New York Years," 186. Schwartz, *Bands of America,* 92–93, has a brief account of the band's arrival and concert in Salt Lake City, with Utah then still a territory. See also Darlington, *Irish Orpheus,* 85–86.

11. Decorations, *San Francisco Chronicle*, 18 April 1876, 3. Reserved seats, notice in *San Francisco Evening Bulletin,* 17 April 1876, 4, and in *Chronicle*, ibid., 4. Invitation to stroll, *Chronicle,* notice for Saturday matinee, 22 April 1876, 4. Nearly 20,000, *San Francisco Evening Bulletin*, 14 April 1876, 4.

12. Notice for concert, *San Francisco Evening Bulletin*, 27 April 1876, 4. *Chronicle*, 27 April 1876, 4.

13. The emperor, *San Francisco Chronicle*, 26 April 1876, 8. His second performance, see notice, *San Francisco Evening Bulletin*, 28 April 1876, 4. For this concert, the San Francisco Handel and Haydn Society and the Oakland Harmonic Society joined the band and performed choruses from Handel and Haydn.

14. "Trivial," *San Francisco Chronicle*, 22 April 1876, 3. Band member (unnamed) on Gilmore, *Detroit Free Press*, 27 May 1886.

15. Schwartz, *Bands of America,* 86–87, has details on the union and its fees.

16. Norton debut, *Herald*, 2 October 1876, 5. Ira Glackens, *Yankee Diva, Lillian Nordica and the Golden Days of Opera* (New York: Coleridge Press, 1963), 30–31, tells of her audition for Gilmore and first performance. At the former she sang "Let

the Bright Seraphim" from Handel's *Samson* and "Caro campagne" from Bellini's *La sonnambula.* At the latter she repeated the Bellini aria.

17. Norton on tour, Glackens, ibid., 23: "Gilmore paid her $100 a week and expenses, including those of her mother." Uniforms, *Times*, 30 September 1878, 8.

18. According to the "sociable" but unnamed band member's account in the *Detroit Free Press*, 27 May 1886, besides the Germans and Americans, Gilmore's core band of fifty consisted of seven Frenchmen, three Dutchmen, two Italians, one Spaniard, one Swiss (the kettle drummer), and one Irishman (Gilmore). Possibly, when Gilmore increased the band to one hundred, the proportion of Americans, because for the most part locally recruited, rose. Sousa's first all-American-born band, Sousa, *Marching Along,* 334. The *Monthly Musical Record,* quoted in Glackens, *Yankee Diva,* 38. The *Musical Standard,* quoted in Glackens, ibid., 39.

19. See Glackens, ibid., 40–41. Also, 87–88, where she receives a caller, Verdi, and sings "Caro nome" for him, "*exactly as written*" (her emphasis). Schwartz, *Bands of America,* 104, suggests that Nordica's parting with Gilmore's band was not amicable: "Lillian and her mother had a clash with Gilmore. Lillian broke her contract."

20. *Times,* 30 September 1878, 8. Also Schwartz, *Bands of America,* 107.

21. On Frank Johnson, Eileen Southern, *The Music of Black Americans: A History*, 2nd ed. (New York: W.W. Norton, 1983), 107–110.

22. Schwartz, *Bands of America*, 130. On this tour Gilmore had twenty-two soloists. R. F. Goldman, *The Concert Band,* 22, has a photograph dated 1885 of the band with anvils, so presumably Gilmore revived the chorus that year; and Darlington, *Irish Orpheus,* 116, records performances, with anvils and artillery, at Manhattan Beach in 1884. The unnamed "sociable" bandsman, *Detroit Free Press*, 27 May 1886.

23. *Detroit Free Press,* ibid.

24. *Detroit Free Press,* ibid., and Herbert L. Clarke, *How I Became a Cornetist* (St. Louis, MO: Joseph L. Huber, 1934; repr., Kenosha, WI: Lebland Educational Publications, 1973), 67.

25. 7th Regiment Band roster, Raoul F. Camus, "Grafulla and Cappa: Bandmasters of New York's Famous Seventh Regiment," 209. Leon Mead, "The Military Bands of the United States," *Harper's Weekly*, 28 September 1899, 785, however, states that for concert performances the band increased the proportion of woodwinds,

26. Schwartz, *Bands of America,* 122. Mead, ibid., lists the "Reminiscences" as one of the numbers typically appearing on the Central Park concert programs, with "the fire alarm, the start, the run, and the falling of the wall."

27. *Musical Courier,* vol. 25, no. 3 (1892), 10; reportedly repr. in *Metronome,* vol. 8, no. 12 (1892), 7. Schwartz, ibid., 131, states the library of Gilmore's Band held some ten thousand pieces, and "Gilmore employed two to three full-time experts who were kept busy making arrangements of new music for the band."

28. *Times*, 4 March 1887, 5. Steinway Hall, at 71–73 East 14th Street, was built in 1866, seated 2,500, had good acoustics, and closed in 1890, two years before Carnegie Hall opened.

29. Joseph Horowitz, *Wagner Nights,* 8.

30. Sousa's first arrangement of Sullivan's music, of selections from *Trial by Jury,* came the year before, in 1877, see Patrick Robert Warfield, "Salesman of

Americanism, Globetrotter, and Musician: The Nineteenth-Century John Philip Sousa, 1854–1893" (PhD diss. Indiana University, 2003), 159.

31. Sousa, on *Pinafore* and audiences, *Marching Along* (Boston: Hale, Cushman & Flint, 1928; repr. 1941), 62. Nine in twelve years includes pirated productions. H. L. Mencken, writing in 1910–1911, agreed, though he put more emphasis on *The Mikado,* see *H. L. Mencken on Music,* selected by Louis Cheslock (New York: Schirmer Books, 1975), 111, 114. "Quite conscious" purpose in England, see Tony Joseph, *The D'Oyley Carte Opera Company, 1875–1982* (Bristol: Bunthorne Books, 1994), 11, 69–71. For discussion of gradual change in the United States, see Levine's *Highbrow/ Lowbrow,* in particular, 84–104, 191–200; also Karen Ahlquist, *Democracy at the Opera: Music, Theater, and Culture in New York City, 1815–60* (Urbana: University of Illinois Press, 1997), in particular 188–200.

32. Ahlquist, *Democracy at the Opera,* "The New Italian Opera and Its Reception," 160–181. Broyles, *"Music of the Highest Class,"* 304.

33. *The Diary of George Templeton Strong,* vol. 2: *The Turbulent Fifties, 1850–1859*, eds. Allan Nevins and Milton Halsey Thomas (New York: Macmillan, 1952), 59. Entry for 29 July 1851.

34. For one who early saw the change coming and seemingly with regret, *The Diary of Philip Hone, 1828–1851,* ed. Allan Nevins (1927; repr. New York: Arno Press and *New York Times*, 1976), 104, 836. See also Katherine K. Preston, "Between the Cracks: The Performance of English-Language Opera in Late Nineteenth-Century America," *American Music* 21, no. 3 (Fall 2003): 356–57, 360–62.

35. Rodolfo Celletti, *A History of Bel Canto* (Oxford: Clarendon Press, 1991), 3, citing three ancient and honorable Italian theorists, G. M. Artusi, G. B. Doni, and G. Della Casa. A passage of pathos, which Verdi scored for two cornets playing mostly in thirds and only lightly accompanied, occurs in Rodrigo's death scene in *Don Carlos,* starting just before "O Carlo, ascolta." For conflicting opinions on the merits of the cornet, see chapter 1, note 15.

36. Clarke, *How I Became a Cornetist,* 64–67.

37. Ibid. See Schwartz, *Bands of America,* 104, for examples of honest dealing.

38. Cipolla, "Patrick S. Gilmore: The New York Years," 186.

39. *Musical Courier*, vol. 25, no. 3 (1892), 10, and quoted in Raoul F. Camus, "Grafulla and Cappa," *European Music and Musicians in New York City, 1840–1900,* 211–12.

40. Leon Mead, "The Military Bands of the United States," *Harper's Weekly,* 28 September 1899, 786.

Chapter Four

John Philip Sousa, the Marine Band, and Sousa's Band

Gilmore's sudden death in September 1892, occurring while he and his expanded, hundred-man band were booked at the St. Louis Exposition, where most of the country's best bands were scheduled to play, not only distressed bandsmen everywhere, but stirred in many, after the initial regret, thoughts of change and advancement. For such a void, at the very top, would surely start a shuffle in positions, personnel, and bookings. Who would lead the band? Would it hold together? At its present size, or in smaller number? And would it continue its tour of American cities, ending the following summer at the Chicago Columbian Exposition, or were those dates and venues now open to others?

Led by its assistant conductor, Charles W. Freudenvoll, the band played out its engagement in St. Louis, but Freudenvoll declined to continue further. He was more familiar than most with the financial prospects of the tour and felt that, lacking the glamour of Gilmore in person, such a large band could not meet expenses. He resigned and was succeeded by D. W. Reeves, the respected leader of the American Band of Providence, Rhode Island. Then Reeves and the band, still using Gilmore's name, started on its round of American cities; but without the great man on the podium they lost public support, and after a few concerts in several cities the rest of the tour was canceled. Reeves returned to Providence, and some players left the band. By spring of 1893, as still more players departed, the band's fate, despite occasional engagements, seemed evermore precarious. Yet in the fall, a remnant of twenty-eight members reorganized, hired others to bring their number up to fifty, and using Gilmore's arrangements and compositions began again to tour as the 22nd Regiment Band. Their leader was the young German-trained cellist, Irishman Victor Herbert, whose first operetta a year later would have a moderate success and start him on a new career, but early in 1897 he, too, left the band, after which it soon expired.[1]

The rival band which ultimately inherited nineteen of Gilmore's soloists, and among them the famed saxophonist Edouard A. LeFebre and the young cornetist Herbert L. Clarke, was a new group, barely a year old, and the creation initially of Gilmore's former booking agent, David Blakely. In 1891, he had split with Gilmore, apparently over the proposed hundred-man-band tour. Gilmore, as always, had dreamed of fielding a full wind symphony that would be the equal of any string orchestra; whereas Blakely apparently saw in the expanded number and increased expense only mounting debt. Having lost Gilmore from his roster, he sought a successor. Ultimately he settled on the leader of the U.S. Marine Band, which had just completed two short tours with him. That band had numbered forty-six plus percussion and a vocal soloist, and its leader, who would become the leader of Blakely's new band, was the thirty-seven-year-old composer and conductor John Philip Sousa.[2]

Sousa had joined the U.S. Marine Band in 1880 in a sudden shift of career for which nostalgia may have been partly responsible. Born in 1854 of a Portuguese father and German mother, he had grown up in Washington, D.C., where his father played trombone in the Marine Band. The couple's eldest son, Philip, as he was called at home, was a precocious, somewhat willful child but exceptionally able in music. One day at an early age, however, he quarreled with his music teacher, John Esputa, and refused to go back. So his father got him a job as a baker's assistant. After three nights of baking, he told his father, "I'd rather die than be a baker," and the father said, "I think you had better make it up with Esputa and start in with your music again." Thereafter Sousa was all musician, studying hard and becoming an able violinist.

When he was thirteen, a circus bandmaster heard him play and offered him a job with the circus. To take it, Philip planned to run away from home and then to write his parents about the marvels of circus life and his happiness therein. He told a friend of his plan, who told his mother, who told Sousa's mother, who told Sousa's father, who told the boy next morning, "When you dress today, put on your Sunday clothes." As it was not Sunday, Sousa was puzzled, but obeyed, and after breakfast his father said, "We will take a walk." They arrived at marine headquarters, entered the commandant's office, and his father enlisted his son in the marine band as an apprentice, a program which included instruction in all phases of music as well as playing in the band. And as young Philip knew, departure from the marines without leave was desertion, so visions of the circus faded. But he was not unhappy. For the past three years on occasion he had played triangles, cymbals, and E-flat horn with the band, and he knew all the musicians in it.[3]

For seven years he stayed with the U.S. Marine Band, studying in particular trombone, fife, drum, and clarinet, while also in his free time playing violin with concert and theater orchestras. Meanwhile, with private teachers, he studied voice, violin, piano, flute, cornet, alto horn, trombone, baritone, and tuba, till there was hardly an instrument on which he was not proficient. Then at age twenty, by which time he had published several songs and piano works, he took a discharge from the marines to play violin chiefly with theater orchestras in Washington and Philadelphia and occasionally with concert orchestras. In 1878 in Philadelphia he played in a concert orchestra led by Offenbach, whose music appealed to him, and then in 1878 he made his arrangement of *H.M S. Pinafore* for the Church Choir Company, conducting the company both in Philadelphia and on tour.[4]

In addition to *Pinafore,* Sousa also made orchestral arrangements for the stage of Gilbert and Sullivan's *The Sorcerer* and *Iolanthe*, and for Sullivan's operetta without Gilbert, *The Contrabandista,* and published potpourris for various solo instruments based on the four operettas. When in 1879 he began to compose his own operettas, completing twelve by 1915, Sullivan's influence was plain; but it would be Sousa's misfortune never to find a librettist to match Gilbert. Still, by 1879, Sousa knew many important people in the world of music, was admired, and could look forward to a steady career in the theater, conducting, arranging, and composing songs, marches, piano works, and operettas.[5]

Yet in September 1880, still only twenty-five, he left all that to accept a position as conductor of the U.S. Marine Band. Besides nostalgia, a reason for the return to Washington and the marines may have been a desire for a more settled life. He had married in December 1879 and his first child was born in the spring of 1881. The marine post offered steady work and income while leaving him time to compose, and while with the marines he published two marches still heard today, in 1886, "The Gladiator," and in 1888, dedicated to the corps and later adopted as its official march, "Semper Fidelis."[6]

Sousa was the U.S. Marine Band's fourteenth leader, the first to be American born, and though young, only twenty-five (he grew a full beard to look older), and never having conducted a military band, he came to the post with an unusually full musical background, not only in theatre music, especially operetta, but also in what was increasingly called "serious" music; music whose aim, some claimed, was not to entertain but to uplift and inspire. With the energy of youth he had played his violin, as well as other instruments, in groups of all kinds. With Esputa and others, as well as in the marine apprentice program, he had studied theory, harmony, counterpoint, and structure; and by 1880 he had already succeeded as an arranger, conductor, and even to some extent as a composer. As such he was the most rounded musician yet to

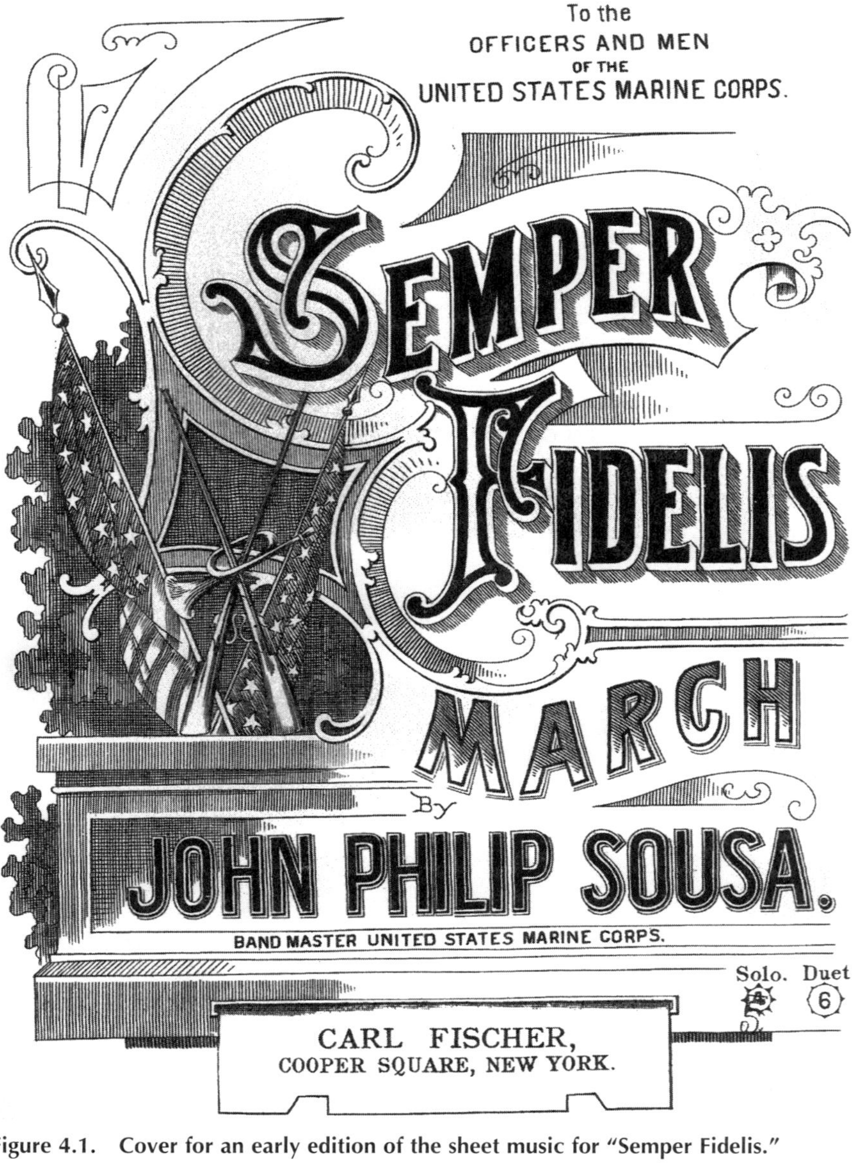

Figure 4.1. Cover for an early edition of the sheet music for "Semper Fidelis."

lead the U.S. Marine Band. The best of his predecessors, Francis Scala, who had led it from 1855 through 1871, had increased its members from roughly twenty to thirty, had improved its playing, and had performed in concerts and at White House functions (chiefly dances), a repertory of which some 88 percent was drawn from Italian opera (see appendix 6).

When Sousa took over, after several short-term successors to Scala, he was startled to discover, as he declared in his autobiography, that the band's repertory still contained "not a sheet of Wagner, Berlioz, Grieg, Tchaikovsky, or any other of the modern composers who were attracting attention throughout the musical world." In fact, though Scala's collection of arrangements, left to the Library of Congress on his death, does not include any of Wagner, he and the band had played the Grand March from *Tannhäuser* at least once, and likely more often. Still, by 1880 the band's repertory was, as Sousa judged, "limited, antiquated, and a good deal of it poorly arranged and badly copied," and he promptly began to rearrange and introduce a host of new composers.[7]

A series of seven outdoor concerts in August 1882, given at Cape May, New Jersey, one of the band's few appearances outside of Washington, suggests the extent of the change (see appendix 7). Among the operatic numbers played were arrangements of Audran, Bizet, Boito, Glinka, Sullivan, and two of Wagner, based on *Rienzi* and *Lohengrin*, as well as five taken from operettas by Offenbach. By 1885, when the band issued a catalogue of its music (see appendix 8), the list also included arrangements of works by Haydn, Mozart, Mendelssohn, and Brahms's Hungarian Dances, as well as six selections of Sousa's favorite composer, Wagner, taken from *Rienzi, Holländer, Tannhäuser,* and *Lohengrin.* Moreover, despite the band's far greater number of marching engagements, a survey of existing concert programs in the years 1888 and 1889 (by which time a Fantasia from *Die Walküre* had been added) shows at least fourteen performances of Wagner excerpts within the twenty-four months.[8]

At first, not all of Sousa's changes pleased his musicians. Some of the older bandsmen, among whom were some of the less skilled, resented his calls for improvement, rehearsals, and more performances, for these often conflicted with "outside" engagements, which paid better. But gradually he succeeded in replacing the older with younger men, better trained and more sympathetic to his goals. Soon he had one of the country's best marching bands. As he described it: "The front file consisted of trombones and basses, finely built young fellows who could step out and keep up a cadence of one hundred and twenty a minute from start to finish."[9]

In 1889, he composed one of his most popular marches for this band, "The Washington Post," commissioned to celebrate not a military "post" but the Washington newspaper, which had run an essay contest and wanted a march for the awards ceremony. This march, in 6/8 time, has a slight syncopation, and proved ideal for the new dance craze, the two-step, and as such it was played across the country and in Europe, increasing Sousa's reputation. Dancing masters, the *Times* reported, were protesting that Sousa's marches had "killed the waltz."[10]

Throughout the 1880s, Sousa and the band played almost entirely in Washington with only an occasional concert in a nearby city. For all its

Figure 4.2. Cover for an early edition of the sheet music for "The Washington Post" march.

improvements, though greatly admired locally, it was still primarily a town band, tied to a single city, numbering no more than thirty-eight musicians, and not the equal of Gilmore's or Cappa's 7th Regiment Band, both larger, with distinguished soloists and national tours. Though Sousa, through military channels, frequently requested permission to take the U.S. Marine

Band on tour—arguing no doubt that "The President's Own Band" should be heard by the country's people—he was allowed to take the band only to the nearest cities, of which Philadelphia was the most important. Programs for two seasons of three concerts each at the city's Academy of Music, in 1889 and 1890, show how his taste was affecting the band's operatic repertory (see appendix 9). In the six concerts, Rossini still led with five excerpts, now followed, however, by Saint-Saëns whose aria from *Samson and Delilah* (1877), "My Heart at Thy Sweet Voice," was sung three times, though the opera had not yet been staged in the United States. Moreover, with a Grand Scene from Massenet's *Esclarmonde* (1889), he may have been introducing the opera to the United States, for it premiered in New Orleans only three years later. And Berlioz was heard twice, both times with excerpts from *The Damnation of Faust*. For contrast, Sousa offered a "humoresque," "The Contest" by Charles Godfrey, in which according to the program: "The band tunes, the principal performers try their respective instruments. The contestants are Messrs. Clarinetti, Cornetti, Piccolini, Fagotti. The manager is Signor Tromboni, the judges, Mr. B. B. Bombardon and Signor Miflat Tuba. The contest is brought to a sudden termination by the unwarrantable interference of the drummers. Cause—jealousy." In the spring, the work was repeated, allegedly "by request."[11]

Then, in the winter of 1891, the chief objector to any tour, the commandant of the U.S. Marine Corps, went on sick leave, and at once Sousa put in his request again and was referred through the chain of command until finally reaching President Harrison. He went first, however, to Mrs. Harrison, and the president upon seeing Sousa began: "Mrs. Harrison tells me . . ." and gave permission.[12]

It was a short, hastily constructed tour, lasting only forty days in the early spring, but it was managed by Gilmore's agent, David Blakely, who on the short notice managed to squeeze in forty-five concerts in thirty-five cities in the Northeast and Midwest. In at least one program Blakely gratefully declared: "The President and Secretary of the Navy have consented to give a leave of absence to the band for a brief tour, in response to many pressing requests, and because they recognize the fact that the people throughout the country should have an opportunity to listen to the band which is maintained by their pleasure and at their expense."[13]

The tour was sufficiently successful so that Blakely and Sousa planned a longer one for the following year, through the north of the country and from the East to the West Coast, with more than seventy-three concerts in thirty-nine cities. In San Francisco the band gave six performances, and in Chicago, seven, in both cities with increasing public support and excitement. At the tour's close, after all the newspaper coverage and pre-performance publicity by Blakely's staff, the U.S. Marine Band, its leader, and his marches (frequently played as encores) had national reputations. Though the origin of his title the "March King" cannot be definitely fixed, it seems to have taken hold in these years and originated, at least in the United States, with the current publisher of Sousa's marches, who used it in his advertising.[14] (See photospread.)

Then one day Blakely took the final step in the creation of the Sousa Band. He went to Sousa with a proposition. First he asked, how much is your annual pay from the marines. To which Sousa replied, "About $1,500," increased a little by private projects and the sale of his marches. (He had been selling them to his publisher, Harry Coleman of Philadelphia, for $35 a piece, with no royalty on future sales.) Blakely, representing a syndicate of businessmen, then asked if he'd like to lead a private touring concert band at a guaranteed annual salary of $6,000 with a 10 percent share of profits in the first year and 20 percent thereafter. Sousa, perhaps disbelieving the riches offered, said only "I'll think it over." Ever since Jullien's tour in 1854–1855 such independence—total freedom to plan the schedule and programs—had been the dream of the more adventurous band leaders, but even Gilmore, who had tried it, had soon retreated into a connection with New York's 22nd Regiment. Yet Blakely, on explaining his plans and figures, was convincing. And on 30 July 1892, Sousa, with an honorable discharge, left the marines and began to recruit his own civilian, concert band.[15]

The contract between the two men had one clause that further reflected the dreams of Gilmore and others. Clause 8: "It shall be the aim and duty of the said Sousa by individual effort, and band rehearsal and practice, and by the preparation and furnishing of music, to make this band equal in executive ability to the band of the Garde Républicaine in Paris." And the next clause had the gist of the contract, the nub of future success: "It shall be the effort of the musical director to make programmes, which, while embodying a good class of music, shall be popular and pleasing, and have regard to business success."[16]

In September 1892, Sousa started on his first tour. He had recruited a band of forty-eight, of which twenty-five were woodwinds, eighteen brass, three percussion, and two vocalists, a balance reflecting Gilmore's example. In other ways, too, Gilmore set the standards to be met. Months before the tour began Sousa had received instructions from one of Blakely's assistants on how to improve his publicity photos:

> Excuse me to say that you are a much better looking man at present than either of the photographs we have on hand. . . . Three photographs we have in question show the beard to be too heavy, and the position is not quite right for an effective three sheet poster. . . . Now, do not delay a moment, but go at once to the photographer and have a full figure taken, including the feet, something near the position of Gilmore enclosed. . . . No photograph is good when both ears are in view. Tell

the artist that the likeness must be perfectly easy and composed, and not to look as though you were "having your picture tuk." . . . Bring the arms as near the body as is easy so as to have all the space we can for the outlines . . . with your left hand between the lapels of your coat as represented, or at the side, close to the body, or folded behind your back. Show the baton in some easy position.[17]

Sousa, though thirty-seven, had much to learn about business and the world outside the military, and one of the first of Blakely's good deeds for him was to get him a new publisher, the John Church Company, who would pay royalties on his works. In its first seven years, the march "The Liberty Bell" (1893) earned $40,000, and "reportedly" in his lifetime he received as royalties on "The Stars and Stripes Forever" "more than $300,000."[18]

Advice also came from interested third parties. The general manager of the Western Pennsylvania Exposition wrote to Blakely (with emphasis as shown): "I am glad you have secured Sousa; you ought to find him a good drawing card. A great deal depends upon his manner with the public, upon his *personal* popularity. . . . Gilmore's secret is simply his *methods* with his audiences. He has a taking way personally which 'catches them.' Do not let Sousa bring with him the stiffness and sternness which military men acquire, and which is apt to stick to them even when in private life. . . . I simply suggest that *you* see to it that he *unbends* before his audiences like the great *Patrick,* otherwise he will fail."[19]

Sousa soon developed a persona that audiences found pleasing. Though relatively short, five foot seven and a half, aided by the podium he evidently appeared taller, for a reviewer in 1891 described him as "a tall, burly fellow in the prime of life, and, unlike most of his fellows in the wide domain of art, he combs his hair carefully." A fitter description than "burly" might be "well built," but whether in or out of uniform, he always sought to look trim, to present a "fine figur' of a man," no doubt partly by nature and partly by military training, but also for what he called "showmanship."[20]

Initially the band toured under a name chosen by Blakely, "Sousa's New Marine Band," but that soon changed to the simpler and more accurate "Sousa's Band." Similarly, the band's uniform passed from moderately ornate, sky blue with gold braid and red-striped trousers, to simpler dark navy blue or black wool, cut to provide a jacket buttoned to the throat, with a little braided embroidery on the collar and cuffs, and an officer's hat. Sousa's uniform was the same, though more carefully tailored, always without pockets, and with gold braid on the collar, cuff, and hat. He used only the plainest wood for his batons, calling them his "twenty-five cent specials," but for his hands he always wore spotless, white, kid gloves. Before he died, in 1932, he reportedly had owned and discarded more than ten thousand pair, an estimate which, considering the band played a total of 15,623 concerts, may be modest.[21]

As conceived by Blakely and Sousa, the band's only purpose was to give concerts, and, as previously noted, in its forty years it marched only eight times. From the start its sole source of income was to be its concerts, a marked difference from most bands, which kept some town, military, or industrial tie to help with expenses. In relying entirely on fees for performance or box office receipts, it also differed from symphony orchestras, which were funded seasonally by sponsors. The band's need to play to survive underlies its astonishing record of performance. The scholar Paul Edmund Bierley reports an estimate that in its first eight years the band "played more concerts than all six of the country's major symphony orchestras put together." But the figures—in 1894 it played 661 concerts, and in 1902, its busiest year, 730—suggest that at least some of these concerts must have been short "sets" of forty or fifty minutes rather than a full concert of ninety or a hundred. Moreover, however good the arrangements, some time must have been lost in travel. In all its tours, seventy-four in North America, four in Europe, and one around the world in 1911 (47,346 miles by train or steamer in 352 days), the band traveled upward of 1,200,000 miles. Yet it still returned a profit, and as Sousa noted, "This was accomplished quite without subsidy, depending entirely on our own drawing-power."[22]

In his programming Sousa, like Gilmore, mixed so-called serious with popular music, always questioning the truth of the distinction. Accused once of playing too much popular music, he responded by offering an entire concert of indisputably popular works all taken from "classical" composers, Mendelssohn, Mozart, Handel, Bach, Haydn, Beethoven, Weber, and Schumann. His declared aim in playing such composers as Wagner, Tchaikovsky, or Dvorak was not to educate the public but to entertain them, and he believed that the public, if exposed to an excerpt from *Parsifal,* soon would come to like it: "Hear enough music and you cannot help appreciating the better kind." But if in performance he felt that his selection of serious music was not holding the audience's attention, he would bring it to a swift close and almost without pause start on something popular, "Annie Laurie," "Dixie," or "The Stars and Stripes Forever."[23]

From his work in the theater and concerts with the U.S. Marine Band, he knew that audiences wanted encores to be popular, and with his own band his typical program might list nine numbers for the concert, but with frequent, unannounced encores (a way of keeping the audience interested) would play twenty. And except for a single intermission, he allowed only a short pause between numbers, for he believed that to hold the audience's attention, the concert should move right along. The bandsmen, having warmed up their instruments offstage, would take their seats, all at once, followed by Sousa, who approaching the podium would smile, bow once or twice, step up, turn, and Crash! Opening number. At the work's close, not leaving the podium, Sousa would call out the encore to the band, turn to the audience, bow once or twice, usually bent slightly to the left and with a straight back—he was proud of his "military back"—turn to the band, and while the applause was still loud, begin. The time between numbers was usually less and never more than thirty seconds, and the encores were seldom longer than three minutes. Moreover, the first encore might be followed by a second, or even a third, while to the side or back of the band a man would hold up a placard with the current work's title. The speed—it was one of the ways Sousa kept the bandsmen alert and amused—often required the men to start playing before they had found the number in their encore books, but after playing, "Dixie" or "Semper Fidelis" more than a thousand times, they could play either by heart. Yet one time when they tried to play the *William Tell* overture without music, they broke down, and Sousa promptly switched to "Semper Fidelis." After 1897, to meet audience demand, at almost every concert they played "The Stars and Stripes Forever."[24]

Any march or number could be varied slightly by the amount of showmanship that Sousa decided to put into a rendering. He believed that audiences like to see the soloists at work, to see the puffed cheek, the suck of breath, the reddened face. So when Herbert Clarke had a cornet solo or Arthur Pryor one on the trombone, the man would rise, come forward—the movement alone roused expectation—and play at stage front. The excitement would increase if not one artist but six, as for the sextet from *Lucia,* stepped forward. But the most exciting of all these movements of players in the midst of a piece was reserved for "The Stars and Stripes Forever." Suddenly six piccolo players would line stage front for their variation on the trio, the march's most memorable theme. After the piccolos had shrieked their descant, alongside them appeared the band's cornets and trombones, and with the band behind them swelling its tone, as the soloists let loose, the audience often rose to its feet, screaming and shouting. Such is the power of a good march, and it seems fair to say: around the world no American music is better known than "The Stars and Stripes Forever."

Another feature of Sousa's encores was often the local school or college song, or a work, whether or not published, by some local composer. He took care in each town or city to find any music of local significance, to get copies of parts if possible, and then perhaps before the concert play through the piece once or twice, but if time was short, in performance play it at sight. The musicians were all good sight-readers and having played so much together had a fine sense of balance; college songs and school marches, after all, usually follow a pattern. As a result, the list of composers played by the band, some 2,030, is studded with unfamiliar names, with works played in only one year. Similarly,

Figure 4.3. Cover for the original edition of the sheet music for "The Stars and Stripes Forever." Old York Road Historical Society.

the compositions of better known contemporary composers changed constantly as their works passed through periods of popularity. The band, for example, played thirty-eight of Victor Herbert's compositions, the choice shifting whenever a new operetta caught the public's ear. One of the more enduring of such selections was the "Italian Street Song" from *Naughty Marietta*, a vocal solo offered every year but one from 1924 through 1931.[25]

In the forty years of leading his band, Sousa in many ways, some probably unconsciously, sought to keep in step with public fashion, even in such a minor matter as the amount of hair on his face. Men's style in that time passed from the full beards of Lincoln and his cabinet, through the moustaches of Teddy Roosevelt and Taft, to faces clean-shaven like those of Hoover and Franklin D. Roosevelt. Starting in the U.S. Marine Band at age twenty-five, in an effort to look older Sousa had grown a full, black moustache, sideburns, and beard, but after obtaining his own band he began to neaten the beard, and by 1910, when he was fifty-six and his hair was graying, he had thinned the sideburns, trimmed the beard and moustache, and, consciously or not, allowed more personality to show. Then during World War I, he volunteered at a dollar a month to train bandsmen for the U.S. Navy. But before reporting for duty at the Great Lakes Naval Training Station, he went to a barber and had all his facial hair shaved off save a neat white moustache and small goatee. Trying to explain the sudden change to his wife, he pleaded that at sixty-two and joining the navy he should try to look younger. Then, sometime before 1922, he eliminated even the goatee, leaving only a trim white moustache, by which time, to most of the younger eyes in any audience, he appeared, perhaps more than he realized, to be a kindly, old grandfather.[26]

On the podium he conducted, as one London newspaper put it, "with great calmness. Many people had, no doubt, expected to witness an exhibition of eccentricities such as the caricatures of the music hall imitators have accustomed them to. They would be disappointed, for though Sousa has mannerisms, he has no extravagances." He hardly ever moved his feet, but his upper body, arms, and face reflected the music. According to Bierley, "He was a proponent of conducting in circular motions and within a small circle. . . . Each of his gestures, which were sometimes almost imperceptible, meant something—the dancing fingers, the delicate hand expressions, the undulations of the wrists, the quick head movements. He swayed gracefully from side to side, leaned forward gently with the tender passages and backward with the strong ones." As a reporter in Duluth once wrote: "Every motion is graceful and expresses exactly what the music conveys. A deaf person might almost watch Sousa and understand the music." And with any new music, his musicians, having a full view of his face, could tell at once whether or not, and how much, he liked the piece. One time, after trying out one of his new marches, a silence ensued, and then Sousa's voice was heard, soft and distressed, "Christ almighty! [a favorite expletive] Did I write that!"[27]

For his skills and because he treated his musicians with respect, encouraging each in turn to share in the spotlight, they liked and trusted him, and despite the grueling schedule many stayed with him for years. If during a concert he heard a mistake—and his ear was remarkably acute—he would not at the time express any displeasure or even comment on it later, but when the piece was played again and if the musician got the passage right, Sousa might place his hand over his heart and smile. And that was it. He was similarly patient and understanding with the public. He enjoyed meeting people, would sign autographs, listen to would-be composers, give interviews to local reporters, and on occasion do battle for what he thought was right. When in 1922, in Binghamton, New York, a group of ministers protested a Sunday concert which charged admission, Sousa, prodded by a reporter, observed that the ministers were being paid for their Sunday work, and in any case, "There is more inspiration in some of my marches than in all their sermons!" But provocation was needed to stir such belligerence.[28]

A clarinetist in the band once summarized its feelings about their leader: "Mr. Sousa may not have been the best conductor in the world, but he was certainly one of them. He was a small man, not a dashing-dapper-dan who could tower over us. And he had a kind, little old pipsqueeky voice, not a big boomy voice to shout commands. But when he stepped up on that podium, something happened. I can't explain it; it just happened. We knew we were playing with the immortals, and no one could touch us." The public felt the same. One time a newspaper reviewer following a concert in Raleigh, North Carolina, stated: "An account of Sousa's concert at the Academy of Music last night is unnecessary, for everybody in Raleigh seems to have been present." Another, in Greensboro, complained that because all the seats had been sold, even those usually reserved for the press, it is "impossible to report on the quality of the concert." But if it was announced that for some reason Sousa would not conduct, box office receipts promptly fell off.[29]

In a chapter of his autobiography, Sousa addressed directly the question of why he preferred a wind band or symphony to the typical string orchestra. A violinist himself, he agreed that "the most aesthetic of the pure families of instruments is beyond question the violin group. In sentiment, mystery, glamour, register, unanimity of tonal facility and perfection in dexterity it more than equals all other families." But the woodwinds, and especially the clarinet, could surpass it "in coquetry, humorous murmurs and the mimicry of animated nature." And the brass, though less diverse than either the violin or the woodwinds, "has the power to thunder forth a barbaric splendor of sound or to intone the chants of the cathedral. Therefore, composers have found a greater diversity of tone color in a multitude of wind instruments, cylinder or conical, single-reed, double-reed, direct vibration or cup-shaped mouthpiece than in the string family alone. All these wind instruments have added to the palette of the orchestrator and have enabled him to use his creative power in blending the various colors."[30]

He agreed that many works of such classical composers as Haydn, Mozart, and Beethoven were composed with a predominant string sound in mind, and such works, he felt, should be left to string orchestras. But many of the more modern composers, such as Richard Strauss, made use of new or improved wind instruments, such as saxophones, and Wagner, for example, "in nearly every instance, enunciates the 'leit-motifs' of his operas through the agency of wood-wind or brass." Among such modern composers there was a clear tendency "to place in the hands of the wood-wind corps and the brass choir of the orchestra the most dramatic effects of the symphonic body." Hence, "there is much modern music that is better adapted to a wind combination than to a string," even if scored originally for an orchestra. In closing he echoed Gilmore, saying, "The string-band and the wind-band are among the brightest constellations in the melodic heavens. The former may be likened to a woman, the latter to a man, for like maid and man, brought together in divine harmony, they can breathe into life the soulful, the sentimental, the heroic and the sublime."[31]

His band's instrumentation, though changing slightly each year as artists entered or left, reflects these thoughts. In the years 1892 through 1931 its roster of musicians (not including Sousa) ran from forty-eight to seventy-six, but in the majority of years it numbered between fifty and sixty-six. In its first six years the ratio of woodwinds to brass was roughly 3–2, typically twenty-seven to eighteen. Then, as the years passed, and as the number of woodwinds slightly increased, that ratio changed to 5–3, or even in some years closer to 2–1. In 1925, for example, when the band was at its largest, he had forty-seven woodwinds to twenty-four brass.[32]

In his continual search for what he considered the best tone, he not only dropped and added instruments but even caused one to be modified. In 1899, displeased with the helicon tuba's too directional sound—it wound around the body and its narrow bell blasted the sound directly forward—he persuaded a manufacturer to construct it with a larger bell opening upward, so that the sound would diffuse over the whole band. This came to be called the Sousaphone, and after 1908, for marching bands where the player was often in a rear rank a bell could be substituted that projected the sound directly forward, over the bandsmen's heads. In addition he often used, and claimed to be the first to use, mutes for cornets and trombones. In the woodwind family, by 1905 he had dropped altogether the Sarrusophone (the double-reed brass with a tone rather like an oboe or bassoon), and after 1921 replaced the E-flat clarinet, whose tone he thought shrill, with two flutes. Every year, the B-flat clarinets, the workhorse of the woodwinds, typically totaled half the section. Sousa's aim was flexibility, a smooth tone, and the ability to play softly. People were astonished that the band, often still mistakenly called a brass band, could aptly accompany a solo violin, which it frequently did in such works as Dvorak's "Humoresque," Sarasate's, "Gypsy Airs," or movements of Mendelssohn's Violin Concerto.[33]

The control of dynamics, the variations between loud and soft, was one of Sousa's skills as a conductor, though unfortunately recordings during the first quarter of the twentieth century, being primitive, do not capture his subtleties. But another skill, his ability to choose and hold a tempo, is better revealed. Leopold Stokowski, from 1912 to 1936 the conductor of the Philadelphia Orchestra, as a young man had attended a Sousa concert and later remarked: "The music swept me off my feet. The rhythm of Sousa stirred me, for it was unique. I tried to analyze my sensations. The music had such wonderful regularity. Someone else might have such regularity but he would not have the enormous drive and push. . . . They say that genius is doing something better than any other person does it. Sousa is such a genius. He is a genius whose music stands supreme as a symbol of the red-bloodedness of humanity." Stokowski articulated for many what seemed Sousa's secret: regularity, with enormous drive and push.[34]

In addition to frequent shifts in dynamics, Sousa also sought to avoid monotony by varying the instrumentation in repeats and sections of the work, an opportunity he thought greater with a wind band than a symphony orchestra, because of the greater diversity of woodwinds and brass. That diversity offered the chance of unusual combinations in "quartets," a phrase he liked but did not limit to four instruments, or even six, eight, or more, as when piccolos, cornets, and trombones lined the stage front. And in hiring his soloists he sought not only artistic skill but something more, showmanship, for he believed, "When personality is missing, the ear is bound to tire."[35]

What Sousa chiefly chose to play over his forty-year career, other than his own works, is set out in appendix 12, but what that appendix cannot show, because it is limited to works he played for fifteen or more years, is his range of taste. He played what he liked tempered by what he knew audiences liked and, regardless of style, by what he thought they might like if given the chance, perhaps first in excerpt, to hear it. Thus, in addition to what the appendix lists, in 1911 he took on his world tour both an excerpt from *The Well-Tempered Clavier* and the air from Bach's Suite in G major, which he had previously played in 1905; a Beethoven minuet (violin solo) that he repeated in 1912, 1913, and 1924; and Richard Strauss's "Till Eulenspiegel's Merry Pranks," which had proved popular in 1907, 1908, and 1910 and which he had in the repertory for nine years. He was always partial to humor in music and believed that bands with their predominance of woodwinds could display it better than string orchestras. He evidently liked Strauss, however, for in eleven years he also scheduled the love scene from the opera *Feuersnot*, taking it on tour in 1905, 1925, 1926, and 1930.

Of Wagner, his favorite composer, he played excerpts from all the operas except the first two, *Die Feen* and *Das Liebesverbot.* Somewhat surprising perhaps was his early testing of excerpts from *Parsifal,* introducing the prelude at a concert at Manhattan Beach, New York, on 15 August 1893. This was not the prelude's first performance, for beginning in 1882 various string orchestras had played it, but it did anticipate the Metropolitan Opera's first production of the work by ten years. And Sousa, considering the amount of other Wagner he played, with ten more operas to choose from, was notably loyal to *Parsifal,* playing excerpts in twenty-seven of his forty years.

Though less frequently, among the works of other "classical" composers he performed Haydn's "Surprise" Symphony, Schubert's *Rosamunde* ballet music, *Marche militaire,* and "Unfinished" Symphony, and Schumann's *Träumerei* in an arrangement featuring solo violin. Of more modern composers he scheduled arrangements of Smetana's overture to *The Bartered Bride*, Percy Grainger's "Shepherd's Hey," and sixteen of Henri Wieniawski's works, all for solo violin, of which the two most often played were a mazurka, "Obertass," and the Polonaise Brilliante in D major.

He also scheduled more of Tchaikovsky than appendix 12 can reveal: selections from *Eugene Onegin*; movements from Symphony No. 6; and in three years the symphonic ballad *Le Voyvoda,* which tells a story, based on Pushkin poem, in which the "voyvoda" (provincial governor) is killed by a pistol shot. The ballad, a descriptive piece, climaxes in a stormy section pierced by a sudden pistol shot. One night in 1926, however, during the opening of the storm the trombones made a wrong entrance, pulled in others after them, and the different parts became thoroughly muddled. To stop the cacophony the pistol man shot his blank, and after a second of silence all the musicians picked up at the same place and proceeded euphoniously to the end. How much, one wonders, did the audience perceive?[36]

Sousa's liking for operetta appears in appendix 12 under Offenbach and Sullivan, but of the latter he played far more than is shown. For seven years he scheduled a ballet suite from the perhaps not so brilliant *Victoria and Merrie England*; for six years performances of the excellent *Di Ballo* overture and of the incidental music for *The Merchant of Venice*; and for three years the incidental music from *The Foresters.* In addition, he repeatedly scheduled selections of all kinds from William Vincent Wallace's operetta (or perhaps opera) *Maritana,* with its best-known song "Scenes That Are Brightest May Charm Awhile"; and from German operettas, he scheduled what many were playing at home on their pianos, Leon Jessel's "Parade of the Wooden Soldiers" and Paul Lincke's "Glow-Worm."[37]

Finally, though playing many of his own works, he did not neglect other American composers. On the so-called classical side perhaps his favorite was George W. Chadwick, of whom he offered ten works in all, with "Symphonic Sketches: Jubilee" the most frequently played and taken on tour in

1904, 1905, and 1908. In addition, he liked the works of Chadwick's pupil Lucius Hosmer, often scheduling and taking on tour in the years 1917–1930 "Chinese Wedding Procession" (saxophone ensemble or band), "Ethiopian Rhapsody," "Northern Rhapsody," and "Southern Rhapsody." Of Edward McDowell, besides seven other selections, he played "The Witches' Dance," Op. 17, on tour in 1922–1924. In four years on tour, 1910, 1911, 1923, and 1924, he offered as a vocal solo Horatio Parker's song "The Lark Now Leaves His Wat'ry Nest." On the more popular side, besides keeping abreast of current songs, such as those from Jerome Kern's *Sally* and *Show Boat,* on a tour in 1900 he introduced ragtime to Europe and scheduled, as a xylophone solo, such standards as Euday L. Bowman's "Twelfth Street Rag." But it must be admitted that his greatest success was not with ragtime, and his effort to keep abreast with jazz, as ragtime morphed into jazz, showed him in the late 1920s beginning to fall behind the country in its changing musical taste, but by then he was over seventy. Yet he still pleased a large portion of the American public and enjoyed worldwide recognition through his marches.[38]

NOTES

1. Schwartz, *Bands of America,* 140–41. Sousa on Victor Herbert, Sousa, *Marching Along*, 345.
2. Sousa, ibid., 98–99, 122–25.
3. Ibid., 1–5, 25–27.
4. Ibid., 63–64, 272. Warfield, "Salesman of Americanism," 40.
5. Sousa's first operetta was *Katherine,* completed in 1879 but never produced, see Bierley, *John Philip Sousa: American Phenomenon*, 41, 225. The Sousa Band, however, played its overture in the years 1894–1896 and 1927, see Bierley, *The Incredible Band,* 403. In all, Sousa completed twelve operettas, with three more left unfinished. His first published and produced was *The Smugglers,* 1882. His most successful, *El Capitan* (1895), survives today in an occasional production and in Sousa's *El Capitan* march, based on the work's melodies. His last operetta produced, in 1913, was *The Glassblowers* (sometimes titled *The American Maid*), revived by Glimmerglass Opera in 2000, after which the production moved to the New York City Opera. For an account of Sousa's work with Sullivan's music, see Warfield, "John Philip Sousa and 'The Menace of Mechanical Music,'" *Journal for the Society of American Music* 3, no. 4 (2009): 433–40.
6. On "Semper Fidelis" I quote from a letter I received, dated 22 April 2010, from the historian, U.S. Marine Band, Master Gunnery Sergeant D. Michael Ressler: "I have never been able to find any letter, Marine Corps order, or any other paperwork that officially names *Semper Fidelis* as the official march of the Marine Corps. It is undeniable, however, that for many years, the march has been accepted as the official march and no one questions the fact. In an article titled 'Sidelights on Sousa's Personality,' published on 9 July 1910, in the magazine *Musical America,* the author wrote: 'This march is

called *Semper Fidelis* (ever true), and has been adopted by the U.S. government as the official "March Past" of the Marine Corps.' This quote establishes that for at least the last 100 years *Semper Fidelis* has held the status of the official march of the Marine Corps. I suspect that this status goes back much farther than that. Sousa appears to have made the claim throughout his life. From all that I have read about Sousa, he was a most honest and honorable man, and I conclude that there must have been some kind of written or oral declaration of the march's official status. In his autobiography *Marching Along* [p. 85], Sousa wrote the following comment, 'It is the official march adopted by the Marine Corps, by order of the General commanding, and I am very proud of the fact that it is the only composition which can claim official recognition by our government.' The march was composed in 1888 while Sousa was still the director of the Marine Band. His reference to 'the General commanding' may be to the Commandant of the Marine Corps in 1888, Colonel Charles G. McCawley. Colonel McCawley may have given the march its official status but the evidence of this has never been found."

7. Band's repertory, Sousa, *Marching Along,* 68. Scala and Wagner, program of concert on 24 June 1867 at the Tremont Temple, Boston, Massachusetts, in the U.S. Marine Band Library, Washington, D.C.

8. Survey of Wagner performances, letter to the author, 12 February 2010, from MGySgt D. Michael Ressler, and I thank him for sharing his survey with me, for a copy of the 1885 catalogue of the band's music, and for copies of many of the band's programs, some of which inform appendixes 7, 8, and 9.

9. Sousa, *Marching Along,* 70.

10. On "The Washington Post," see Warfield, "Salesman of Americanism," 324, 329–35; Sousa, *Marching Along*, 117–18; Bierley, *American Phenomenon,* 47–49. The Sousa Band played it often, see Bierley, *The Incredible Band,* 406. Dancing masters, *Times*, 10 September 1899, 16.

11. "President's Own," an argument later made by Sousa's agent, see Warfield, "Making the Band: The Formation of John Philip Sousa's Ensemble," *American Music* 24, no. 1 (Spring 2006): 35, quoting David Blakely's letter to the assistant secretary of the treasury. Programs in the U.S. Marine Band Library, Washington, D.C. Philadelphia concerts, see appendix 9. "The Contest," on 19 April 1890.

12. Sousa, *Marching Along,* 98. Also, Warfield, "Salesman of Americanism," 236n4.

13. Program for the afternoon and evening performances at the Music Hall, Cleveland, Ohio, 11 April 1891; in the U.S. Marine Band Library, Washington, D.C.

14. Sousa, *Marching Along*, 111.

15. Ibid., 122–24, 333. In greater detail, Warfield, "Salesman of Americanism," 452–55.

16. Bierley, *The Incredible Band,* 22. Also, Warfield, "Salesman of Americanism," appendix B.2, 560.

17. Initial number of Sousa's Band, see Bierley, *The Incredible Band,* 251. R. F. Goldman earlier, in *The Concert Band* (1946), 59, puts the number at forty-nine (not including the vocalists or conductor) and gives a slightly different instrumentation. On his photograph, Warfield, "Salesman of Americanism," 446.

18. Royalty on "Liberty Bell," Bierley, *John Philip Sousa: American Phenomenon,* 61, and on "The Stars and Stripes Forever," R. F. Goldman, "John Philip Sousa,"

in *Selected Essays and Reviews, 1948–1968,* ed. Dorothy Klotzman (Brooklyn: Institute for Studies in American Music, 1980), 219. Estimated annual income from royalties, Bierley, *The Incredible Band,* 17.

19. Warfield, "Salesman of Americanism," 40.

20. Warfield, "John Philip Sousa and 'The Menace of Mechanical Music,'" *Journal of the Society for American Music* 3, no. 4 (Winter 2009): 451, quoting the *Daily Telegram*, Worcester, Massachusetts, ca. 2 April 1891. Showmanship, Bierley, *American Phenomenon,* 138.

21. On baton and gloves, Bierley, *American Phenomenon,* 133.

22. Eight times, Bierley, *The Incredible Band,* 45. Number of concerts, ibid., 4n8. Number of tours, Bierley, ibid., 89, 143; Sousa, *Marching Along,* 338; and Keith Brion, "The Uneasy Silence of History," 13, in *Sousa Marches, Played by the Sousa Band, The Complete Commercial Recordings*, (Crystal Records, CD461–3, 2000).

23. For the "popular" program by "serious" composers, see Sousa, *Marching Along,* 295: a vocalist sang "Batti-Batti" from Mozart's *Don Giovanni;* a violinist played Mendelssohn's concerto; and the band played Handel's "Largo" (from the opera *Serse*), Bach's Loure (from his third violincello suite), Haydn's "Surprise" Symphony, Beethoven's *Leonore* Overture No. 3, Weber's "Invitation to the Dance," Schumann's "Traümerei," and Mendelssohn's "Wedding March." "Hear enough music," ibid., 132. Frank Byrne, "The Recorded Sousa Marches—Story and Sound," 30, in the recording *Sousa Marches* by Crystal Records, identifies the source of this quotation as a 1927 article by Sousa, "World's Greatest Composers Will Develop Here."

24. Concert to move along, Bierley, *The Incredible Band,* 14; Bierley, *American Phenomenon,* 139–40. No "warming up" onstage before an audience, see Bierley, *Marching Along*, rev. ed., 335n. Ten seconds, Bierley, *The Incredible Band,* 12, 270. Breakdown in *William Tell* overture, Schwartz, *Bands of America,* 294.

25. Unknown composers, Sousa, *Marching Along,* 242–43, 303. Number extrapolated from Bierley's *The Incredible Band,* appendix V. Herbert's operettas, ibid., 363, and Sousa on Herbert, *Marching Along,* 345.

26. Facial hair, looking older, Schwartz, *Bands of America,*144; looking younger, ibid., 265. Schwartz states that for the navy Sousa shaved off all but the moustache. Bierley, however, in *American Phenomenon,* 15 and 80, has photographs of him with the goatee while in the navy, but one photo on page 84, taken in 1923, shows him without it. Other photographs on 82–83 show him as an older man no longer in the navy but wearing his naval uniform to conduct, without his goatee. Bierley, *The Incredible Band,* 78, shows a drawing of him (1922) without the goatee. It would seem, therefore, that he shaved it off sometime soon after leaving the navy. He was discharged in late January 1919, Bierley, 81.

27. Conducting style, "no extravagances," Schwartz, *Bands of America,* 198, quoting the London *Daily Mail*, 23 February 1903. "Circular motions," Bierley, *American Phenomenon,* 135. "Deaf person," Bierley, *The Incredible Band,* 10, quoting the *Duluth Herald,* 23 May 1893. And Bierley, *American Phenomenon,* 134–35. Also Warfield, "Salesman of Americanism," 500. "Christ Almighty," Bierley, *The Incredible Band,* 135. Favorite expletive, Schwartz, *Bands of America,* 301–02.

28. Hand on heart, Bierley, *American Phenomenon,* 133. Sunday concert, Bierley, *The Incredible Band,* 34.

29. Clarinetist on Sousa, quoted in Bierley, *American* Phenomenon, 130. The clarinetist was Edmund A. Wall. Raleigh concert, 4 January 1899, and Greensboro concert, 4 March 1924, Bierley, *The Incredible Band,* 136.

30. Sousa, *Marching Along,* 329.

31. Ibid., 329, 332. For Gilmore's remark, see close of chapter 3.

32. Instrumentation, Bierley, *The Incredible Band,* 251–252.

33. Sousaphone, Bierley, *American Phenomenon,* 146; Sousa, *Marching Along,* 334; and R. F. Goldman, *The Concert Band,* 144. Sarrusophones, see Clappé, *The Wind-Band and Its Instruments,* 82–84; also, Bierley, *The Incredible Band,* 249; and R. F. Goldman, *The Concert Band,* 48.

34. On Stokowski, Schwartz, *Bands of America,* 262, quotes the remark at greater length. Bierley, *The Incredible Band,* 41, opens his first chapter with the remark as an epigraph and gives its origin in a speech by Stokowski in Philadelphia on 15 May1924. See also Oliver Daniel, *Stokowski* (New York: Dodd, Mead, 1982), 821.

35. Though no source seems sure when the statement was made, it clearly was part of Sousa's belief in how to keep an audience attentive. See Bierley, *The Incredible Band,* 248–49, and Bierley, *American Phenomenon,* 143, where in a footnote Bierley cites "an unidentified clipping in the 1925 Sousa Band press book."

36. "Le Voyvoda," Bierley, *The Incredible Band,* 140. On the ballad, see David Brown, *Tchaikovsky: The Final Years, 1885–1893* (New York: W.W. Norton, 1991), vol. 4, 293–98. For another quite different occasion when firing a shot saved the day, see Schwartz, *Bands of America,* 294–95.

37. Sullivan's *The Foresters* was based on Tennyson's poetic drama abut Robin Hood. It never played in London and opened in New York on 17 March 1892, running only until mid-April. For a harsh judgment on it, see Gervase Hughes, *The Music of Arthur Sullivan* (London: Macmillan, 1960), 24, 26. More favorable, *Times*, 18 March 1892, 1, and 20 March 1892, 13.

38. See Gunther Schuller, *Early Jazz: Its Roots and Musical Development* (New York: Oxford University Press, 1968), 89, asserting that Louis Armstrong, on 28 June 1928, established "the general stylistic direction of jazz for several decades to come." By then Sousa, born 6 November 1854, was seventy-three and a half.

Chapter Five

John Philip Sousa

Summers in Coney Island and Winters in Rochester, New York

The business affairs of Sousa's Band were managed by David Blakely's office in New York, which, though it frequently moved, always settled in the theater and music district on the city's west side, even for several years renting rooms in Carnegie Hall. The office was never grand, and because much of the work was contracted to advance and publicity men out of town, the permanent staff was small. Headquarters, however, had cabinets with timetables for every passenger railroad in the country, data on the size and shape of theaters all across the country, and information on hotels near the theaters, as well as records of communications back and forth with out of town agents. Telephones not yet being common, much of the business was done by telegraph.[1]

For Sousa, the fact that the office was in New York to some extent tied him to the city, and for some twenty years while continuing to live chiefly in Washington (where his three children were born), he kept an apartment in New York where he and his family stayed, until finally in 1915 he first rented and then bought three acres and a house at Sands Point, Port Washington, Long Island. Another tie to New York was the city's position as the country's chief exchange for hiring musicians, which in turn was a reason that rehearsals for tours were held there, with those in the 1890s usually needing twelve days. Moreover, even though the band, unlike Cappa's 7th Regiment Band or even Gilmore's, with its tie to New York's 22nd Regiment, had no military sponsor in the city, in its first decade it became associated with New York in the public's mind, in part because of steady summer engagements at Coney Island, the site in the 1890s not only of the city's most famous amusement park but also of its most luxurious seaside resort.[2]

The island, a five-mile sandbar facing the Atlantic Ocean and supposedly named by the Dutch after its numerous rabbits (*konijn*), is now an island in name only, though it used to be separated from Brooklyn's southwestern mainland by a tidal creek, long since filled in. Moreover, today only the western half of the island bears its famous name; the eastern part, which in the late nineteenth century blossomed as a seaside resort, has three residential communities, west to east, Brighton Beach, Manhattan Beach, and Corbin Place. But at the close of the nineteenth century these were the sites of three large hotels, each standing on its own expansive acres and divided from the Coney Island of crowds, noise, cheap food, and roller coasters by Ocean Avenue, and more potently, by fences, gates, and private police.

The three hotels, Brighton Beach, Manhattan Beach, and the Oriental, all rose at roughly the same time, 1878. The first was created by a group of Brooklyn businessmen and catered primarily to the upper middle class of Brooklyn, the substantial burghers and professional people. The Manhattan supposedly drew a more *recherché* crowd, celebrities and big businessmen and their wives, and the Oriental was the *ne plus ultra* of exclusivity. The latter two were created by the owner of the Long Island Rail Road, Austin Corbin, who earlier had bought up lots at the eastern end of the island. By 1880 his resort had two hotels, the Manhattan Beach and the Oriental, each offering splendidly furnished suites, large public rooms, surrounding parks, music and bathing pavilions, a paved esplanade along the beach with lamps and benches, and behind the hotels the Coney Island Jockey Club Racetrack, or as it came to be called, Sheepshead Bay Racetrack. Corbin's east end was private property, fenced and guarded as such, with the two hotels open only in summer, charging the highest prices. Corbin's property connected directly to Brooklyn, Manhattan, and Staten Island by ferries and by the public rail lines, the last part of which was a Corbin-owned private railroad, "the Culver line" (electrified in 1899 and eventually part of New York's subway system). The Brighton Beach Hotel similarly had a rail connection to the city's subway lines, music and bathing pavilions, and a racetrack. For city dwellers the multiple lines made possible a brief visit to the shore to bathe or to hear a band. To remind those living or working on Manhattan Island of Coney's seaside charms, Corbin put up a large electrified sign at 23rd Street and Broadway, said to be New York's first and for several years a city "sight." It claimed to have fifteen hundred lights, all suggesting in swathes of color a balmy day "Swept by Ocean Breezes."[3]

Initially at Manhattan Beach Corbin hired the Dodworth Band, after which for fourteen years Gilmore's had been the chief musical attraction, usually playing at least two concerts a day in July and August. Sometimes, however, Gilmore had other engagements or regimental duties, and Corbin, for a substitute, had sought to engage Sousa and the U.S. Marine Band. Sousa had been willing, but his superiors in the corps had not, and nothing came of the opening. But on Gilmore's death in September 1892, by which time Sousa had left the marines to form his own civilian band, Corbin and Blakely quickly came to agreement and Sousa filled Gilmore's place at Manhattan Beach for July and August 1893. In anticipation, the *Times* assured its readers: "It was no easy task to find a successor to Gilmore, but the management believes that Sousa . . . will meet all the requirements. . . . He is no fanatic in the matter of classicism, yet he is not so disposed as was Mr. Gilmore to revel in the effects of thunderous volumes of sound. Critics are prone to say of him that he possesses in large measure that magnetic quality which fetches audiences and performers into sympathy."[4]

While he was on tour, before coming to Manhattan Beach, some critics questioned his mixture of serious and popular music, and seven concerts in Boston's huge Mechanics Hall, 4–7 May, show the extremes of his programming, popular and serious (see appendix 10). The occasion, perhaps his closest to a Gilmore "Jubilee," was the Columbian Exposition, celebrating the four hundredth anniversary of the discovery of the Americas, and the event, for which he was the musical director, included not only his own concert band but a group of professional vocalists, a chorus, and a full orchestra (with its own conductor) featuring a section of seventy young women playing strings. The popular extreme included as the exposition's opening number Gilmore's march and song "Columbia," and to conclude each concert, Sousa's "Salute to the Nations," which employed besides the band and orchestra, a corps of Scottish bagpipers playing "The Campbells Are Coming," an Irish fife and drum corps for "The Wearing of the Green," and other representative groups for Spain, France, Italy, and Germany, all ending with "The Star-Spangled Banner" and a "tableaux vivant of Columbia Triumphant." The serious extreme was the second concert, a matinee on 5 May, which, except for the final "Salute to the Nations," was given entirely to excerpts from Wagner's operas. A critic for the *Boston Herald* feared this was "possibly an overestimate of the strength of the Wagner cult hereabout," and its audience of only 2,500 was perhaps the smallest of the series. Yet in comparing Sousa's Band to the French Garde Républicaine, he ranked Sousa's higher: "Combined with the wonderful purity of tone, absolute control of the instruments, and light and shade seldom known, save in orchestral shading, the new band of Sousa has a brilliancy and vitality that even the French band does not altogether equal." And a week later, at a similar exposition in St. Louis, a critic for the city's *Star* explicitly judged the new band a worthy successor to Gilmore's, in part because "There is a daintier finish to its presentations, a more poetic rendition, a finer tone-quality than was the case with Gilmore."[5]

Nevertheless, in New York and at Manhattan Beach there were many who doubted, and perhaps some who, out of loyalty to Gilmore, hoped otherwise. But Sousa's opening concert, played in the hotel's pavilion, which could seat perhaps three thousand, and with others listening from the hotel's verandah or lawns, went well. The *New York Corn Advertiser* reported: "There were hundreds of people who came down to that first concert determined not to like the new band or its leader, but those who came to scoff remained to praise, for Mr. Sousa and his splendid band made an instantaneous and unqualified success. The band stands today as the best organization of its kind on this continent, and no other leader could so well fill the place of Gilmore as does Mr. Sousa. His modesty is a great point in his favor and at once won the hearts of the audience."[6]

The next day, a Sunday, Sousa as usual featured a hymn, presenting a soprano soloist accompanied by "cathedral chimes" in "Nearer My God to Thee." The program began with the overture to Wagner's *Flying Dutchman*; continued with Miska Hauser's "Slumber Song," with an oboe soloist; Liszt's Hungarian Rhapsody No. 2; Valentine's prayer from Gounod's *Faust*, sung by a baritone; and Sousa's own symphonic poem *The Chariot Race* (1890). According to the *Herald,* "Every number was encored," and most likely by another hymn. For Sunday concerts or religious holidays, Sousa frequently played a medley of hymns and sacred music, which he titled "Songs of Grace and Songs of Glory." The hymns might vary according to season; so, too, might selections from the Hebrew Ritual or the Greek Orthodox Church; and more than once he included an arrangement of what he titled for the newspaper announcements "Prelude to Verdi's *Requiem."* What comprised this "Prelude," however, is uncertain, for the term is not Verdi's.[7]

Most of the audiences for these performances were reported to number in the thousands, and the musical part of the evening was usually followed by an extravagant fireworks display which in 1893 featured "The Siege and Storming of Vicksburg." For that event, in which Sousa's Band may not have been employed, the *Times* announced, "Five hundred infantry, two squadrons of cavalry, and two batteries of artillery will participate in the mimic fray, and the lake within the inclosure is now being deepened to accommodate the ironclad gunboats, and other craft which will share in the assault. . . . As a prelude to the artillery duel and the advance of the storming columns, tableaus and incidents illustrative of life in the South before the war will be presented. One hundred jubilee singers will join in the rendition of favorite camp-meeting hymns and other melodies."[8]

At this time at the Brighton Beach pavilion, on musical evenings at least, there were no such frivolities. The conductor there was Anton Seidl of the Metropolitan Opera and New York Philharmonic leading an orchestra made up mostly of men from those two institutions, and the programs were weightier. Seidl, a Hungarian, who before coming to New York had worked with Wagner in Bayreuth, was one of the great Wagner conductors of the day, and his programs were uncompromising. The weekly *Spirit of the Times* in 1890 commented: "Here is the light, airy, popular program which is expected to attract crowds to hear Seidl's concert, this evening," and listed: "1. Overture to the *Flying Dutchman*; 2. *Waldweben*; 3. *Lohengrin*; 4. *Siegfried Idyll*; 5. Intermission of ten minutes; 6. Overture to *Tannhäuser*; 7. Song from *The Meistersinger*; 8. "Good Friday," from *Parsifal*." The journal doubted the audience would be large, but the craze for Wagner was then at its height, and in Brooklyn was supported by a Seidl Society, organized by and chiefly for women. For working women the society provided "not only free or inexpensive railroad and concert tickets, but child care," and for ladies "without escorts," special seating and travel arrangements. As the Wagner historian Joseph Horowitz notes, Seidl, with his long hair, romantic looks, and priestly manner, seemed more "an Artist" to women; Sousa, scorned for his tight-fitting uniform and white gloves, was "a populist entertainer."[9]

Unlike Brighton Beach, the emphasis at Manhattan Beach and the Oriental was very much on society and exclusiveness. Corbin, a Yankee from New Hampshire, began to exclude Jews from his hotels in 1879 and sought chiefly Christian businessmen and English nobility. The *Herald,* for one, often named the "well-known people" currently on show at the two hotels and in reporting the arrival of a titled couple, remarked:

> Society at Manhattan Beach was reinforced last week by Sir William and Lady Brooks . . . [whose suite at the Oriental] had been especially reserved for them on receipt of a telegram from Saratoga. . . . Lady Brooks, who long reigned in England as a society beauty, begins to show the ravages of age, but there are traces of a superb figure and magnificent coloring. She is tall, fair and slender. She dresses in dark colors and has one of the sweetest of voices. She took several long walks while at the Beach with an English woman's enthusiasm for exercise and went in bathing several times. She is a most graceful swimmer. Sir William is robust, ruddy, smooth faced and about fifty years old with a most un-American accent and the typical Englishman's desire to fuss and fume as much as possible.[10]

Sousa's success at Manhattan Beach evidently pleased Corbin, for thereafter the band became the resort's chief musical attraction. In its first five seasons it performed a total of fifty-four weeks, and played every summer through 1901, except for 1898 when Sousa was ill and nearly died from typhoid fever and pneumonia. Apparently everyone agreed that without him the band could not sustain a two-and-a-half-month season at a single stand, and in his place the hotel offered a series of short engagements by less famous competitors. Earlier, however, Sousa had sealed his tie to Manhattan Beach by introducing in 1894 a march dedicated to Corbin, "Manhattan Beach." It promptly proved one of his more popular works and was published, as then was usual for his marches, in at least eighteen arrangements for a variety of instruments.[11]

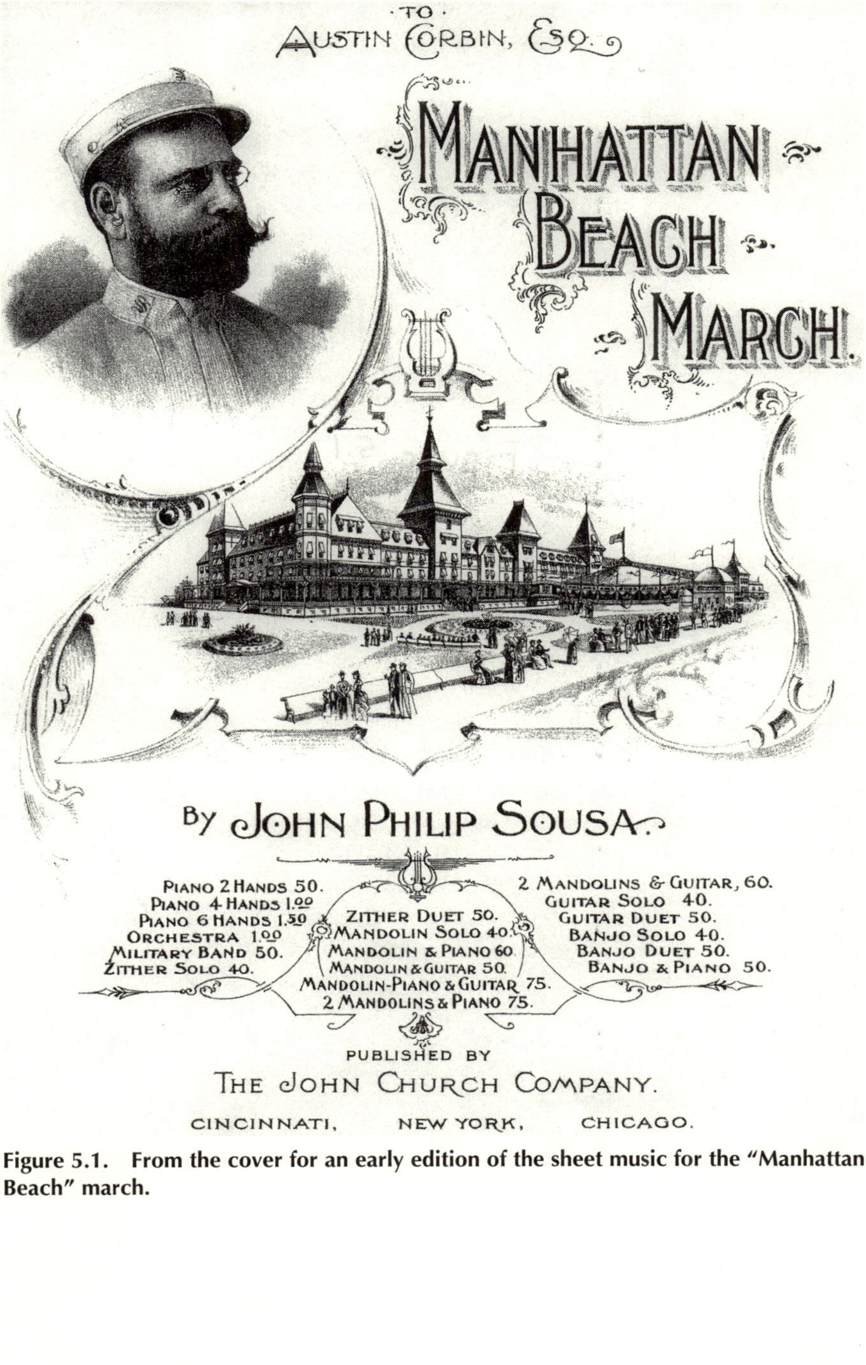

Figure 5.1. From the cover for an early edition of the sheet music for the "Manhattan Beach" march.

At this time Sousa's position in American music was high, perhaps even dominant, not only as a conductor but also as a composer. Besides his band concerts and his marches, his operetta *El Capitan,* premiered in 1896, was a big success, playing in theaters all across the country for more than a decade, and occasionally thereafter. Two more operettas followed in the next two years, *The Bride Elect* (1897) and *The Charlatan* (1898), and though neither matched the record of *El Capitan,* both provided excerpts that were still in Sousa's active repertory thirty years later and in band repertory today.[12]

Then one morning in December 1896, while with his wife on vacation in Europe, Sousa read in the *Paris Herald* a report of Blakely's sudden death in November in the New York office. Hastily he booked passage on the *Teutonic* and while on board and in agitation, for he had a Blakely-organized tour scheduled, he began to hear a new piece playing in his head: "Suddenly, I began to sense the rhythmic beat of a band playing within my brain. It kept on ceaselessly, playing, playing, playing. Throughout the whole tense voyage, that imaginary band continued to unfold the same themes, echoing and re-echoing the most distinct melody." Stirred by the sight of New York Harbor and the American flag, on reaching home he set to work, completed the march on Christmas Day, titled it "The Stars and Stripes Forever," and introduced it at the Academy of Music in Philadelphia on the afternoon and evening of 14 May 1897.[13]

The evening concert was his fiftieth in the city, and he offered the new march to mark the occasion. His announcement in the *Public Ledger,* however, had promised that it would be played at each concert, and the next day the *Philadelphia Inquirer,* reporting a large audience at both "not withstanding Outside Attractions" (chiefly the unveiling of a new statue of Washington at an entrance to Fairmount Park), stated that at both concerts the march was "enthusiastically received." Soon audiences in excited response to its strains began to stand whenever it was played, which for a time became the custom.[14]

As the century came to a close, the *Musical Courier,* noting Sousa's success not only with marches but with his light operas, exclaimed:

> It is Sousa in the band, Sousa in the orchestra, Sousa in the phonograph, Sousa in the hand organ, Sousa in the music box, Sousa everywhere. The American composer is the man, not of the hour or of the day, but of the time! Such a fame, prestige and popularity as John Philip Sousa has achieved through his own efforts could not be of an ephemeral nature, because it is founded upon the broadest lines of intellect, originality and unconquerable force.[15]

Though Sousa's typical repertory for the summer crowd at Manhattan Beach veered toward the popular, that of his winter tours was typically more serious. To offer an example for the corresponding years, and limited to one annually repeated visit, consider his programs for the sixteen concerts he gave in Rochester in the years 1894–1901 (see appendix 11). Happily, because the band always played in the same locale, the Lyceum Theatre, its programs were not skewed by weather, acoustic problems, or other temporary local peculiarities. In the sixteen programs, each usually announcing nine or ten numbers and adding always as many short and popular encores, Sousa scheduled forty-four operatic selections by twenty-five composers, with another four of the selections played twice in the eight years and one, the sextet from *Lucia* arranged for six brass soloists, offered four times. Thus on average at any concert, the audience heard at least three operatic numbers with these typically placed at important points, to open or close the performance or before the intermission.

Wagner was the composer most often performed, with twelve excerpts of seven operas, *Tannhäuser* through *Parsifal,* omitting only *Das Rheingold* and *Die Meistersinger.* Yet elsewhere in these years Sousa played excerpts from these two and also from the two operas preceding *Tannhäuser, Rienzi* and *Der Fliegende Holländer.* Thus in his active repertory at this time he had selections from all eleven of Wagner's well-known operas. In Rochester, at least in the last two years covered in appendix 11, he played no Wagner, which may be a matter of chance or possibly he perceived a slight decline in the public's interest. Outside New York, as the smaller audience in Boston for his all-Wagner concert (1893) suggested, the veneration for the composer was weaker, in part no doubt because the smaller cities lacked New York's huge German immigrant population, but also in part because they lacked resident opera companies. Or, if they had one, it was not led by an Anton Seidl, supported by a Seidl Society, and so of Wagner they heard only the occasional excerpt played by a touring band or orchestra.

In his last two seasons at Rochester, Sousa offered in place of Wagner a slight increase in the works of Italian operatic composers, Verdi, Boito, Ponchielli, Leoncavallo, and Giordano. Donizetti's sextet from *Lucia,* arranged for three cornets or trumpets, two trombones, and a bass tuba, was played in four of the eight years, and was the work most frequently performed. Rossini, however, now appeared only once, with the overture to *William Tell,* though elsewhere Sousa was still playing the overture to *Semiramide* and other excerpts from that opera. Similarly elsewhere, he offered excerpts from Rossini's *Stabat Mater,* seemingly performed, depending on the band's current roster, with either vocal, cornet, or trombone soloists. A curiosity of the Verdi selections was the first appearance, in 1901, of the overture to *Aroldo,* which Sousa continued to play into the 1920s and which, except for him, and to a lesser extent E. F. Goldman, was otherwise unknown. For instance, it never was performed at the Metropolitan's Sunday Afternoon concerts, 1883–1946, and after 1863 the opera seems not to have been heard complete in the United States until a concert performance in New York in 1961.[16]

Another such rarity and equally successful for Sousa was Ponchielli's overture to his opera, *I promessi sposi,* which on occasion replaced the better known "Dance of the Hours," from *La Gioconda.* On the other hand, though he kept Boito's "Night of the Classical Sabbath," from *Mefistofele,* steadily in his repertory, after only two seasons he dropped the opera's prologue, possibly for the lack of a bass singer. Lastly, among the operatic numbers were six, by such composers as Giordano, Goldmark, and Humperdinck, which had received their world premieres in 1893 or later. In these years, therefore, he often was scheduling music which many in the audience were hearing for the first time.

Though the reasons are not clear, Sousa's annual summer stand at Manhattan Beach ended with the 1901 season. According to his autobiography the decision was his: "Manhattan Beach was rapidly changing. The crowd, though appreciative, was not a wealthy one and I saw the writing on the wall which proclaimed, 'This is the end.'" Corbin had died in 1896, killed with his coachman in a carriage upset. According to the *Times,* "Just as they were moving out of the yard, the horses, which were being driven without blinders for the first time, shied and all the occupants were thrown down an embankment against a stonewall." Perhaps with Corbin dead the resort lost some of its managerial energy and social cachet; perhaps, too, as Brooklyn's population, swollen by immigration, doubled in the years 1890–1910, the steady approach to Coney Island of lower and middle income houses and a simultaneous expansion of the island's west end amusement parks spoiled the east end's sense of exclusiveness. Whatever the reason, the whim of fashion shifted to other resorts, and in 1911, the year after horse racing closed at Sheepshead Bay, the Manhattan Beach Hotel was razed. By then, however, Sousa had established himself and the band as the chief summer attraction at the Willow Grove Park, north of Philadelphia.[17]

NOTES

1. Bierley, *The Incredible Band,* 42–45.
2. Rehearsals. Bierley, *American Phenomenon,* 161–62, and Schwartz, *Bands of America,* 149–50; on the "first" rehearsal, 1893, Schwartz, 156–57.
3. The Culver Line, *Times,* 13 May 1893, 9. The electric billboard, Nathan Silver, *Lost New York* (New York: Wings Books, Random House, 1967), 66–67, and Joseph Horowitz, *Wagner Nights,* 210.
4. Following his European tour in 1878, Gilmore started at Manhattan Beach in 1879, Cipolla, "Patrick S. Gilmore: The New York Years," 187. Sousa at Manhattan

Beach, Sousa, *Marching Along,* 138. *Times,* 13 May 1839, 9; also *Times,* 27 May 1893, 9.

5. Opening concert, *Boston Herald,* 5 May 1893, 9; Wagner concert, ibid., 6 May 1893, 7; and 2,500, *Boston News,* ibid., 2. Comparison to French band, *Boston Herald,* 5 May 1893, 9,and *St. Louis Star*, 13 May 1893, quoted by Warfield, "Salesman of Americanism," 501, and also favorable reviews in Syracuse, Buffalo, Duluth, Kansas City, Des Moines, and the *St. Louis Chronicle.*

6. *New York Corn Advertiser,* 3 July 1893, quoted in Warfield, "Salesman of Americanism," 517–18, and again in "Making the Band: The Formation of John Philip Sousa's Ensemble," *American Music* 24, no. 1 (Spring 2006), 59.

7. *Herald,* 3 July 1893, 4. A page-long synopsis for the *Chariot Race*, signed "Ben-Hur," is in the program for Sousa's Philadelphia concert with the U.S. Marine Band, 9 May 1891; program in the U.S. Marine Band Library, Washington, D.C. Verdi *Requiem* "Prelude," twice in Boston, for the Columbian Exposition, the *Boston Herald,* 7 May 1893, 15. Also in Kansas City, Warfield, "Salesman of Americanism," 539, citing program for 14 May 1893. The *Kansas City Star,* the next day, reported: "The potpourri of religious songs and hymns, given in the afternoon, was one of the most potent numbers heard here in many months." Uncertainty of the "Prelude," Verdi's *Requiem* opens with a twenty-seven-bar passage asking requiem for the dead, which runs roughly two minutes and is easily recognized. One can hear it played at the start of "Songs of Grace and Songs of Glory" on the American Classics album *Music for Wind Band* (Naxos, 8.559059), which features Keith Brion, a Sousa specialist, and the Royal Artillery Band. In contrast, when Brion and the Razumovsky Symphony Orchestra on the American Classics album *Sousa "At the Symphony"* (Naxos, 8.559013) recorded a similar "Sacred Songs" medley and started it "with a section of Verdi's *Requiem,*" the excerpt was taken from bars 21 through 26 of Verdi's opening, ran only thirty seconds, and required a sharp ear to pinpoint the source. The discrepancy suggests that Sousa perhaps kept two versions of his introductory excerpt, longer and shorter, using whichever fit better in his program—just as he often changed the hymns in the medley. I thank Byron Hanson, archivist at Interlochen, for this point.

8. Siege of Vicksburg, *Times,* 13 May 1893, 9.

9. On Anton Seidl and the Brighton Beach concerts, Horowitz, *Wagner Nights,* 199–212. Horowitz quoting the *Spirit of the Times,* 26 July 1890, ibid., 201–02; on women and Wagner, ibid., 195, 199, 205; artist not populist entertainer, ibid., 302. On the increasing role of women in musical organizations of all sorts, Broyles, "Art Music from 1860 to 1920," 216–17, 227–32; and on the Seidl Society, 230. For more on Seidl and the Seidl Society, in greater detail, see Joseph Horowitz, *Moral Fire: Musical Portraits from America's Fin de Siècle* (Berkeley: University of California Press, 2012), 83–85, 125–27, and 138–161.

10. Lady Brooks, *Herald,* 2 July 1893, 13; other socialites seen on the hotel piazzas, *Herald,* 3 July 1893, 4. The *Herald,* 7 July 1893, 4, listed the people seen at the Manhattan Beach and Oriental hotels, but remarked of the humbler Brighton Beach piazzas only that they were "well filled."

11. Fifty-four weeks, five seasons, Schwartz, *Bands of America,* 166, citing an 1899 program which gave statistics on the band's activities. It estimated that by then the band had played more than 3,500 concerts in more than four hundred cities. Sousa's eighty-day stand at Manhattan Beach, Bierley, *The Incredible Band,* 20. Published arrangements of his works were usually for two-, four-, and six-hands at piano, for orchestra or military band, and for various combinations of mandolin, zither, guitar, or banjo. For the vocal edition of "The Stars and Stripes Forever," for which Sousa had written words, the John Church Company published only a single arrangement, for voice and piano. Sousa in *Marching Along*, 324, suggests that during the Spanish-American War, the two most popular songs sung by Americans were "There'll Be a Hot Time in the Old Town To-Night" and "The Stars and Stripes Forever."

12. *El Capitan,* for example, Goodspeed Opera Company in the 1970s, and recently Canton Comic Opera (concert performance) in 2005 and Ohio Light Opera Company in 2010. Sousa, *Marching Along,* 150. As excerpts from *The Bride Elect*, Sousa offered not only its principal march but other songs presented as vocal solos, and in thirty-one of the band's forty years scheduled a potpourri, "Selections," which ran almost eleven minutes, unusually long for Sousa, but an excerpt he would not have continued unless audiences had liked it.

13. Blakely had died of apoplexy in his office in Carnegie Hall on 7 November 1896. The *Herald,* 8 November 1896, 9, described him as "the manager of Sousa's Band." Also, Sousa, *Marching Along*, 157. Dating "The Stars and Stripes Forever" 25 December 1896, see Bierley, *The Incredible Band,* 20.

14. The premiere, *Public Ledger* (Philadelphia), 15 May 1897, 19, and the *Philadelphia Inquirer,* 16 May 1897, 11. See also Sousa, *Marching Along,* 301. Audience standing, Schwartz, *Bands of America,* 162, and Bierley, *American Phenomenon,* 143. Also, Patrick Warfield, "The March as Musical Drama and the Spectacle of John Philip Sousa," *Journal of the American Musicological Society* 64, no. 2 (Summer 2011).

15. Editorial, "The Era of Sousa," *Musical Courier* 37, no. 1, 4 July 1898, n.p.

16. On *Aroldo,* see George W. Martin, "The Metropolitan Opera's Sunday Evening Concerts and Verdi," *The Opera Quarterly* 19, no. 1 (Winter 2003): 16–27, and Kaufman's chronology, *Verdi and His Major Contemporaries,* 464–65. R. F. Goldman, *The Band's Music* (New York: Pitman, 1938), 400–410, lists the excerpts from Verdi's operas then current for bands. Besides the usual, *Aida* and so forth, were the overtures to *Giovanna d'Arco* and *Aroldo,* and excerpts from *Nabucco*, *I Lombardi, Attila, Macbeth,* and *Don Carlos.*

17. "The end," Sousa, *Marching Along,* 232. Corbin's death, *Times,* 5 June 1896, 1.

Chapter Six

John Philip Sousa

Willow Grove Park, Pennsylvania

Sousa in his statements and his writings was not much given to critical comparisons, yet sometimes a mild remark may imply one. Thus when he ascribes his liking for Willow Grove Park to the fact that "its first consideration is music," it suggests that he was happier with the park's concept and policies than with those at Manhattan Beach. He approved of the way the Willow Grove "management endeavors to obtain every year the best the country affords. Such organizations as the Chicago Symphony, the Damrosch Orchestra, the Russian Orchestra, and famous bands like Conway's, Pryor's, Creatore's and Banda Rossa have played there. All this can be heard without paying a penny." And though dismayed to discover at his first meal at the park's casino that he could not have wine with his dinner, he saw purpose in the ban: to keep the focus on other pleasures. Besides, he was not forced to go entirely without, for in the town of Willow Grove the Mineral Springs Hotel, where he often stayed, served liquor. As on most issues, Sousa's attitude about drink was relaxed. Apparently both by nature and conviction he inclined to "live and let live," though not in all matters—on one occasion he fired a musician for anti-Semitic remarks—and in 1926, after Prohibition had come into force (1920) he expressed his feelings about it musically in two humoresques, "Follow the Swallow" and "The Mingling of the Wets and Drys." These got him into trouble that year at the Methodist Camp Meeting at Ocean Grove, New Jersey, where the elders, hearing that he had scheduled the latter, based on drinking songs, protested. Sousa then substituted with the former, and though previously a fixture at the camp meeting, he was not invited back.[1]

Unlike Manhattan Beach, which had its "Ocean Breezes," Willow Grove Park was man-made, the creation of a trolley line, the Philadelphia Rapid Transit Company, which extended its electrified line some sixteen miles into the city's countryside and then sought riders to use it, particularly on the weekends. Accordingly, the company bought two farms, almost a hundred acres, and designed a park with three lakes, three picnic areas with tables, benches, hot and cold water available, some grounds set aside for sports (chiefly baseball), and a few amusements—such as a carousel, a scenic railroad (mostly at treetop height), and a trolley ride around the park's perimeter. There were also a few refreshment stands and the casino for dining, but most imposing was the music pavilion beside the large, four-acre lake. To landscape the park, the Transit Company had planted some 7,500 trees, 3,500 assorted shrubbery, 4,000 privets, and 5,000 flowering plants, and the picnic groves were attractive and always well picked up. In addition, all visitors to the park were advised, and on occasion warned by park guards ("manly fellows" in grey uniforms), to dress and behave properly. Unaccompanied ladies were promised a park safe for themselves and children and provided with a large pavilion with changing rooms, lavatories, and rocking chairs on the porches. The Transit Company touted Willow Grove not as an amusement park but as one for pleasure, a quiet day in the country with an opportunity, in summer months, to hear good music.[2]

As a historian of the park noted, "It is important to keep in mind that most Philadelphians had never been out of the city," and for many the trip to Willow Grove was itself an adventure. The ride out from the center of Philadelphia took an hour and twenty minutes and along the way passed several grand estates, such as those of John Wanamaker and Joseph Wharton (who founded the business school). The cost—with no admission charged for the park—was fifteen cents one way, and a guide book described the line's roadway as a "magnificent serpent-like boulevard sixteen miles in length, hard and smooth, kept in perfect state by a large force of men, and forming a panorama of rare rural scenery." In addition to the trolley line, the town of Willow Grove was a stop on the Reading Railroad, and so people from as far west as Harrisburg or Hershey could easily reach the park and stay overnight in the town's hotels. From its first season in 1896 it daily drew crowds by the thousands, especially women, children, Sunday School groups, reunions of all sorts, and picnickers. The three groves reportedly could accommodate 25,000 persons.[3] (See the photospread.)

For the park's first summer season the music attraction was a trombonist and his band, "Innes and His Famous Fifty." Frederick Innes, after playing with Gilmore, had started his own touring group and adopted Gilmore's style of programs, mixing popular and classical numbers. He also had submitted designs to Willow Grove for the park's band shell which had risen close to the shore of the largest lake, a building of considerable size containing not only the shell proper (40 feet high, 50 feet in diameter, and bracketed by tall Ionic columns) but surrounding offices and changing rooms (see photos).

The audience sat in open air on wooden benches, while others lolled on the surrounding lawns or listened from rowboats on the lake. Happily, the shell's acoustics proved excellent, and from Decoration Day, 31 May 1896, to the close of the season, on 20 September, Innes and his men played, weather permitting, every afternoon and evening. According to the park's historian, "Monday night was public request night, and Friday evenings were strictly classical"; on all other occasions the programs offered "a mix of classical music, operatic selections, marches, songs and lighter classics."[4]

Seemingly, though in a later season, the Innes band or one like it was the example recalled by H. L. Mencken in an article for the *Baltimore Sun* in 1911:

> Gilmore had toured the country, and Sousa had toured the country, and other professors of the brass had followed them—but at $1.50 a seat. Here was a band that played for nothing in a huge summer park, where anyone able to pay a few cents car fare was welcome to listen all he cared.
>
> The result was a palpable hit—an enormous popular success. I once saw a crowd of 15,000 at Willow Grove packed close about the shell and listening to this excellent band. It played, not silly ragtime, but honest music. The sextet from *Lucia,* performed by two trumpets, two trombones, a baritone and a tenor, was its *pièce de résistance*—and the sextet from *Lucia* is still the masterpiece of all true Italian bands. It played, too, the quartet from *Rigoletto,* the overture to *William Tell,* the pilgrims' chorus from *Tannhäuser,* the soldiers' chorus from *Faust,* the great march from *Aida,* the tower scene from *Il trovatore* (as duet, as I recall it, for trumpet and trombone), the wedding music from *Lohengrin,* elaborate arrangements of *Don Giovanni, The Barber of Seville, Traviata, Carmen, Cavalleria Rusticana* [then the favorite of the hour], *Stradella* and *Lucrezia Borgia.* Going further, it tackled the familiar ballet suites, the time-honored overtures. And after a while it plunged boldly into Tschaikovski's *1812* and other such things of fuming and fury.[5]

After Innes, for its second season, the Grove offered Walter Damrosch and the New York Symphony, and to the surprise of some his more classical programs proved popular: on Monday nights a complete symphony, and on Fridays, all Wagner. Indeed, so popular was Damrosch and the symphony that the park's historian could assert: "He set a new standard for outdoor summer music in America and stimulated a popular appreciation of Classical music. The founding of the Philadelphia Orchestra in 1901 would be attributable in part to the popularity Damrosch had brought to symphonic music." Soon parks elsewhere, which in the twenty years 1887–1907 were said to have increased in number "from two to two hundred," began to imitate Willow Grove in their summer programs.[6]

Undoubtedly a reason for the success of the music programs was the still primitive state of recordings and radio broadcasts, for neither were yet cheap or plentiful. For most people the pleasure, the excitement, of music played by professionals could be had only at a live performance, and Willow Grove, amid pleasant surroundings, offered two concerts a day. By 1899 the park had adopted a policy of offering a variety of musical groups over the summer, including for the longer stands usually a symphony orchestra and a nationally known band. The following season, urged by Damrosch, it built a roof reaching outward from the band shell, a pavilion supported by narrow pillars, open at the sides and back but reducing the dissipation of sound while providing four thousand listeners with some slight protection from wind and rain. Those not under the pavilion continued to sit on the surrounding lawns, and in fair weather usually numbered in the thousands.[7] (See the photospread.)

Sousa's first season at Willow Grove was 1901, his last at Manhattan Beach, and he opened a short stand on Decoration Day, introducing for the occasion his latest work, "The Invincible Eagle." As a composer he was prolific in several forms of music, excepting symphony and chamber works, and in addition to 15 operettas (three left unfinished), at his death he left a catalogue—to mention only the larger categories—of 70 songs, 322 arrangements, and 136 marches, with a few more of the last left untitled and seemingly unperformed. Some of the marches no doubt are better than others, but among the twenty-five most frequently played is "The Invincible Eagle" which, like "Manhattan Beach," has a particular association.[8]

In addition to the park, Sousa liked the town of Willow Grove and its countryside where in off-hours he could ride horseback, shoot skeet (he was an excellent shot), play golf, or even pitch an inning or two in the band's baseball games. His musicians equally liked it, and for many of them the town became a summer home, a place where for five or six weeks they could rest from travel and be joined by wives and children. With success at the park assured, Sousa returned annually through 1926 except for the year 1911 when he and the band toured round the world. He did not play at the park in 1927 but did return for a single day (three concerts) in 1928, his final performances in the park. In all, at Willow Grove Park he played a total of 2,751 concerts.[9]

Historians generally note 1910 as the climactic year for bands in the United States. Soon thereafter a decline in audience began, which in turn began to limit opportunities for touring as venues shut down or turned their attention elsewhere. There were many reasons, one of the chief being the rise of the automobile, which though it had a long history began a swift advance in 1911 when Henry Ford won a court case freeing it from a restrictive patent. Then in 1914 he began to mass-produce cars on assembly lines and in 1915 to make loans to people buying his Model T, by which time the annual sale of cars in the United States had risen from roughly 4,000 in 1900 to 895,000, and by

1925 to 3.7 million, opening for many a wider choice of countryside than one park at the end of a trolley line.[10]

Similarly, recordings were steadily improving in sound and number, and in 1912, for example, the Victor Talking Machine Company published its first *Victor Book of the Opera,* which offered the "Stories of Seventy Grand Operas" with "Descriptions of Seven Hundred Victor Opera Records." Among them were many with Caruso singing, and "allegedly," according to a historian, the Victor company gave him "a gold record in 1911, when they realized that they had sold over a million copies of his records." Though Sousa paid musicians higher wages than did most of his colleagues, he never had a tenor to match Caruso.[11]

Moreover, he was never comfortable with recordings. At first he spoke out vigorously against them, publishing in *Appleton's Magazine* in 1906 what has been called his "most celebrated—and vitriolic—article," "The Menace of Mechanical Music." He opened, "Sweeping across the country with the speed of a transient fashion in slang or Panama hats, political war cries or popular novels, comes now the mechanical device to sing for us a song; or play for us a piano, in substitute for human skill, intelligence, and soul." Warning that "it is the living, breathing example alone that is valuable to the student and can set into motion his creative and performing abilities"; he foresaw a day when "the tide of amateurism cannot but recede, until there will be left only the mechanical device and the professional executant." The article was accompanied by satiric drawings, one of which showed a boy, in utter disbelief, calling to his mother to come to the drawing room to see a man "playing the piano with his hands!" Furthermore, for Sousa the recording process was too mechanical to be artistic; it broke the tie of performer and audience, dulled all nuances, and dimmed the color and timbre of instruments.[12]

The article caused a stir, and editors and readers took sides. In one reply that the magazine published, the writer rejoiced at the prospect of banishing from our homes "the horrors of scales and exercises," insisting "the mechanical reproduction of songs by correct methods will only stimulate him [the amateur] to sing the more and enable him to sing the better." Good recorded performances in the home, he predicted, would surely increase the public's interest in music. Words flew without persuasion, and the argument continues.[13]

Late in life, Sousa relented slightly about recordings, but only slightly. Of the 1,770 pieces issued on recordings labeled as by "Sousa's Band," almost all were played by bands with only a nucleus of his musicians aided by pick-up players, and of the recordings Sousa conducted only eight, of which only six were issued. All of these were performances of his marches and made between 1917 and 1923, with even the last of them made three years before an "electrical" process in recording, with microphones, replaced the "acoustic." In the latter, the band typically was smaller than usual, numbering at most between thirty and forty-five (instead of fifty to seventy), and all sat huddled before a large horn collecting the sound which then passed through a diaphragm to a stylus and onto a wax disc—the master, from which the commercial, shellac records were made. The gramophone, in playing these, essentially reversed the process. But the recordings did not reproduce the sound of the band in live performance, and to Sousa's ear surely seemed imperfect, as they did also to members of the band, and perhaps even to some of the public.[14]

Nevertheless, what passed on Victor labels as "Sousa's Band" made many recordings of operatic excerpts, as did also other bands, and on occasion an operatic rarity would be added to the backside of a familiar excerpt. The first edition of *The Victor Book of the Opera* (1912), for instance, has a pairing of "Selections from Aida" by Arthur Pryor's Band with the "Grand Trio" from Verdi's *Attila,* featuring the cornet, trombone, and euphonium soloists of Bohumir Kryl's Band. At that time *Attila* was hardly a familiar opera, seemingly not staged in the United States since two performances in San Francisco in 1872. And in the book's 1919 edition, for example, there is a pairing of the well-known Pilgrims Chorus from *Tannhäuser* with the then almost unknown Grand March from Verdi's *Don Carlos,* not staged in New York since 1877 and still awaiting a premiere at the Metropolitan. Though the recording was by "Sousa's Band" and he personally liked the music, he did not conduct.[15]

But if Sousa was unwilling, others were not, and one who in these early years made many recordings was his former solo trombonist Arthur W. Pryor, who also had served as Sousa's assistant conductor from 1895 to 1903. In that last year, he left Sousa to form his own band and began six highly successful years of touring, during which he and his men developed a national reputation. But after 1909, Pryor gave up extensive touring to concentrate on engagements close to home, and filled in much of the freed time by making recordings. In the 1912 edition of the *Victor Book of the Opera*, Pryor and his band are listed with selections from at least thirty-four of the seventy grand operas; additionally, he is thought to have conducted some 75 percent of the nearly 1,200 Victor recordings credited to the Sousa Band. For those under his own name, most of Pryor's excerpts were taken from French and Italian operas, and some of his arrangements, though startling in conception—such as "Celeste Aida" offered as a trombone solo—because of his skill, are beautiful. In earlier years he had worked for a time as the director of an opera company in Denver, and he reportedly preferred "slow, lyric ballads and operatic arias to the fast, spell-binding display pieces that Sousa insisted he perform first." On just what basis he recorded with Sousa's Band, or just how the Victor company could label the records as such when Sousa was not conducting is not clear, but personally the two men remained friends for life, and at Sousa's funeral Pryor was one of the pallbearers.[16] (See the photospread.)

Furthermore, along with the increase in automobiles and recordings, yet another technological advance threatened the primacy of music at parks like Willow Grove: the radio broadcast. On 13 January 1910 a double bill of *Cavalleria Rusticana* and *I Pagliacci,* with Caruso and Pasquale Amato in the latter, was broadcast from the Metropolitan stage. Only a few heard the performance, but among radio fans the feat stirred great excitement, and developments soon followed. As a historian of radio notes, the Chicago Civic Opera for its 1921–1922 season had an arrangement with the local radio station KYW by which "all performances, afternoon and evening, six days a week, were broadcast—and nothing else." To which he added: "At the beginning of the season there were thought to be 1,300 receivers in the Chicago area. No sets were yet in the stores, but people began clamoring for them. . . . By the end of the opera season 20,000 sets were reported in operation in Chicago." Nationally, in 1922 the sales of radio sets and parts reached $60 million, and in 1924, $358 million. With music increasingly available at home, fewer sought it in parks.[17]

Neither Sousa nor Willow Grove could control such vast social changes, and the park met the new conditions by steadily leasing space to more concessions of all sorts, which charged fees. Acre by acre the lawns gave way to shooting galleries, food and ice cream shops, a movie theater, roller coasters, snap-the-whips, and a huge ballroom (10 cents a couple per dance). By 1914 Willow Grove was changing from a pleasure to an amusement park—"Life is a lark at Willow Grove Park"—and though the better bands and symphony orchestras continued to play in the music pavilion, they soon ceased to be the park's main attraction, and the park began to charge for seats near the stage.

By the 1926 season the Transit Company had signed a contract with a dance band leader, Meyer Davis, giving him control of the park, and according to its historian, Davis "was not in favor of the free public concerts." In an effort to boost revenue he brought in "beauty pageants, leg and ankle contests, and other racy spectacles," and offered raffles for cash prizes. Sousa's contract, however, had already been signed, and 1926 thus became his last full season at the park. He also at this time reportedly advised Edwin Franko Goldman, an independent band leader in New York, against touring. Public interest was declining.[18]

As reconstructed by the scholar Paul Edmund Bierley, that last full season ran "fifty-seven days, from Sunday, 18 July through Sunday, 12 September," and totaled 228 concerts. The number was reached by playing four short concerts a day, about forty-five minutes each, beginning at 2:30, 4:30, 7:45, and 9:45, each without an intermission. "Every program was different, although some selections were repeated at later dates." From programs of the concerts kept by a band member who noted encores on the programs, Bierley could reconstruct "without guesswork" ninety-four concerts, including all encores, and a survey of these suggests how, by the mid-1920s, Sousa's repertory was changing.[19]

Among the operatic numbers, for example, there was less Wagner, only seven excerpts in the ninety-four concerts, but twelve of Verdi. One reason may be that excerpts from Wagner tend to run long and the concerts were short; whereas for Verdi, in these years Sousa had an excellent soprano, Marjorie Moody, whose most frequent numbers were "Caro nome" from *Rigoletto* and "Ah, fors' è lui," from *Traviata.* To such vocal excerpts, Sousa added orchestral selections from *Aida, Trovatore,* and, more unusual, from *Don Carlos.* He had introduced the last as early as 1895 and through 1927 scheduled it in twenty-two years, giving the music at that time far more exposure than any opera company or symphony orchestra. Moreover, at least for these Willow Grove concerts he seems, in a mild attempt at updating, to have increased the number of excerpts from the more recent Italian operas by Puccini, Giordano, and Leoncavallo, while reducing the number by Rossini and Donizetti.

The greatest change in the programming, however, taking the ninety-four concerts as a fair sample, was the number of them featuring Sousa's own compositions, twenty-eight in all, almost one in three. But then with programs short, marches suited. He was always sensitive to what the audience wanted, and evidently now, in what many may have realized was his last full season, the people wanted to see him and to hear his music. And the pattern for "The Stars and Stripes Forever" seems to have been once a day, most often in the fourth and closing concert.

Another important change was the appearance eight times, averaging once a week, of a Sousa fantasy first introduced in 1925 and titled *Jazz America,* which featured the band's saxophone octet, usually made up of four altos, two tenors, a baritone, and a bass. How much, if any, of the piece the players improvised is not clear. Sousa with great success had introduced Paris to ragtime in his 1900 tour, and in 1919, to acknowledge the increasing interest in jazz, he had composed a humoresque, "Showing Off Before Company," which would begin, either to open the program or as first after intermission, with no one onstage. A musician would wander in, riffing on his instrument, then another, and another, playing at first in response to each other and then together, and like *Jazz America* this reversal of Haydn's Farewell Symphony was a popular success. Sousa at first had thought that jazz was a fad likely soon to disappear, and the jazzing of classical tunes distressed him, but by 1926 he was in his seventy-second year, and like many in his generation he found the decade of the 1920s, with "flappers," jazz, and Prohibition, hard to understand.[20]

He was more comfortable with operetta, and in the ninety-four-concert sample of Sousa's last season, he played excerpts from Victor Herbert's works nineteen times, with "Ah, Sweet Mystery of Life" and "Italian Street Song," both from *Naughty Marietta,* each having six performances. Harking back to his early experiences with Gilbert and Sullivan, he scheduled nine excerpts from Sullivan, including the rarely heard incidental music to Tennyson's *The Foresters* (1892), as well as five from works by Offenbach. He also on occasion played a musical comedy song, such as "Look for the Silver Lining" from Jerome Kern's *Sally,* or "Do, Do, Do" from Gershwin's *Oh, Kay!* This last, sung by Marjorie Moody, he played at a concert on 27 August, six weeks before the show had its "try-outs" in Philadelphia.[21]

He seems to have taken to Gershwin, both to the music and the lyrics, for his humoresque on "Swanee" is warm-hearted, boisterous, amusingly orchestrated, and full of Sousa's regularity, drive, and push. An audience member who heard it played as an encore in 1920 reported:

> Under his pen this number became a transcription of the south with mocking birds, whippoorwills, piccaninies, cowbells, steam whistles, Swanee Rivers flowing all through every section, in minors, majors, diminished, augmented, persuasively in the oboe, humorously in the saxophones, triple-tongued in the cornets, and majestically by the ensemble. So that instead of a two minute one-step, we had a ten-minute paraphrase of this rollicking, romping dance number.[22]

Whether by nature or early experience, Sousa seems always to have been partial to theater music, vocal or dramatic, more so than to dance band music that often had rhythm but no particular story. Moreover, his seventy songs indicate a strong response to texts, and as he wrote in his autobiography: "The chief aim of the composer is to produce color, nuance, and change of dynamics, and to emphasize the story-telling quality."[23]

To close his 1926 season at Willow Grove, at the day's fourth concert beginning at 9:30 p.m., he opened with his jazz humoresque, "Showing Off Before Company," followed as an encore by his *El Capitan* march; then a second humoresque, "The Mingling of the Wets and the Drys," succeeded by a new song he had composed, "There's a Merry Brown Thrush," with a text by the Massachusetts poet Lucy Larcom. The encore was "Annie Laurie," and then "The Stars and Stripes Forever" and "The Star-Spangled Banner." As was increasingly usual in his later years, his program featured a work in the currently popular musical style, a reference to a current social issue, a work set to an American poem, and in its marches, a heartfelt burst of patriotism.

As always, educational projects appealed to him, and so in 1930 he accepted an invitation to visit the National High School Orchestra and Band Camp (today Interlochen Arts Camp), founded by Joseph Maddy in 1928, which, like most arts programs at the time, was struggling to survive the Depression. He was to conduct the gathered high school bands in two Sunday concerts, but as often happened he did more. Arriving on Friday and greeted by the band on the hotel verandah, he agreed to lead it in "The Stars and Stripes Forever," and that night in an impromptu concert conducted several more of his marches. At the scheduled rehearsal on Saturday, apparently on request, he spoke about himself, remarking that in World War I, at age sixty-two, he had volunteered to join the navy. The camp's yearbook records: "He tells us how he became a musician and how he 'won the war by shaving off his beard.'" The scheduled Sunday concerts, at which he conducted four of his marches, set a new record for attendance, eight thousand. The following year he came again, and did more. He premiered a new march, "Northern Pines," dedicating it and its royalties to the camp, and this time conducted, besides six marches (four of his and two by others), the *Rienzi* overture, the finale to *Tristan und Isolde,* his own suite *Three Quotations* and his own *Presidential Polonaise.* For this concert the bass drummer in the National High School Band was seventeen-year-old Frederick Fennell, who in his obituary in the *Times*, seventy-three years later, would be named as "arguably the most famous band conductor since Sousa."[24]

Yet the technical and social changes of the decade were overtaking him, and he and his band were the last to support themselves exclusively by touring. Most others had given up such independence and survived, if at all, by submitting themselves to some sponsor, a town, a dance hall, a regiment, the radio, or some fraternal group. A sign of the shifting public interest occurred in programs for Sousa's 1927 tour. That year, for the first time, some of the concerts, limited to forty minutes, were followed by a movie or even by other musical groups. But for the 1928 tour, billed as his "Golden Jubilee," the movie format was limited to a week in Chicago and another in Rochester, New York, while elsewhere he gave 219 full concerts in twenty-eight states in the country's Northeast, Midwest, Texas, California, and the Southwest.[25]

The remaining tours, 1929 through 1931 were shorter, in part because Sousa in 1929 for the first time brought his band to a live radio broadcast. Initially, he had refused to play on the radio, wanting always to have direct contact with the audience so that he could gauge its response, bring a long piece to a swift close, change the tempo with a march, and insert encores at will. That direct contact with the audience was important as well to his musicians, one of whom claimed never to have tired of playing "The Stars and Stripes Forever," because, knowing his part so well, he could watch the mounting excitement of the audience, a pleasure that did not stale.[26]

Sousa had received frequent requests to broadcast and finally in 1929 he relented, declaring through the *Boston Herald:* "I have, therefore, finally concluded that people want to hear us and that it would be foolish to fail to utilize this great modern invention which makes it possible for millions instead of a few thousand to listen to a concert." But he was not comfortable with it. As Bierley noted: "Sousa was also surprised to learn that he had no control over the broadcast format. The choice of selections had to be approved each week by a network committee. After writing his own list of selections on the studio blackboard, he would usually find some were erased, shortened, or switched around by the advertising representative to allow for an introduction, commercial messages, a sign-off, and special announcements." And encores were forbidden. Yet he and his band, a pick-up group recruited in New York because of union rules, made thirty-five live broadcasts and three prerecorded. Audience response was strong.[27]

A memorable broadcast took place in Reading, Pennsylvania, on 9 March 1932. Sousa was to conduct the town's Ringgold Band in a concert celebrating the band's eightieth birthday. Founded in 1852, the Ringgold Band today is one of the country's oldest. In winter it still performs a schedule of roughly a concert a month and in May through September some seventeen or more at festivals, parades, and picnics. It most famous leader (1901–1923) was Monroe A. Althouse, also a successful composer, and by Ringgold tradition every concert must start with an Althouse march. Ultimately, however, the band's eightieth anniversary concert was led by Arthur Pryor, because three days earlier, Sousa, aged seventy-seven, had died of a heart attack. Yet earlier that day he had led the band in rehearsal, and so it happened that the last piece he conducted was "The Stars and Stripes Forever." His death ended his band, for without him and with the country deep in the Depression, the musicians recognized that no band could hope to sustain itself on tour by fees and ticket sales alone. Sousa's Band, with Sousa conducting, had been the attraction.[28]

At Willow Grove, the managers, once again the Transit Company, in 1934 dedicated its spectacular new fountain in its largest lake to Sousa, and from time to time had memorial Sousa concerts. The last, on 16 September 1956, in which the U.S. Navy Band paid tribute to Sousa, was also the last performance of any group in the music pavilion.

For three more years the pavilion stood unused, and then was torn down. Meanwhile, in other ways the park had steadily modernized. Looking back, its historian reports, "By the 1930s the airships ride had converted from gondolas to airplanes; by the early 1950s, the planes would give way to rocket ships"; and looking forward, there were ever more concessions, new rides,

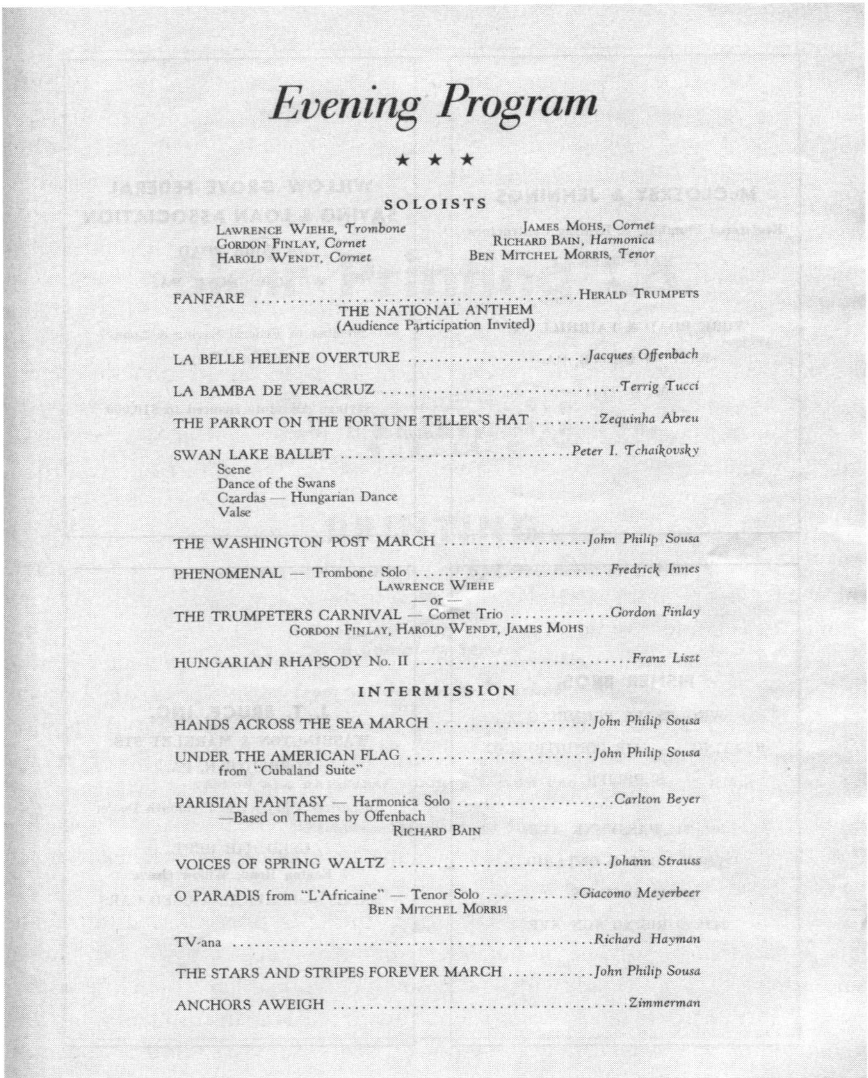

Evening Program

★ ★ ★

SOLOISTS

LAWRENCE WIEHE, *Trombone*
GORDON FINLAY, *Cornet*
HAROLD WENDT, *Cornet*
JAMES MOHS, *Cornet*
RICHARD BAIN, *Harmonica*
BEN MITCHEL MORRIS, *Tenor*

FANFARE .... HERALD TRUMPETS

THE NATIONAL ANTHEM
(Audience Participation Invited)

LA BELLE HELENE OVERTURE .... *Jacques Offenbach*

LA BAMBA DE VERACRUZ .... *Terrig Tucci*

THE PARROT ON THE FORTUNE TELLER'S HAT .... *Zequinha Abreu*

SWAN LAKE BALLET .... *Peter I. Tchaikovsky*
Scene
Dance of the Swans
Czardas — Hungarian Dance
Valse

THE WASHINGTON POST MARCH .... *John Philip Sousa*

PHENOMENAL — Trombone Solo .... *Fredrick Innes*
LAWRENCE WIEHE
— or —
THE TRUMPETERS CARNIVAL — Cornet Trio .... *Gordon Finlay*
GORDON FINLAY, HAROLD WENDT, JAMES MOHS

HUNGARIAN RHAPSODY No. II .... *Franz Liszt*

INTERMISSION

HANDS ACROSS THE SEA MARCH .... *John Philip Sousa*

UNDER THE AMERICAN FLAG .... *John Philip Sousa*
from "Cubaland Suite"

PARISIAN FANTASY — Harmonica Solo .... *Carlton Beyer*
—Based on Themes by Offenbach
RICHARD BAIN

VOICES OF SPRING WALTZ .... *Johann Strauss*

O PARADIS from "L'Africaine" — Tenor Solo .... *Giacomo Meyerbeer*
BEN MITCHEL MORRIS

TV-ana .... *Richard Hayman*

THE STARS AND STRIPES FOREVER MARCH .... *John Philip Sousa*

ANCHORS AWEIGH .... *Zimmerman*

Figure 6.1. Program for the last concert in the shell at Willow Grove Park, played by the U.S. Navy Band "in a tribute to the Immortal John Philip Sousa" on Sunday, 16 September 1956. Old York Road Historical Society.

new games, and new foods, along with a more relaxed dress code: men were no longer required to wear jackets. Only the ban on liquor held firm. As the years passed, and the outlying grounds and picnic groves were sold, the lakes filled in, and the lawns paved over, the park abandoned any idea of cultural programs. In 1976, having passed into private hands and needing repairs, it closed, became embroiled in a lawsuit, and was demolished and sold. In its place, in 1982, arose a shopping mall.[29]

In assessing Sousa (for Sousa in his last year, see photos) it is easy to become fixated on "The Stars and Stripes Forever," to believe it is all that need be remembered, in part because it was so attractively conceived: in a time of personal trouble, expressing love of country, dated Christmas Day 1896, and, in the year of his death, the last work he conducted. Moreover, of all his works, it is the most closely tied to the country in peace and war, and the one which the U.S. Congress and President Reagan in 1987 declared the country's "national march."[30]

Nevertheless, Sousa's position in our music's history rests on more than one march, or even on many, though he is credited with raising what had been merely "functional music," used to move soldiers or people from one place to another, "into the realm of art." In other forms, too, he has a place. As a historian of American operetta has noted: *El Capitan* bodes "well to be the most enduring American comic opera of the nineteenth century," carefully noting, however, that Victor Herbert's most popular operettas all premiered in the next century. Still, *El Capitan* has had several successful revivals, with the latest staged by the Ohio Light Opera Company in 2010. Two others, *The Bride Elect* and *The Charlatan* exist today chiefly in suites and excerpts, but a third, *The Glass Blowers or The American Maid*, was resurrected in the summer of 2000 by the Glimmerglass Opera Company, at Cooperstown, New York. A reviewer for *Opera* described it as "a convoluted saga of class disparity, amorous diversity, economic stress and social upheaval at the time of the Spanish-American War . . . held together by an always elegant, occasionally eloquent parade of ballads, waltzes, mazurkas, cakewalks, choral and orchestral interludes and comic routines, not to mention snap-your-fingers-and-tap-your-toes marches. The music is clever and spiffy, graceful and gutsy, amusing and charming, as needed." And the following year the production moved to the New York City Opera, where it won an equally favorable report in the *Times*. Though it may be too much to say, as did the Glimmerglass program, that Sousa may be considered the "father of American opera and musical theatre," he has a place in its history.[31]

Moreover, besides the marches and operettas, some of his nonvocal works, waltzes, suites, and humoresques, are attractive, but because composed for bands, which today give fewer concerts, are seldom heard unless rearranged for orchestra, which occurs most often for summer "Pops" festivals. Some works also may suffer from Sousa's folksy titling. His *Coeds of Michigan* (1925), for example, an appealing, five and a half minute waltz suite, might please some persons more if titled *Valse romantique,* Op. 37. But that was not Sousa's way. As the *Musical Courier* had noted in 1898, "As a conductor Sousa is of the people and for the people," and in setting program titles for his touring audiences he spoke the language of the people.[32]

In one area of composition, however, he had a relative failure, one that caused him pain. His songs, all seventy of them, were seldom sung. This was true in his lifetime, and is so today. Yet he never stopped composing them. They were, according to Bierley, "especially close to his heart. Most of them do have a simple beauty and are perhaps more reflective of his innermost feelings than is generally known. He was never able to understand why they did not become widely popular. His associates noted that he was visibly saddened by this situation and that the person who approached him on the subject of his songs had made a friend for life."[33]

His compositions aside, Sousa has a significant place in the history of American music as a conductor, educator, and businessman. To take the last first, his forty years of touring without subsidy, relying only on fees and box office receipts, is an accomplishment that no musical group of fifty or more musicians has ever matched. Bierley bluntly states that Sousa's Band "was the most successful organization of its kind in the history of entertainment"—which perhaps is true.[34]

No doubt he was blessed in the timing of his career, 1892–1932, for all but the last three years, which endured the Depression, were years of growth and prosperity in the United States. Even in its wars the country was lucky, for the Spanish-American War produced some heroic exploits and less than 400 deaths in battle, and even World War I, which the country entered late, the fatalities numbered only 53,402, which was small compared to the millions lost by the major European countries. In these years the United States became a world power, bursting with confidence, and that "clarion call of America" is, in Sousa's words, "the keynote" of his marches. In 1927 a reviewer wrote: "A concert by Sousa's Band is more than a mere concert—it is a dramatic performance, a stirring lesson in patriotism, and a popular musical event, all on the same program."[35]

But if in the timing of his life and his patriotic feelings Sousa happily represented the ethos of his age, his accomplishments as a conductor and educator were quite personal. In his band he created what many consider to be the greatest band the world has ever heard, and a study of how he conducted his marches, built chiefly on reports of his musicians, shows that he didn't play them exactly as they were published, for as he told one of his flutists: " Mr.

Lefter, if everybody played it the way it's written, then everybody's band would sound like Sousa's Band so we make some changes now and then just to make it a little bit different." Clearly in leading his marches, he made small changes in tempo, dynamics, shading, and nuance, so that his performances indeed were unique. Perhaps his most notable stylistic tic was what he called "spacing the notes." One historian describes it this way: "Except for sustained passages, the Sousa Band played their notes slightly shorter or crisper so as to create an impression of cleanly separated rhythmic patterns." To which another adds: "The separation between short and long notes makes long notes seem even longer and gives additional rhythmic emphasis . . . [which] gives a lighter character to the marches and emphasizes their dance-like qualities." And seemingly that same virtue shone in his conducting of waltzes, songs, and humoresques.[36]

As a conductor, he had a style that people found appealing. A critic for the *Syracuse Standard* wrote: "Anybody who has seen the sheer delight of a little girl playing mother with her dolls can appreciate the pleasure Sousa takes in leading his famous band. . . . He is the very personification of masculine grace. With the most delicate skill imaginable he modulates his volume of sound, and even when he calls out three trombones, two double basses, all the drums and the cymbals for a tremendous blast, he does it with a quick half-arm movement that expresses as much as if he had jumped four feet in the air." And in Duluth, a critic noted: "Sousa is an ideal leader. He is not overly demonstrative and no violence characterizes his movements, but every motion is graceful and expresses exactly what the music conveys." Sousa once compared himself to a strolling musician, "who is, in fact, a little band all in himself. That is what I am constantly trying to do—to make my musicians and myself a one-man band! . . . So, when I stretch out my hand in the direction of some player, I give him the music I feel and, as I beckon to him, the music leaps back at me. But the element which welds us all into one harmonious whole is sympathy—my sympathy for them and theirs for me."[37]

Lastly, as an educator, in our musical history he is the most important of many band leaders who helped to spread some familiarity with opera. Especially when he went on tour, many in his audience were not symphony subscribers or opera goers, but persons less practised in their musical tastes. For them, as Sousa declared in his autobiography, "I have always selected my programmes according to my own conception of the dictates of good taste. Of course, this disregard of precedent and tradition gives rise to a good deal of criticism—generally from affronted musicians, not from the public." One such high-minded critic in New York, W. J. Henderson of the *Times,* flatly stated that "opera is the lowest form of music" because tied to a text.

"The highest form of music," he argued, "is naturally one in which the laws of musical art find their fullest demonstration. This form can only be one of absolute music." Yet Sousa, who was certainly a sensitive musician, continued regularly to include operatic numbers and songs in his programs because he and his audiences liked them. The human voice is, after all, a much loved instrument, and for forty years, roughly two generations, while introducing many in his audiences to the more demanding and enduring orchestral music of the classical world, he often included for them, in addition to selections and overtures from opera, vocal excerpts.[38]

As an educator Sousa did not talk his points, but he made the sound of the piccolo unforgettable for audiences, some of whom may not have known the instrument's name, by bringing his piccolo players front stage for the trio in "The Stars and Stripes Forever." Similarly, no one who heard a cornet solo by Herbert Clarke or watched Arthur Pryor slide his trombone in and out could forget the sight and the sounds. It need take nothing away from the later achievements of Walter Damrosch or Leonard Bernstein as musical educators to suggest that Sousa did as much or more in his forty years as they did in their shorter stints, or that in his day, when a conductor had to bring the music in person to the distant audience, the job was more arduous.[39]

What he accomplished in entertaining and educating Americans in music can hardly be overstated, for in his day no other musical organization was comparable. When Mahler came in 1909 to conduct the New York Philharmonic, for example, except for an occasional concert in Brooklyn and Philadelphia it had never played outside of Manhattan, and in that year Mahler took it on its very first tour, to New Haven, Springfield, Providence, and Boston. And though he greatly increased the orchestra's number of concerts per year, the total compared to Sousa's schedule was tiny. In 1908–1909 the orchestra played eighteen concerts, in 1909–1910, forty-six, and in 1910–1911, sixty-five. But 1911 was the year Sousa went around the world, a tour of 352 days, a journey of 47, 346 miles, and, despite days of silence spent in travel, played 486 concerts.[40]

Moreover, though Sousa's was the outstanding professional touring band, there were others playing weekly or daily concerts at parks, halls, and bandstands around the country until changing times in the 1920s began to make them obsolete. And many of these, whether in imitation of Sousa or merely responding to what seemed the day's custom, played excerpts from opera, and not just Rossini, Wagner, or Verdi. But today there are fewer such musical groups or educators at work, and in many parts of the country only the eyes of the very old will light up at the mention of a bandstand—"We would go, the whole family, take a picnic, and hear the concert!" It seems we as a people have lost something, but then, nothing lasts forever.

NOTES

1. Sousa, *Marching Along,* 229. Mineral Springs Hotel, Old York Road Historical Society, *Willow Grove Park* (Charleston, SC: Arcadia, 2005), 29. The book has many well-produced and informative photographs. See also Bierley, *The Incredible Band,* 26, 35, 49–51. Firing musician, Bierley, *The Incredible Band,* 47. Sousa on wine, *Marching Along,* 229, 202–203. Ocean Grove, *Times,* 8 May 1927, sec. 2, p. 4; also Bierley, *American Phenomenon,* 105.

2. *Willow Grove Park,* 39; see also 78 for rules at the dance hall, such as: Gentlemen not admitted unless accompanied by at least one lady; No dancing on Sunday; and on Fridays a dancing contest with prizes awarded.

3. The term "historian" personifies what was evidently a group effort by members of the Old York Road Historical Society, *Willow Grove Park,* 12, 43.

4. Ibid., 35. For a description of Frederick N. Innes and his band, see Schwartz, *Bands of America,* 97–98, 126–28, 179–84. *Willow Grove Park,* 34–35.

5. *H. L. Mencken on Music,* 119. Though Mencken here speaks highly of the operatic selections, in "From a Letter to Isaac Goldberg," in this same book, 202, he confesses: "I seldom go to the opera; it is to music what a bawdy house is to a cathedral. The spectacle of fat women sweating, with their mouths wide open, is very offensive. I believe that most of the best music written is in the form of symphonies for grand orchestra."

6. On Damrosch, *Willow Grove Park,* 45. Schwartz, *Bands of America,* 234, quotes Innes as reminiscing, ca. 1906: "When I first went into the business as a band director, there were just two summer places employing bands of the first class. Today it is safe to say there are two hundred." Schwartz then lists fifty-one of the most important, located in twenty-one states and Washington, D.C.

7. *Willow Grove Park,* 52–53, 46.

8. See Bierley, *American Phenomenon,* 225–34. Also Frank Byrne, "Sousa Marches: Principles for Historically Informed Performance," in *The Wind Ensemble and Its Repertoire,* eds. Frank J. Cipolla and Donald Humsberger (Rochester, NY: University of Rochester Press, 1994), 145, on "136-plus" marches, because of some untitled and apparently unperformed marches found in Sousa's papers placed after his death in the Library of Congress.

9. No Willow Grove concert in 1927, Bierley, *The Incredible Band,* 35; total concerts, ibid., 49.

10. "Automobile Industry," *Columbia Encyclopedia,* 6th ed. (New York: Columbia University Press, 2000).

11. John R. Bolig, *Caruso Records: A History and Discography* (Denver: Mainspring Press, 2002), 15.

12. *Appleton's Magazine,* vol. 8, no. 3, 8 September 1906, 278, 279, 281. Illustrations drawn by F. Strothmann. "Vitriolic," Warfield, "The Menace of Mechanical Music," 431.

13. *Appleton's Magazine*, vol. 8, no. 5, 8 November 1906, 638–40. The writer was Paul H. Cromelin. The classical pianist Charles Rosen, *Piano Notes: The World of*

the Pianist (New York: The Free Press, 2002), 160–73, offers an exceptional discussion of the pros and cons of recordings, including such statements as: "Records have altered the listening habits of the music lover perhaps beyond repair. The intense concentration that the art of music sometimes requires has become harder to command." On the morality of splicing tapes: "True irresponsibility—to the public, to the music, to one-self—is to make an inferior record." On rock recordings: "A record of rock music is not a reproduction, but a creation. . . . We may even say that a rock concert is generally a reproduction of a record, and often an inadequate reproduction." For E. F. Goldman's opinions on the impact of radio and phonographs, see *Band Betterment,* 9.

14. Bierley, *The Incredible Band,* 78; see also, Bierley article, "John Philip Sousa: Salesman of Americanism," accompanying the recording *The Original All-American Sousa!,* Keith Brion and his New Sousa Band (Delos 3102; 1990–1992), 15–20. Bolig, *Caruso Records,* 16–17. For a succinct account of pre-electric recordings, see article by Barrymore Laurence Scherer, *Wall Street Journal,* 18 January 2005, p. D-9. Bierley, *The Incredible Band,* 88, tells of an old band member who upon hearing a replay of a broadcast by Sousa's Band remarked: "Oh—The boys were having a bad day!"

15. For *Attila* trio, see Ellen S. Johnson, "The Paul E. Bierley Band Record Collection Featuring John Philip Sousa," in *The Wind Band and Its Repertoire,* 220, 221. Metropolitan premiere of *Don Carlos,* 23 December 1920. The *Victor* book does not list the conductor.

16. Pryor, see essay on his life and art by Daniel E. Frizane accompanying the recording *Arthur Pryor: Trombone Soloist of the Sousa Band* (Crystal Records, CD451). For Sousa on Pryor's skill in the years 1892–1903, no one "on earth to equal Arthur Pryor," *Marching Along,* 323. Sousa conducts only six recordings, Byrne, "Sousa Marches," 148. Pryor's preferences, Frizane, *Arthur Pryor,* 7.

17. Erik Barnouw, *A Tower in Babel: A History of Broadcasting in the United States to 1933* (New York: Oxford University Press, 1966), 27, 88, 114. By 1924, Schwartz, *Bands of America,* 289.

18. *Willow Grove Park,* 75; and 70: "Beginning in 1913, the park removed a section of the public benches in front of the stage and installed more comfortable seating for which there was a charge. The concerts were still free, but there was a price for the nicer seats." Leg contests, 86. Advice to Goldman, 85.

19. Programs as reconstructed, Bierley, *The Incredible Band,* 310. The band member was percussionist John Joseph Heney who in 1931 toured with Sousa as a xylophone soloist and in 1926 as a member of the saxophone octet and also of the clarinet trio, see 215, 310.

20. On Marjorie Moody, Bierley, ibid., 69, 262–69. *Jazz America,* Bierley, *American Phenomenon,* 178, has a photograph of an octet; and *The Incredible Band,* 35, of the sextet for the 1919–1920 tour, two altos, two tenors, one baritone, one bass. Ragtime, *The Incredible Band,* 24, and *American Phenomenon*; playing "Smokey Mokes" and "Whistling Rufus," 17–18; and for a comment by Debussy on the band's ragtime, 136. Jazz, *American Phenomenon,* 18–19. "Showing Off," Warfield, "The March as Musical Drama and the Spectacle of Sousa," 305. Sousa on jazz, *Marching Along,* 357–58.

21. Tennyson's *The Foresters,* a poetic drama about Robin Hood. Gershwin's *Oh, Kay!* in Philadelphia opened at the Shubert Theatre, 18 October 1926. On "Look for the Silver Lining," Alec Wilder, *American Popular Son: The Great Innovators, 1900–1950* (New York: Oxford University Press), 50–52.

22. The *Musical Messenger,* 20 December 1920, report by Ed Chenette, "Sousa's Band," on the concert of 5 November at the Hibbing Armory, Hibbing, Minnesota. Humoresques on "Swanee" and on Kern's "Look for the Silver Lining" on the recording *John Philip Sousa "At the Symphony"* (Naxos, 8.559013). On the song "Swanee," Hamm, *Yesterdays,* 346–47.

23. Sousa, *Marching Along,* 332. Warfield, "The March as Musical Drama and the Spectacle of Sousa," 297, 299, 302.

24. Interlochen Center for the Arts, yearbooks for 1930 and 1931. I thank Byron Hanson, archivist at Interlochen, for the information, including the illustration of the young Frederick Fennell. *Times* obituary, 9 December 2004, C-11.

25. Movie concerts, Bierley, *The Incredible Band,* 191, and for a typical movie concert, 308. On the 1928 tour, Bierley, ibid., 192–93.

26. Schwartz, *Bands of America,* 162, quoting Frank Sullivan, saxophonist.

27. Bierley, *The Incredible Band,* 86, quoting the *Boston Herald,* 8 April 1929, on why finally willing to broadcast. Sousa's discomfort with broadcasting, ibid., 88. Union rules, ibid., 88: "Local 802 of the American Federation of Musicians had a 'six-month wait' rule before outsiders could perform in New York. Many musicians were freelancers and had irregular schedules so a different group would perform every week."

28. "Last work conducted," Bierley, *American Phenomenon,* 92. An attempt in 1934 to revive the band as "Sousa Men's Band" collapsed after a single, free concert in Rockefeller Center's Sunken Plaza in New York City, ibid., 189. Also the *Times,* 3 May 1934, 14, 18.

29. End of music pavilion, *Willow Grove Park,* 110. Rocket ships, ibid., 100; shopping mall, ibid., 126.

30. President Reagan signed the bill on 11 December 1987; the Senate had passed it on 6 November, and the House on 1 December. *USA Today,* 2 December 1987, 4, reported that Congressman Morris Udall, Dem-Ariz., had remarked that unlike other favorite patriotic songs, the march was "entirely our own." ("The Star-Spangled Banner," for example, is sung to music composed in 1771 by an Englishman, John Stafford Smith, for a poem titled "To Anacreon in Heaven"; and "Hail to the Chief" originates in an old Scottish boating song.) For a history of earlier attempts to win congressional action on "The Stars and Stripes Forever," and reasons for failure, see Bierley, *American Phenomenon,* 217.

31. "Realm of art," Byrne, "Sousa Marches," 141. For Sousa on "the art" of composing marches, see *Marching Along,* 358–60. His role in operetta, Gerald Boardman, *American Operetta: From* H.M.S. Pinafore *to* Sweeney Todd (New York: Oxford University Press, 1981), 59. Revivals of *El Capitan,* e.g., Goodspeed Opera Company (Connecticut) in the 1970s; and more recently, Canton Comic Opera (Ohio; a concert performance), 2005. On *The Glass Blowers,* Martin Bernheimer, *Opera* 51, no. 12 (December 2000): 1432. *Times,* preview article, 7 July 2000, sec. E, 1: "This side

of Sousa's career has been undervalued." See enthusiastic review, *Times*, 8 August 2000, sec. E, 1. *The Glass Blowers* at the New York City Opera, see *Times* preview, 14 April 2002, sec. 2, 25; and an enthusiastic review, 18 April 2002, sec. E, 1. Glimmerglass Opera Program, 2000 Festival Season, 41. The program note claims that the original production in 1913 was "the first instance of film integrated with live actors in a Broadway show." The film depicted the American victory in the Spanish-American War at Santiago, Cuba, on 3 July 1898.

32. For Sousa currently heard at summer pops concerts, see article by Keith Brion accompanying *John Philip Sousa "At the Symphony"* (Naxos records, 8.559013), 6. Editorial on Sousa, *Musical Courier,* vol. 37, no. 1, 4 July 1898, n.p.

33. Sousa's songs, Bierley, *American Phenomenon,* 124. R. F. Goldman, "John Philip Sousa," in *Selected Essays and Reviews, 1948–1968,* 210, states: "These songs range from the humorous to the sentimental, and it must be admitted that they are not distinguished. But it is typical of composers to love their least-favored works."

34. Bierley, *The Incredible Band,* 144.

35. Sousa, *Marching Along,* 364. Bierley, *American Phenomenon,* 139, quoting the Seattle (Washington) *Post-Intelligencer*, 1 October 1927.

36. Byrne, "Sousa Marches," 142, quoting several musicians on Sousa's style of conducting. Bierley, *The Incredible Band,* 221, identifies the flutist as Joseph Grove Lefter, who played "one or more of 1930 tours." Later Lefter became the leader of the St. Petersburg (Florida) Municipal Band. Spacing the notes, Byrne, "Sousa Marches," 150, and quoting Bierley.

37. Warfield, "Salesman of Americanism," 500, quoting several newspapers on Sousa's conducting. See also, "Sousa's Band," by Ed Chenette, *Musical Messenger,* 20 December 1920. Sousa, *Marching Along,* 340.

38. Affronted musicians, Sousa, *Marching Along,* 340. W. J. Henderson, "Themes and Topics in the Musical World," *Times*, 24 December 1899, 17.

39. On Damrosch, see George W. Martin, *The Damrosch Dynasty: America's First Family of Music* (Boston: Houghton Mifflin, 1983), 362–74. On Bernstein, see Horowitz, *The Post-Classical Predicament,* 144–63.

40. Shanet, *Philharmonic,* 209, 211, 216, 222.

Chapter Seven

The Rise of Dance Bands

Herbert L. Clarke and the Long Beach Municipal Band

Following Sousa's death in 1932, no more bands toured in his fashion: with fifty or more players, for most of the year, funding itself on receipts for live concerts. The chief reason, aside from there being no leader of equal rank, was the country's Depression that not only increased costs but by closing venues narrowed opportunities. In addition to the economic distress, which roiled the country's economy from 1929 to the start of World War II, there was the steady advance in the technologies of radio, recordings, and movies. Initially, each of these had strengthened the cause of the concert band, but soon they began to undermine it, supporting to a greater extent a derivative, the dance band, to which they soon gave a competing life of its own.

The first of the new mediums to make itself felt in this contrary fashion was radio, to which Sousa finally had submitted, leading his first studio broadcast, on 6 May 1929, for the General Motors Family Party program aired by the National Broadcasting Company. Later he told the *New York Times* that until then, "I had never heard a radio concert." But others, in their millions, had, and increasingly what they had heard had been not a broadcast of a two-hour, live concert but a shorter airing of a café's small dance band, whether broadcast live from the café or a radio studio.[1]

A leader who early made such use of radio was Vincent Lopez, a pianist with a dance band of ten members he grandly called his "Pennsylvania Hotel Orchestra." In 1921 he had begun a weekly 90-minute show over station WJZ, broadcasting from Newark, New Jersey, to much of the New York City area. In the next few years, as the reach of broadcasting expanded, the Lopez "orchestra" became one of the country's best known bands, largely by radio. His theme song, "Nola," a novelty piano piece by Felix Arndt, which Lopez played with bravura, soon became a favorite, and in homes across the country amateur pianists, often with simplified versions, struggled to master its triplets just as thirty years earlier their parents had struggled to achieve the slight syncopations of Sousa's "Washington Post" march.

Ultimately, Lopez, and many other bandleaders, would find security in frequent long engagements to a single employer, initially in his case at the Hotel Pennsylvania, in New York City, and then later at the Hotel Taft, which touted its proximity to Times Square as "Top of the Great White Way." There he and his orchestra, starting in 1941, played for twenty years. In the early 1950s he hosted a popular radio show titled *Shake the Maracas*, during which for small prizes members of the audience were invited to express themselves in rhythm.[2]

Another band, typical of some that prospered during and after the Depression, was led by Guy Lombardo (born in Ontario, Canada), whose Royal Canadians offered "The Sweetest Music This Side of Heaven." For thirty-three years, starting in late 1929, they played for dance and dinner patrons of the Roosevelt Grill in the Hotel Roosevelt, New York, and then from 1962 until 1976 at the Waldorf Astoria. The band, which included four Lombardo brothers with Guy the eldest, usually numbered eleven and, like the Lopez band, besides piano and percussion employed mostly saxophones and brass. Lombardo's New Year's Eve radio broadcasts, climaxing in "Auld Lang Syne," became for many the only proper accompaniment to the hilarity, tears, drink, and regret that marked the passing of the old year. Even today many people starting to sing it will adopt, consciously or not, Lombardo's style and tempo.[3]

A similar group was the Casa Loma Orchestra, led most famously after 1937 by Glen Gray, a saxophonist. Throughout the mid-1930s it played regularly for radio's *Camel Caravan,* and the show's theme song, "Smoke Rings," led smokers of all cigarette brands, on lighting up, to croon the opening bars, or to parody them: "Oh, watch me blow, three rings in a row. Puff. Puff. Puff!" By the mid-1930s, however, though a large audience continued to enjoy sentimental songs and dreamy dance numbers, popular music and dance was "hotting up" with jazz and swing bands playing for jitterbugs, or for the more sedate, the Big Apple dance routine.[4]

Few social customs changed more radically in the early decades of the twentieth century than dancing. Traditionally, it was a gathering of a community, whether geographical or social. In the countryside it usually featured square dancing, such as the Virginia reel in which the dancers line up facing each other and perform prescribed movements. At balls and cotillions in the city, the waltz and quadrille often dominated, with the dances separated by frequent promenades. The quadrille, for example, was danced by sets of two, four, or eight couples, with the music typically in five varied movements, and with the maneuvers, as in square dancing, specified. Even the waltz often was danced with the couples moving in a single large circle around the edge of the floor. Then in 1911, the year of Irving Berlin's "Alexander's Ragtime Band," a craze for ballroom dancing began, inspired chiefly by the skill and grace of Irene and Vernon Castle; others soon sought to emulate them in the latest fling, the one-step, two-step, or turkey trot. By the end of World War I, with women dressing more simply and the less-demanding fox-trot now almost universal, dancing had become a more frequent, less formal pleasure, moving from barns and ballrooms into cafés, nightclubs, or dance halls, and spurring the rise of dance bands. Moreover, the dancing now was by individual couples, in far closer personal contact, starting and stopping on whim, and moving in whatever style they chose and without reference to others, while the music was all but continuous. Hence the bands were restricted to works with a steady beat, small shifts in volume, and a familiar or easily followed tune—programs in which excerpts from opera had little or no place.[5]

Equally menacing to the concert bands, their operatic repertory, and their tours was the increase in the number and quality of recordings. In the 1920s and early 1930s the band profiting most from this steady improvement was the Paul Whiteman Orchestra, another group of eight to fifteen players, with a home base in the Palais Royal, a large New York café-nightclub on Times Square. Yet in its touring this band somewhat resembled Sousa's, frequently leaving New York in the late spring and summer months when the nightclub closed for refurbishing. Initially Whiteman toured through New York, New Jersey, and New England, often following concerts with sessions for dancing, but in 1925, he and the orchestra visited thirty-eight states, and in 1926 he took it to England, Germany, France, and Holland. Whereas the smaller dance bands, "combos," typically had five to ten musicians, with some playing more than one instrument (and the larger bands, ten to twenty), Whiteman, for concert or theater engagements, began to engage as many as twenty-five musicians, or even in 1927, for a stand at the Paramount Theatre in New York, thirty-five.

An early recording that displays his style was "Whispering," which had on its back side "The Japanese Sandman." It was released in November 1920 and by the end of the next year it had sold nearly two million copies, almost double the number of most "hits." He recorded it with a band of ten, including himself on the violin, giving one chorus of "Whispering" to a solo trumpet and another to a rare instrument, a slide whistle. The effect of the latter on this particular tune was so infectious that for many years anyone hearing the melody would instinctively purse his lips and start to whistle. Assisted by a remake in 1928 with a band now numbering sixteen, the recording held the rank of all-time best seller until 1944.[6]

Whiteman and his larger band, playing more concerts than most, also could do more with orchestral music, and like Sousa he occasionally made arrangements of operatic classics, such as the "Song of India" from Rimsky-Korsakov's *Sadko,* the "Meditation" from Massenet's *Thaïs,* and a fantasy based on the Polovetsian Dances from Borodin's *Prince Igor.* In the 1920s he became famous not only for programs mixing symphonic music with jazz, but also for "jazzing" some of the classics, and the public soon titled him the "King of Jazz."[7]

An unusual recording, because it needed both sides of a twelve-inch platter, was of a work he had commissioned to show the influence of jazz on symphonic music, Gershwin's *Rhapsody in Blue,* which he had presented at a concert in New York's Aeolian Hall on 12 February 1924. Though some critics were hesitant in praise, the piece had a great success with the audience, and Whiteman promptly played it twice more, first in the Aeolian and then in the larger Carnegie Hall. He also took it on tour and later issued two recordings of it, the second in 1927, using the new electrical process.

Then in 1930, the first feature-length movie musical filmed entirely in Technicolor, *King of Jazz,* featured Whiteman and his orchestra in a sort of variety show with girls, dancers, and comedy acts, climaxed by a performance of the *Rhapsody.* That climax caused the Technicolor crew considerable difficulty. Color in film was then primitive and had no blue, only red and green. After many trials, the sequence was shot against an all gray-and-silver background, which allowed a green that reportedly "gave the illusion of peacock blue." With the *Rhapsody* played in concerts, on the radio, in recordings, and in a movie, by 1930 there can hardly have been a music lover who had not heard it often. Five years later the composer-critic Virgil Thomson called it "the most successful orchestral piece ever launched by any American composer."[8]

Like Sousa, however, Whiteman was criticized by some for his mixed programs, and especially for his jazzy treatment of "classics." The most virulent attack, following his tour of England in 1926, came from Ernest Newman, one of England's leading critics, who launched his assault in both the New York and London *Times:*

> Your typical jazz composer or jazz enthusiast is merely a musical illiterate who is absurdly pleased with little things because he does not know how little they are. . . . Mr. Whiteman . . . would not have "Onward, Christian Soldiers" jazzed because this is a majestic tune with religious association, but the "Peer Gynt" suite and the "Poet and Peasant" overture, why not jazz them? . . . All we musicians can do is to say to him and them, "jazz hymns, ancient and modern,—most of these are hardly above your own intellectual level—but keep your dirty paws off your betters."[9]

With Whiteman at the moment unavailable, on a train to Los Angeles, New York reporters asked Gershwin to comment, for only months earlier on the band's European tour Whiteman had played the *Rhapsody* in all four countries. Gershwin, however, declined: the attack was on Whiteman, and for him to answer. His reply, when it came, was measured and raised a question that made some at least of the so-called serious musicians and critics uneasy. After explaining that he had not wanted to jazz "Onward, Christian Soldiers" for reasons that were more ethical than musical, he went on to ask:

> Why are there so few masterpieces written along accepted symphonic lines today? I believe it is because that form became so studious that it grew decadent. If jazz should ever become dependent upon theory it will lose its virility. What critic is so self assured that he can prophesy what musical structure will be ten years from now? It is only by disregarding the conventional main routes that we reach new destinations. Let supposedly astute critics take off their high hats long enough to recognize the possibilities in a brown derby.[10]

Though Sousa had not jazzed the classics, he had received similar criticism for mixing serious and popular music in his programs, but perhaps because his public support was so overwhelmingly strong, and because (unlike Whiteman, Lombardo, or Lopez) he was outstanding also as a conductor and composer, the attacks were not so savage. Yet he, too, had seen and sought to accommodate a new audience that was developing, one which seemed to seek a different sort of music from that which he typically programmed.

In the course of these changes, which diminished the opportunities for excerpts from the classics or opera, another threat to that repertory appeared in what was becoming by the mid-twenties an increasingly rigid form of popular song composed often chiefly for dance. Composers, seemingly in response to what they felt the public wanted, now typically offered an introduction or "verse," usually of little interest and seldom played (Hoagy Carmichael's "Stardust" being a well-known exception); then the tuneful chorus in which the main theme is stated, immediately repeated, and followed by a "release," which led to a reprise of the main theme. Or in poetic shorthand, *aaba*.[11]

Moreover, inasmuch as the song's chorus usually was the only part familiar to dancers, it was the part most frequently played, often without its "verse." But the chorus alone, even if repeated, made a number too short, and so bands arranged medleys, in which they would string together, by a few bars of transition, the choruses of two or three songs. In this skill the Lombardo band was exceptional, never playing successive choruses in the same key, at the same tempo, or with the same instruments, and varying, on last minute decisions by Guy, the choruses chosen. In this way he could respond to requests or what he sensed was the crowd's current mood.[12]

The rigidity of the popular song formula, however, fit less well the needs of the Whiteman band, which for concerts wanted a repertory of longer, more individual numbers. In the 1930s, he and his band, playing less often, went into a slow decline, and eventually broke up, with Whiteman becoming the music director for the ABC radio network. Another reason for the band's decline, however, may be that after 1924 it lost its home base, the Palais Royal, where it had a contract to play through the winter. In that year the government raided the nightclub, charging it with serving liquor (which it certainly did) in violation of the Constitution's Prohibition Amendment. The lockout (the club never reopened) forced Whiteman still more onto the road for short stands, leaving him and his concert band especially vulnerable to the Depression.

Dance bands, with only ten or eleven players, had the easier time. Expenses were less, and after repeal of Prohibition in 1933, they had an obvious, potent role in drawing people into bars, clubs, and dance halls where liquor could be served. Professional concert bands had no such function, and across the country in the early 1930s they swiftly declined in number. Among the few that survived, opposing the trend toward popular song and dance music, the decrease in their operatic excerpts to some extent can be followed in the programs of the Long Beach (California) Municipal Band, which by the late 1920s had become the West Coast's most renowned concert band.[13]

Though Long Beach, California, the chief port for Los Angeles and blessed with fine beaches, had enjoyed a succession of small bands in its early years, music became more important in 1909 when the city council agreed to fund in part a municipal band. In the course of the next decade the band increased its number of players from roughly twenty to thirty, began to prosper, then went into decline. Meanwhile the city's population had grown from 12,000 in 1909 to 145,000 in 1923. That year the city council, faced with the question of whether to go forward with the band or drop it, voted to increase support and to seek for it a nationally known leader who simply by his presence would focus attention on Long Beach. The council's aim, as the scholar James T. Madeja has uncovered, was to have a band which "not only entertains when people arrive, but is of itself the means of bringing thousands of visitors to Long Beach."[14]

The search was short. Choice was limited, and of the two leading candidates one, it happened, had moved to Los Angeles in the spring, seeking a soft climate for his ill wife. He was Herbert L. Clarke, aged fifty-five and still considered by many to be the world's greatest cornetist. In addition, besides having assisted both Gilmore and Sousa in managing their bands and having conducted Sousa's Band in many of its recordings, in the last five years he had burnished his reputation as a director and conductor by creating out of little the best concert band in Canada. This was the Anglo-Canadian Leather Company Band of Huntsville, a company town of 2,000 in central Ontario. All members of the band were employed in the Anglo-Canadian Leather

Company whose founder, Charles O. Shaw, was himself a fine cornetist—rather remarkably so because he had false teeth, upper and lower. A rich man with a desire to play in a top-notch band, he gave Clarke an unlimited budget and unfettered control of all aspects of management, including the right to add at will more players. The band, which never marched, soon numbered seventy-five, gave concerts on Sundays, playing occasionally in nearby towns, and went to Toronto for the annual Canadian National Exhibition, where it played such works as Tchaikovsky's Fourth and Sixth Symphonies and Rimsky-Korsakov's *Scheherazade,* with Shaw as first cornet. Quickly becoming internationally famous, the band, or more truly a wind symphony, would seem to have been everything Clarke could desire, yet because of his wife's health, in 1923 he had not renewed his contract with Shaw but left for Los Angeles where he had opened a cornet school, enrolling fifty students.[15]

In Huntsville, Shaw or the Anglo-Canadian company had paid Clarke $15,000 annually; in Long Beach, however, the council could muster only $7,200. But it could offer him the nucleus of a concert band, which presently had twenty-three members, a promise to cover the expenses of enlarging the number at once to thirty-five, and allow Clarke a free hand in hiring and firing. Clarke, at first, was inclined to distrust municipal support, fearing it might shift with each election and too easily be swayed by popular whim. There are, after all, always some who dispute the use of any public money to support the arts, and among taxpayers in Long Beach the number at times was sizeable.[16]

Yet the challenge stirred him, and impressed by the council's spokesmen Clarke took the job, announcing to the public that he hoped to expand the band eventually to sixty and to turn "the skeleton of a military band" into "a musical organization second to none." He started work on 16 November with his first rehearsal scheduled for the 23rd and the first concert for the 30th, by which time he already had increased the band to thirty-five. For the opening concert an audience of three thousand filled the municipal auditorium with nearly as many turned away. Outside the hall, hundreds listened through the open doors, and a second concert with the same program was promptly announced. Thus Clarke's opening week began to acclaim, and in the course of his first full year, as *Jacobs' Band Monthly* reported, he conducted "539 concerts and led the band in 9 parades," as well as performing "nearly 200 solos." As the city council had hoped, Clarke by his name and skills swung national attention to Long Beach.[17]

Like Sousa, Clarke believed that a symphonic or wind band could play as well as a string orchestra, or better, because, as he once said, it was able to be "more colorful, more forceful, richer in tone quality, and more majestic than the orchestra." And he, as well as others, felt he had proved as much with the

Anglo-Canadian band. Also like Sousa, but in his mentor's tradition and not as a blind follower, he scheduled more orchestral pieces than did the dance bands. For his opening concert, for example, Clarke's program (see appendix 13) included two Hungarian dances by Brahms, the overture to Gomes's opera *Il Guarany*, and by several composers of operettas a march, a waltz, and a ballet suite. In addition he offered the "Bells of St. Mary's" by A. E. Adams, the *Southern Rhapsody* by Hosmer, as well as his own "Nereid" with himself the soloist and a new work he had composed, "Long Beach Is Calling." In all, except for the lack of a vocalist, this was a program very much in the Gilmore-Sousa tradition, and with all the works, except for the two by Clarke, in Sousa's current repertory.[18]

Moreover, by the end of the year he had enlarged the band to fifty, recruiting mostly woodwind players and thus changing the band's instrumentation from predominantly brass to woodwind. The latter now numbered twenty-six (fifteen clarinets), the brass, twenty, and harp and percussion, four. Furthermore, playing usually in the city's auditorium or in its Lincoln Park, the band now had a regular schedule of two long rehearsals a week and two performances daily, six days a week, fifty weeks a year.

Its popularity soared, and in February 1924 a local radio station broadcast a concert nationally. Soon another local station was airing the two daily concerts, and in 1930 a third station undertook to broadcast them across the Pacific, reaching New Zealand and Australia. Thus the Long Beach Municipal Band, which soon was invited for special occasions to other cities in the West, became at first a rival to Sousa's Band and then, after Sousa's death, at least for the West Coast and Pacific, its chief successor.[19] (See photospread.)

Clarke, meanwhile, recognizing that tourists came to Long Beach for the sun, air, and beaches, and so, unlike the audiences in Huntsville, were not so ready to focus attention on serious music, increasingly omitted the weightier pieces for the more immediately catchy. An exception, however, was a success in 1926 with Handel's *Messiah.* Sung by a choir of 150 and accompanied by the band, the performance proved so popular that Clarke repeated it annually for the next fifteen years. More typical, however, was the fate of a program for band alone (forty-six players) that he presented in 1927, consisting of Tchaikovsky's Symphony No. 6, Wagner's overture to *The Flying Dutchman,* and Rimsky-Korsakov's symphonic suite *Scheherazade.* Apparently there were no reviews of the program or reports of its reception, but Clarke did not repeat it, or schedule another like it.[20]

In the economic depression, however, the city's support shrank, and Clarke had to reduce the band from forty-six to thirty-five. Soon he and his men had to take cuts in salary and accept long periods of unpaid leave, with the longest being three months in 1933 and two in 1938. Soon thereafter he began to lose musicians to World War II, ultimately having to replace twelve players, a third of the band. In his last years—his final concert was on 31 January 1943—he struggled to maintain quality, but always with less, and though he did not complain publicly, he privately found these later years disappointing. Nevertheless, for what he had achieved both in Huntsville and Long Beach, he was celebrated among bandsmen as one of the country's great leaders. At his death, on 30 January 1945, he was buried beside his wife in the Congressional Cemetery, Washington, D.C., and by his request, close to Sousa.[21]

His successor at Long Beach was B. A. Rolfe, best known for having originated radio's *Your Hit Parade*, a program sponsored by the American Tobacco Company, owners of Lucky Strike cigarettes. Each Saturday night from 1935 to 1958 the Lucky Strike Dance Orchestra would play what reportedly were then the country's most popular songs, taken chiefly from "standards," show tunes, or current band novelties, with the week's number one song held secret until the program's finale.[22]

Rolfe, starting in 1943, at once began to shift the band's repertory toward the hit parade format, increasing the number of song or dance numbers in the popular "verse" and "release," or *aaba* form. Inevitably there was less room for anything more purely orchestral or operatic. He also gradually changed the band's instrumentation, replacing some wind instruments with more brass, and in addition changed the band's seating. Under Clarke, as under Gilmore and Sousa, the band had sat in a semicircle, facing the conductor, but under Rolfe the musicians, as in a dance band, faced the audience and often the back of the conductor, who for long periods did little more than wave his baton and beat time. Consequently there was less nuance to the performance, fewer shifts in tempo, dynamics, instrumentation, and phrasing. The tourist audiences at Long Beach, however, seemed to delight as much in the new format as the old, and the band, though its instrumentation and repertory soon were quite different, continued to be one of the country's larger and better known concert bands.[23]

The changes, however, not only altered the programs of the future but more gradually even the perception of those of the past. In 2010, for example, the band, in planning its summer programs to celebrate its one hundredth anniversary as a municipal band, divided the past into periods of differing length, assigning to each period composers whose works, it was implied, were the most frequently played—thus, for the period, 1909–1924, "George M. Cohan, George Gershwin and other composers from Tin Pan Alley"; for 1924–1937 (all Clarke years), "Ragtime and Dixieland jazz [and] George Gershwin"; and for 1937–1950 (until 1943 Clarke years), "the music of the famous big bands such as Tommy Dorsey, Benny Goodman, Count Basie and Glenn Miller, [and] 'The Andrews Sisters.'" Though the scheduling correctly reflects the rise and vitality throughout these years of American popular song, whether musical comedy, dance, or jazz numbers, by omission it misrepresents the interest in orchestral and operatic arrangements, which for most of these years had been strong.[24]

With Clarke's death and the change in the Long Beach band's repertory, one of the last direct links to the wind symphony, concert band tradition of Gilmore and Sousa broke. Clarke had played first cornet for both men, had served both as an administrative assistant as well as a musician, and had shared their hope to elevate bands into something more than "a band of brass to penetrate the Babel" of the streets, to something more than a purveyor of waltzes, polkas, fox-trots for dancers, and to something more than what was becoming increasingly popular, a band whose chief purpose was to entertain a stadium crowd at halftime and as much by marching maneuvers as music.

For all three men, Gilmore, Sousa, and Clarke, the ideal had been something else. As Sousa once had said: "There is much modern music that is better adapted to a wind combination than to a string, although for obvious reasons originally scored for an orchestra. If in such cases the interpretation is equal to the composition the balance of a wind combination is more satisfying." And Clarke once stated his goal to be "a 'wind' orchestra that will introduce to the music-loving public a symphonic rendition of musical selections equal to the greatest of the present string orchestras." Their purpose was high and even after Clarke's death in 1943 some bands pursued it but often in diverse and partial ways and increasingly without selections from operatic music.[25]

NOTES

1. *Times,* "Sousa Marches in Radio 'Parade,'" 22 September 1929, sec. 12, 14. Reportedly, the initial 6 May broadcast was heard as far afield as the U.S. Navy base in Antarctica.

2. Photograph of Lopez and orchestra, with instruments, 1922, see Charles Hamm, *Yesterdays,* 381. And *Jacobs' Band Monthly*, 3 July 1925, "An Interview with Vincent Lopez" by Lloyd Loar. For Lopez's serendipitous start with radio, see Barnouw, *A Tower of Babel,* 87. Felix Arndt, "Nola: A Silhouette for the Piano" (1915). Besides its original edition, the Sam Fox Publishing Co., New York, also issued the song in these other versions for pianists: Simplified Edition, Popular Piano Edition, Fox Trot Edition, Song Edition, Piano Duet (Four Hands), and Piano Duet (Two Pianos). On Lopez and "Nola," see Don Rayno, *Paul Whiteman: Pioneer in American Music*, vol. 1: *1890–1930* (Lanham, MD: Scarecrow Press, 2003), 76, 88. For *Shake the Maracas*, see Craig's Big Bands and Big Names.com, www.bigbandsandbignames/lopez.html.

3. Booton Herndon, *The Sweetest Music This Side of Heaven: The Guy Lombardo Story* (New York: McGraw-Hill, 1964), 93–100, 149–51. Also www.bigbandsandbignames/GuyLombardo.html.

4. The Casa Loma Orchestra was active from 1927 to 1963. "Smoke Rings" (1932) had music by H. Eugene Gifford and lyrics by Ned Washington. Also, David Joyner, "Jazz from 1930 to 1960," *The Cambridge History of American Music* (Cambridge: Cambridge University Press, 1998), 418–19.

5. Changes in dancing, Jeffrey Magee, "Ragtime and Early Jazz," *Cambridge History of American Music,* ibid., 404.

6. Rayno, *Paul Whiteman,* Palais Royal, "New York's largest café," 43, 45, 49, 51, 382 (16 September 1920); annual redecoration, 73, 382 (2 July 1921); and size of Whiteman's orchestra, 45, 49–50, 53, 64, 79, 100, 115, 127, 165. For tours, see entry in Rayno's General Index for "Whiteman, tours," 748. "Whispering/The Japanese Sandman," two million, Rayno, *Paul Whiteman,* 448, 613; best seller, Paul Whiteman, *Records for the Millions,* ed. David A. Stein (New York: Hermitage Press, 1948), 8.

7. Some other arrangements of classics or opera: Tchikovsky's *Marche Slave* and *1812* overture; "Cho-Cho-San," Puccini's *Madama Butterfly*; Anton Rubinstein, "Kamenoi-Ostrow"; Liszt, *Liebestraum*; Saint-Saëns, "My Heart at Thy Sweet Voice" (*Samson and Delilah*); and MacDowell, "To a Wild Rose." On his musical success with a *Wagnerian Fantasie,* see Rayno, *Paul Whiteman,* 61–62, quoting a critic for the *New York Clipper* (see also Rayno, appendix 2, 386–87, for a list of New England tour engagements and programs). The recording of "Song of India" sold more than two million copies, see Whiteman, *Records for the Millions,* 68.

8. *Rhapsody in Blue,* Rayno, *Paul Whiteman,* 79, 88, 91, 134, 145, 152, and 153. The *King of Jazz* film, ibid., 242, 246–47. *A Virgil Thomson Reader,* ed. John Rockwell (Boston: Houghton Mifflin, 1981), 23, quoting an article published in *Modern Music,* November 1935.

9. E. Newman, *Times*, 12 September 1926, p. 1, col. 6; also Rayno, *Paul Whiteman,* 141–42.

10. Rayno, ibid., citing *Variety*, 15 September 1926, 52. Whiteman as a jazz artist, see Gunther Schuller, *Early Jazz* (New York: Oxford, 1968), 192.

11. On the "release," Wilder, *American Popular Song: The Great Innovators, 1900–1950* (New York: Oxford University Press, 1972), 56, and ibid. he states that *aaba* became the principal form of American popular song in the years 1925–1926.

12. Lombardo and his medleys, see Herndon, *The Sweetest Music,* 48–49.

13. For this demise of important concert bands recorded graphically, see Schwartz, *Bands of America,* 308.

14. *Jacobs' Monthly Band*, April 1936, 29. Madeja, "Life and Work of Herbert L. Clarke (1867–1945)," 204.

15. "World's greatest cornetist," *Times*, 1 February 1945, 23; also *Herald-Tribune,* ibid., 14. The other candidate was Giuseppe Creatore (1871–1952), a trombonist and conductor who in 1902 shot to fame in New York with his own band of sixty, recruited in part in Italy and with which he successfully toured until the early 1930s. See Schwartz, *Bands of America,* 212–23. On C. O. Shaw: first cornet, *Musical Canada,* vol. 11, no. 9, September 1921, 7–9; his teeth, Clarke, *Jacobs' Band Monthly,* April 1940, "The Road to Success," chap. xix, 6; Shaw's previous study with Clarke, Madeja, "Life and Work of Herbert L. Clarke," 186. Shaw's contract with Clarke, Madeja, ibid., 187–88. The band's size, schedule, programs, and audiences: Clarke,

"The Road to Success." Clarke's resignation, Madeja, "Life and Work of Herbert L. Clarke," 198; Clarke's cornet school in Los Angeles, ibid.

16. Salary, Madeja, ibid., 201; terms of contract, ibid., 205, 211.

17. "Second to none," ibid., 207, quoting an article in the *Long Beach Press*, 1 December 1923, 13, 18. *Jacobs' Band Monthly*, July 1925, 8.

18. "More colorful," Madeja, "Life and Work of Herbert L. Clarke," 200, quoting an article in the *Long Beach Press*, 16 December 1923, magazine section, 3. For Sousa's repertory in these years, see Bierley, *The Incredible Band,* appendix V.

19. Radio, Madeja, "Life and Work of Herbert L. Clarke," 213–14, 216.

20. Success of *Messiah* and uncertain reception of the all-classics concert, ibid., 220.

21. Cuts in salary and forced vacations, ibid., 223. Disappointment and players lost to the war, ibid., 233. *The Musical Messenger,* March 1920, 4, for Clarke on Sousa as "without any doubt the greatest bandmaster ever known." On wanting to be buried close to Sousa, ibid., 13, and see Madeja, "The Life and Work of Herbert L. Clarke," 236. Clarke on Sousa as a man, Madeja, ibid., quoting an article in *The Independent* (Long Beach), 27 January 1947, 13. Also, *Jacobs' Band Monthly,* April 1932, 8, and ibid., March 1932, 40: "The band world has lost one of its most distinguished and picturesque figures."

22. Hamm, *Yesterdays,* xxi.

23. Clarke privately declared that with the new seating the band's volume seemed diminished: "It sounds like 10 or 12 men instead of 36 players." See Madeja, "Life and Work of Herbert L. Clarke," 235.

24. See http://www.longbeach.gov/park/recreation/lb_municipal_band.asp.

25. Sousa, *Marching Along,* 332; Clarke, see Madeja, "Life and Work of Herbert L. Clarke," 200, quoting *The Evening Telegram* (Toronto), 30 August 1921, 17.

Harvey B. Dodworth. Oil Portrait by Charles Waldo Jenkins, 1857. The New-York Historical Society, #1950.78.

Patrick S. Gilmore. University of Maryland Libraries.

John Sullivan Dwight. From a painting by Caroline Cranch, 1884, in the possession of the Harvard Musical Association.

Herbert L. Clarke, the young cornetist, undated. Interlochen Center for the Arts.

Gilmore bust, sculpted by Dennis B. Sheahan, 1887, which presently sits in the concourse connecting the Interlochen library to its classrooms and administration building. Interlochen Center for the Arts.

Sousa, circa 1890. U.S. Marine Band Library.

Early Years at Willow Grove. Old York Road Historical Society.

Early Years at Willow Grove. Old York Road Historical Society.

The New
Willow Grove Park
(In the Chelten Hills)
FESTIVAL CONCERTS BY
INNES And His Famous Fifty.
Saturday, August 29, 1896.

Thursday, July 7th, 1904
Official Programme Concerts
Willow Grove Park
BUTLER
Concerts Afternoon and Evening
BY THE LADIES' MILITARY BAND
HELEN MAY BUTLER, Directress.

Season 1899.
Willow Grove Park
(In the Chelten Hills)
DAILY CONCERTS BY
Walter Damrosch and His Famous Orchestra
Afternoon and Evening.

CONCERTS
Official Programme
Willow Grove Park
SIG. CREATORE
CONDUCTOR
SEASON 1901. ELEVENTH WEEK.
AUGUST 5th to 11th, INCLUSIVE.
Every Afternoon and Evening.
Royal Italian Band
GIUSEPPE CREATORE, Conductor.
CHANNING ELLERY, Manager.

Four bands that played at Willow Grove. Old York Road Historical Society.

Sousa at Interlochen in 1931, the summer before he died. Interlochen Center for the Arts.

Arthur Pryor. Old York Road Historical Society.

Clarke as an older man, undated. Interlochen Center for the Arts.

A community band, on tour in 2000, meets the pope. G. Hoehn Collection.

Edwin Franko Goldman, 1932, at Interlochen. Interlochen Center for the Arts.

Richard Franko Goldman, young and old, both undated. University of Maryland Libraries.

Richard Franko Goldman, young and old, both undated. University of Maryland Libraries.

Frederick Fennell, 1931, in his first season at Interlochen' summer camp. Interlochen Center for the Arts.

Members of the American Broadcasters Association preparing for a concert at Interlochen on 8 August 1936. Herbert L. Clarke, playing a cornet, can be seen in the front row, the only man wearing a jacket. Interlochen Center for the Arts.

Frederick Fennell, 1989. Interlochen Center for the Arts.

Chapter Eight

The U.S. Marine Band and Contemporary Civilian Bands

After World War II even the limited touring practiced by Clarke and the Long Beach Municipal Band became rarer. Not only did radio and television broadcasts substitute for concerts on tour, but the expense of travel soared even as the expectations of musicians for time off between concerts, pay for rehearsals, and salaries all rose, aided by the increasing power of their labor union. Even the number of concerts at home gradually decreased. At Long Beach, for example, by the summer of 2010 these had dropped from Clarke's twice a day, seven days a week, to four a week. Similarly, as the size of the bands diminished, often as an economy, their instrumentation changed, for they tended to drop woodwinds and so become brassier. While for many the repertory, as had happened at Long Beach, shifted away from orchestral or operatic arrangements toward popular song.

Even dance bands, or at least those of them that captured the most notice in print and on the airways, changed their style in the postwar years. An era of "crooners" opened, in which the vocalists were more important than their backup bands. Before the war there had been Rudy Vallée and Bing Crosby, but during the 1940s and 1950s came a surge of Italian-American singers led by Russ Columbo and Louis Prima. Joining them soon were Frank Sinatra, Vic Damone, Frankie Laine, Tony Bennett, and many others. For fifteen or twenty years, or until the arrival of the Beatles in the mid-1960s, they dominated popular music. But their story, like that of the Beatles and of later pop music, is so far removed from the concept of a concert band as considered here that it becomes a different genre and beyond the scope of this study.

Nevertheless, despite the changing conditions and competition a number of civilian concert bands still managed to flourish, among them the Goldman Band in New York, the Allentown Band in Pennsylvania, and the Racine Concert Band in Wisconsin. There was also the U.S. Marine Band, which,

Figure 8.1. U.S. Marine Band full-dress uniforms as they were in 1875. The picture was used as a frontispiece to the program for the band's 180th anniversary concert, 10 July 1978. U.S. Marine Band.

though neither civilian nor self-supporting, in some respects came closest to realizing the ideals of Sousa and Clarke. In the later part of the twentieth century it had a corps of 143 (of which 40 were women): 122 musicians, with a supporting staff of 15 (library, public affairs, operations, administration, supply, recording lab), a drum major, and 5 officers.[1]

Like the Dodworth Band in New York a hundred years earlier, the U.S. Marine Band today can field a variety of groups as needed. For indoor concerts it offers typically a band of sixty to sixty-five, depending on the instruments scored for the scheduled works, and of that total, usually half are woodwinds of which seventeen are clarinets: fourteen B-flat sopranos, and one each of E-flat sopranino and alto, and one B-flat bass. It also, however, can supply a single harp for a solo recital, or a string quartet (eighteen of the musicians are string players), a brass quintet, jazz combo, dance band, chamber orchestra, or symphonic band. It is thus an extremely versatile organization, and though the army, navy, and air force have bands similarly organized, their schedules typically are less varied.

For its concerts, the marine band does not limit itself to relatively short pieces. Among its longer arrangements from opera that have recently been played were a Grand Fantasie from Wagner's *Die Walküre* (15 mins.), the ballet from Verdi's *Don Carlos* (15 mins.), and perhaps longest of all a *Carmen Symphony,* an orchestral summary of Bizet's opera with the references appearing in proper order (34 mins.) And though the Verdi ballet has been performed only once, in 2000, the band's historian, MGySgt Michael Ressler, estimates that the Wagner Fantasie has been performed in summer concerts, formal concerts, and radio broadcasts at least twenty-five times since 1941; and the *Carmen Symphony*, introduced in 2004, eight times, with seven of these on tour in 2007. Moreover, all three works have been issued on recordings. As for the number of performances of all kinds, in any year these typically number more than eight hundred, of which roughly three hundred are at the White House. No civilian band playing today achieves even a quarter of that total.[2]

Also, in the tradition started by Sousa in 1891, the U.S. Marine Band has toured the United States every year except during World War I, the Depression, and World War II. Over the years the duration of the tours has changed. In mid-twentieth century, they averaged about sixty-three days, but now more typically, thirty-one. In earlier times the public bought tickets to the tour concerts; today these are free, but the cities visited, or their residents or businesses, are required to underwrite part of the cost. In addition to these national tours, the band also has played abroad. In 1985 it gave two concerts in the Netherlands, in 1986 it went to Ireland, and in 1989 to Norway; then in 1990, for nineteen days to the Soviet Union, and in 1992 to London for a Festival of Music in the Royal Albert Hall. Though all these tours, whether abroad or at home, were relatively short, they fortify the band's claim to a national and international reputation, so that the *Washington Post* with some justice could declare in 1987, "The U.S. Marine Band demonstrated once again that it is not only the best in the land but very likely the best in the world." Blunter still, *Time* magazine in 1998 declared, "The best the world has ever produced."[3]

Moreover, for many of its concerts the band continued to include arrangements of orchestral and operatic numbers. Years earlier, in 1924, the marine band had given a commemorative concert to celebrate the twenty-fifth anniversary of its reorganization, originally planned by Sousa but only achieved by congressional act in 1899. As a consequence of the act the band had expanded its number from thirty to sixty, at which time William H. Santelmann, the band's leader, had decreed that all bandsmen, except the soloists, must also be able to play a string instrument, thus allowing the band to field a symphony orchestra as well as a wind band. Since 1902 most of the band's performances inside the White House have been as a symphony orchestra.[4]

The program at that 1924 commemorative concert had begun with the orchestra performing Henry Hadley's *In Bohemia* overture, Saint-Saëns' Cello Concerto No. 1, Bruch's Concerto in G minor for Violin, Strauss's *The Blue Danube Waltz,* and Elgar's *Pomp and Circumstance.* Then, in part 2, as a wind band it offered arrangements of Wagner's overture to *Tannhäuser*; Verdi's "Celeste Aida" set for trombone solo; Rachmaninoff's Prelude in C-sharp minor; Hayden Millars's fantasy, *Le Rêve d'Amour,* set for cornet solo; and Liszt's Hungarian Rhapsody No. 2.[5]

This sort of programming, reminiscent of Sousa, has continued through the years. At a sesquicentennial concert, 1798–1948, besides many marches the band played a duet from Offenbach's *Geneviève de Brabant,* the Wedding March from Wagner's *Lohengrin,* the Wedding March from Mendelssohn's *Midsummer Night's Dream,* and the largo from Dvorak's *New World Symphony.* At a 180th anniversary concert, in 1978, it offered Berlioz's overture *Le Carnaval Romain*, a galop from Offenbach's *Geneviève de Brabant,* and *Das Liebesmahl der Apostel* by Wagner, a work originally composed for male chorus. Five years later, repeating the Offenbach, the band then offered a baritone vocalist in "King Heinrich's Call" and "Evening Star" from Wagner's *Lohengrin,* and also performed a suite from Stravinsky's *The Firebird.* In that same year, 1983, to mark the centennial of Wagner's death it offered an all-Wagner concert, which was scheduled at the concert hall of Kennedy Center for the day and month of Wagner's death, 13 February, but because of a blizzard was postponed to 9 March. Though the band's programs were not always so operatic in origin, there seldom was one that did not include an arrangement of an overture, an aria, or a dramatic work by an opera composer, such as Richard Strauss's *Till Eulenspiegel's Merry Pranks.*

A CONCERT OF THE MUSIC OF RICHARD WAGNER
ON THE CENTENNIAL OF THE COMPOSER'S DEATH
CONCERT HALL, KENNEDY CENTER FOR THE PERFORMING ARTS
SUNDAY, FEBRUARY 13, 1983, AT 8:30 P.M.

LIEUTENANT COLONEL JOHN R. BOURGEOIS, CONDUCTING
MR. PAUL HUME, HOST AND CONCERT MODERATOR

PROGRAM

"The Star Spangled Banner" . . . . Francis Scott Key
(arranged in Wagner style by John Philip Sousa*)

Huldigungsmarsch (1864)†

Eine Faust Overture (1840) . . . . arr. by O. Hackenberger

Trauersinfonie on Themes from Weber's "Euryanthe" (1844)†

Scene from "Lohengrin" (1846-48)
"King Heinrich's Call" . . . . arr. by John R. Bourgeois*
Michael Ryan, Baritone

Aria, "O du mein holder Abendstern," from "Tannhäuser"
(1843-44) . . . . arr. by Thomas Knox*
Michael Ryan, Baritone

"Das Liebesmahl der Apostel" (1843) . . . . arr. by M. Pohle

- INTERMISSION -

Scenes from "Der Ring des Nibelungen"

Das Rheingold (1853-54)
"Entrance of the Gods into Valhalla"

Die Walküre (1854-56)
"Ride of the Valkyries"

Götterdämmerung (1869-74)
Siegfried's Funeral March . . . . arr. by Howard Bowlin*
and Redemption . . . . arr. by John R. Bourgeois*

Siegfried (1856-69)
Siegfried Fantasie . . . . arr. by A. Seidel

*Member U.S. Marine Band
†Original Band Composition

Figure 8.2. U.S. Marine Band.

Today, however, the U.S. Marine Band in touring and number of performances compared to civilian concert bands is an exception. Perhaps closest to it, at least in some respects, is the Allentown Band (Pennsylvania), equally honorable and almost as ancient, for it is the oldest civilian concert band in the United States. Dating with certainty to 1828, it seems also to have performed as a fife and drum corps at least as early as 1822. The band now numbers sixty-five, owns its own rehearsal hall, is self-governing, and recruits its members from amateur musicians in the Lehigh Valley. Besides public concerts, it plays at such events as church picnics, dedication ceremonies, college commencements, and offers free educational concerts for young students to schools in the valley. It also has recorded extensively, appeared on television, and recently made three brief tours to Switzerland and Austria.

Moreover, it has a unique tie to other bands through Lucien Cailliet (1891–1985), who served as its associate conductor from 1934 until 1969. Cailliet, born and trained in France, in 1919 had joined the Philadelphia Orchestra as a clarinetist, saxophonist, and arranger. As an arranger he became increasingly important as he composed more than 140 works, many of them arrangements of operatic music still played by many bands today; for example, "Elsa's Procession to the Cathedral" from Wagner's *Lohengrin,* the overture to Verdi's *Nabucco,* "Musetta's Waltz" from Puccini's *Bohème,* "One Fine Day" from Puccini's *Butterfly,* and the waltzes from R. Strauss's *Rosenkavalier*. Of orchestral music he made a much-played arrangement of Sibelius's *Finlandia,* and in the popular repertory he perhaps is best known for his "Variations on the Theme, Pop! Goes the Weasel," which he dedicated to the Allentown Band.[6]

In New York City another civilian concert band, the Goldman Band, founded in 1911 and active until 2005, became increasingly important over the years as it sought, chiefly when led by the Goldmans, father and son, to develop a repertory of original works for band and to rely less on arrangements of theater or opera music. That development, however, needs a chapter to itself, and will follow.

More typical of the country's civilian town bands after World War II were the Detroit Concert Band and the Staten Island Musicians Society Concert Band or, as it sometimes was called, SIMS. Of these the older was SIMS, which pursued the Gilmore-Sousa-Clarke tradition of a wind symphony but in a much moderated style. Made up principally of Italian-Americans living on Staten Island, throughout the summers it gave two park concerts a week on the island as well as occasional performances in parks in New York City's other four boroughs. Funded chiefly by the city and the Musicians Trust Fund, and paying its players at union rates, it usually numbered about fifty, with at least ten clarinets in place of a symphony orchestra's violin section.

As was traditional in most bands, the first cornet was revered by all, whether justly or not, as the leading soloist; the only stringed instruments were double basses (a practice discussed in the next chapter), and any melodic cello line usually went to the euphonium (baritone tuba of large bore). The band sat in the orchestral semicircle around the conductor, and its repertory, at least as late as the mid-1970s, also was traditional, featuring many arrangements of classical music (see appendix 14) but mixed now with current show tunes and popular songs. According to the band's conductor for the period 1972–1976, Victor DeRenzi (later the artistic director and chief conductor of the Sarasaota Opera Company), "Much of the non-classical music had minimal artistic value and was chosen for the quality of the arrangement rather than for the music itself." And finally, there were the military marches, many of substantial merit, such as those by Mendelssohn, Meyerbeer, and Delibes, three by Prokofiev, and many by Sousa.[7]

The Detroit Concert Band, founded by the cornet soloist Leonard B. Smith in 1946 and led by him until 1991, became the better known, largely because of its leader's reputation as a soloist, conductor, composer, and arranger, and because of its many recordings. Like SIMS, it was primarily a local band, giving concerts throughout the summer at various locations in and around Detroit, even as Smith also conducted the Blossom Festival Concert Band, near Cleveland, from 1972 until 1997. For many band lovers he was not only the successor to Herbert J. Clarke, in whose arrangement of Arban's *Carnival in Venice* he starred, but also to Sousa. He died in 2002.

Many of the band's recordings were made in the 1970s, when it usually numbered slightly more than fifty, and of these perhaps the chief set is the five-disc *Gems of the Concert Band,* presenting seventy-nine selections of traditional concert band repertory. Included are such operatic numbers as Wagner's Prelude to Act III of *Lohengrin,* the sextet from Donizetti's *Lucia di Lammermoor,* and the quartet from Verdi's *Rigoletto.* Among works less usual in band recordings are the overtures to Thomas's *Raymond* and Mendelssohn's *Ruy Blas*, Samuel Coleridge-Taylor's rhapsodic dance, *Bamboula*, and Emil Mollenhauer's fifteen-minute reduction of Verdi's *Manzoni Requiem.*[8]

More of a biological sport among bands, but an example of both their variety and vitality, are the windjammer bands dedicated to the preservation of traditional music of the circus. Their parent, Windjammers Unlimited, Inc., was founded in 1971 and today has some 575 members who gather in groups here and there to give an occasional concert. Windjammer bands play annually at a winter meeting in Sarasota, Florida, with concerts at the Ringling Museum, and then at weekly or monthly summer meetings spread across the country, wherever organized.

Merle Evans (1894–1988), known as "the Toscanini of the Big Top," was the band leader for the Ringling Brothers Barnum & Bailey Circus for fifty years, 1919–1969, and reputedly in that term led more than 22,000 performances. Then, after officially retiring, returned from time to time to lead more. Meanwhile he recorded and directed other bands in the United States and Europe, often programming works of Bach, Beethoven, and Brahms. Circus music in his day had a large repertory of some 2,400 works, all of them clued to some particular act and so requiring an ability to make swift changes. In a typical ten-minute act, for example, there were apt to be upward of fourteen cues, and in the full three-hour performance more than two hundred. And each act, of course, wanted signature music, with tone and tempo to suit: clowns, something bright and jolly; the lion tamer, something soothing; and the elephant man, something to stir the elephant's slow shuffle. On the other hand, what served the elephant was not appropriate for those standing astride galloping horses.

In 1942, for example, the elephants, Evans, and his bandsmen had a problem. The front office had commissioned Igor Stravinsky to write what became his *Circus Polka,* and it included a "Ballet for Elephants," of which the circus then had thirty-seven. The head elephant man, told by the front office to say the elephants liked the music, told reporters that they didn't give "a damn" about it. He said elephants worked best to music with a strong beat, but he hadn't found any beat in Stravinsky's music. Conductor Evans stated the problem more musically: It "was all chopped up—three-quarter time for two measures, two-four time of three measures, three-eight for five and so on." His solution was to sandwich the music "in between Weber's 'Invitation to the Waltz' and Ponchielli's 'Dance of the Hours.' We had to run those elephants in with music they knew or they'd never get started. And we had to get 'em out when their turn was over."[9]

As his solution suggests, circus music often used excerpts from opera. In the repertory of 2,400 works, the leading category was marches, 1,500; followed by overtures, 300; and then by operatic selections, 200. A specialty was 75 trombone smears. At a Ringling performance in San Diego in July 1978, for example, snippets were played from works by Verdi, Borodin, Gounod, Saint-Saëns, Suppé, Smetana, Rimsky-Korsakov, and Tchaikovsky. And finally, for the man shot from the cannon, as the cannon rolled into place, a theme from *Star Wars,* and after the shot, a fanfare adapted from Wagner's *Das Rheingold.*[10]

But playing circus music in concert today is hardly the same as during a performance of old. Windjammer concerts are necessarily nostalgic, for today the Ringling circus is not all that it once was and tends to use only jazz-rock-pop music. Smaller circuses sometimes even have such music pretaped. One tradition, however, seems to have held: "The Stars and Stripes Forever" is reserved for emergencies, a signal to all hands, though hopefully not to the audience, that something has gone wrong, an animal loose, an aerial artist left dangling, or Fire![11]

THE ASSOCIATION OF CONCERT BANDS, INC.
Presents the 1998

COMMUNITY BAND & CHOIR OF AMERICA

On The Legendary S/S NORWAY
NORWEGIAN CRUISE LINES

BAND CONDUCTORS
DR. LELAND A. LILLEHAUG
Sioux Falls, South Dakota USA

JAMES CHRISTENSEN
Villa Park, California USA

CHOIR CONDUCTORS
LARRY LARSON
Oklahoma City, Oklahoma USA

RON STATON
Oklahoma City, Oklahoma USA

You are invited to attend a concert

SAGA THEATER S/S Norway
Wednesday, July 15 & Sunday, July 19 3:00 pm

WORLD'S FAIR EXPO 98 Lisbon, Portugal
Tuesday, July 14 3:00 pm

Figure 8.3. For this cruise the band numbered fifty-seven, not including the two conductors and a manager, and the choir numbered thirty-one, of whom twenty came from California. G. Hoehn Collection.

Still another variant of concert bands is the growth of self-described "community bands." These typically are staffed by amateurs, gathered for some civic occasion, and perform and rehearse usually without pay. They have a corporate representative, the Association of Concert Bands, founded in 1977 "to encourage and foster adult concert community, municipal, and civic bands and to promote the performance of the highest quality traditional and contemporary literature for band."

As well as civic occasions, however, such bands are often organized for trips, such as one put together in 2000 and titled the "Community Band of America 2000." Its members boarded a small ocean liner, the *Costa Atlantica*, and on a twelve-day crossing sailed for Italy where the chief concert was scheduled for 25 October in Rome, to be played in the grand piazza before St. Peter's during a public audience held by Pope John Paul II. The band included fifty-seven professional, semiprofessional, and amateur musicians from eighteen states with a background of playing in thirty-two different community concert bands, as well as two conductors, Col. John R. Bourgeois, emeritus, of the U.S. Marine Band, and Col. Arnald D. Gabriel, emeritus, of the U.S. Air Force Band. Many of the musicians brought family members with them, so in all the group totaled 164. The musicians paid all the tour's expenses, played without pay, and besides rehearsals aboard ship gave two concerts, one at sea for the other passengers, and the other, in Rome.[12]

At Vatican City some seventy thousand people had gathered in the piazza for the Jubilee Year Audience, and the band played "Glory, Glory, Hallelujah" as the pope mobile brought John Paul to the dais from which he addressed the crowd in nine languages. The bandsmen had assumed that the pope's arrival concluded their part in the ceremonies, and were surprised when an official in the Swiss Guards asked them to continue. They then played Cailliet's arrangement of Verdi's overture to *Nabucco,* and when they reached the theme for the chorus of longing, "Va, pensiero," they were startled again, for many of the seventy thousand began to sing. Fearing that perhaps they had interrupted the event, they again looked for guidance and again were told to continue. So they launched into various medleys, including one of Gershwin tunes. For those familiar with the songs this led to some startling moments. Just as the cardinals from around the world were kissing the pope's ring, the band found itself launching into "It Ain't Necessarily So," and when the pope began to bless wedding couples in regalia, it was playing "I Got Rhythm." Throughout, the Swiss Guards stood tall and unsmiling.[13] (For the papal audience, see photospread.)

Lastly, consider another civilian concert band, the Racine Concert Band, of Racine, Wisconsin, which in 1994 received the Sudler Silver Scroll, a high honor for bands. The Racine band was younger than Allentown but older than SIMS. Formed in 1851 by German immigrants, the city of Racine in 1923 began to contribute to the band's support, initially at a 100 percent of expenses, but today covering about 35 percent; businesses (advertising and concert sponsorship) provide about 50, and individuals,15. In summer the band performs ten outdoor concerts, and in winter, indoors, three. The musicians are paid for rehearsals and

THE PRESIDENT'S OWN

Colonel Michael J. Colburn, Director

UNITED STATES MARINE BAND
Sunday, January 10, 2010 at 2:00 P.M.
Center for the Arts Concert Hall
George Mason University
Colonel Michael J. Colburn, conducting

Sousa Season Opener

John Philip Sousa*	March, "The Federal" (1910)
Karl Goldmark transcribed by Victor Grabel	In Springtime Overture, Opus 36
Arthur Pryor transcriber unknown	"Air Varie" *SSgt Samuel Barlow, trombone soloist*
Richard Strauss transcribed by Mark Hindsley	*Till Eulenspiegel's Merry Pranks,* Opus 28
	INTERMISSION
John Philip Sousa*	March, "Yorktown Centennial"
John Philip Sousa*	*Dwellers of the Western World* (1910) The Red Man The White Man The Black Man
Giacomo Puccini transcribed by Edgar L. Barrow	Musetta's Waltz from *La Bohème* *SSgt Sara Dell'Omo, mezzo-soprano*
Emmanuel Chabrier transcribed by Emil Mollenhauer	España Rhapsodie
	SSgt Sara Dell'Omo, concert moderator

*Member, U.S. Marine Band

The Marine Chamber Ensembles will perform Sunday, January 17 at 2:00 P.M. in John Philip Sousa Band Hall at the Marine Barracks Annex in Washington, DC. The program will feature the works of Higdon, Schickele, Saint-Saëns, and Ewazen. Please join us afterward for an open house.

For future concert information, call (202) 433-4011 or visit www.marineband.usmc.mil.

Figure 8.4. U.S. Marine Band.

unless rehearsed cannot play the concert. Operatic numbers would seem to have had a steady place in the band's repertory, for Del Eisch, the band's conductor from 1974 to 2001, when asked for his "five favorite pieces," listed Rossini's overture (arr. Tobani) to *L'Italiana in Algieri;* Vaughan Williams's *English Folk Song Suite*; Rimsky-Korsakov's (arr. Leidzen) Procession of Nobles from the opera *Mlada;* Holst's First Suite in E-flat; and any Sousa march.

Asked further how he felt about the future of adult (nonstudent) community bands, Eisch replied with both pleasure and a warning:

> The outlook is bright for community concert bands. Statistics show a steady growth over the past thirty years. It behooves conductors now to keep in proper perspective a programming balance between entertainment and education. Our audiences still want to be entertained. As conductors we need to suppress our desire to always be on the "cutting edge" with the newest publication. Keep the programming in balance and our audiences will continue to come.[14]

There lay the rub, in the tension between entertainment and education. It emerges clearly in the history of the Goldman Band, which by the 1920s was beginning to make itself known. Thirty years later, admirers would say that the band's founder and leader, Edwin Franko Goldman, was Sousa's successor as a composer, conductor, and organizer. But, as the program in 2010 for the U.S. Marine Band's "Season Opener" suggests, Sousa was neither displaced nor forgotten.

NOTES

1. The figures for the U.S. Marine Band and many of its programs discussed in this chapter were sent to me in a series of letters throughout the year 2010 by the band's historian, Master Gunnery Sergeant D. Michael Ressler.

2. The Grand Fantasie from *Die Walküre* was arranged by Arthur Seidel and depicts principally Siegmund's "Spring Song" to Sieglinde (act 1) and "Wotan's Farewell" as he surrounds Brunnhilde with a ring of magic fire (act 3). The Verdi ballet music from *Don Carlos* was arranged by Donald Patterson. The *Carmen Symphony* was first created by José Serebrier, who followed the musical order of the opera except for the final number which he felt needed voices and for which he substituted the gypsy dance from act 2. For the U.S. Marine Band it was arranged by Donald Patterson. See Recordings, the first two on *Grand Scenes,* Boston Records, 1051; the *Carmen Symphony,* Naxos, 8.57027.

3. *The Washington Post,* 2 April 1987, review by David Johnson of a concert on 31 March. *Time* magazine, 20 July 1998, article by Hugh Sidey, "Glory Raised High by Horns," commenting on the band's two hundredth anniversary celebrated the week before.

4. See the historical program note to the 1924 concert, written by Major Edwin North McClellan, then historian of the corps. Copy in the U.S. Marine Band Library.

5. The program for the 1924 concert, with its fifteen pages of notes, pictures, roster of the band and patrons, makes a small pamphlet. Copy in the U.S. Marine Band Library.

6. The Allentown Band, see its history at http://www.allentownband.com, and the review of its recording of Cailliet arrangements, a 180th anniversary issue, in Windjammers Unlimited's, *Circus Fanfare*, vol. 38, no. 4, August 2008, p. 31.

7. For material on SIMS, I thank Victor DeRenzi, interview during the summer of 2010.

8. Walking Frog Records, *Gems of the Concert Band: The Legacy of Leonard B. Smith*, WRF 306.

9. Gene Plowden, *Merle Evans: Maestro of the Circus* (Miami: E. A. Seemann, 1971), 136–37.

10. See *Circus Fanfare,* the journal of Windjammers Unlimited, Inc., vol. 38, no. 4, August 2008: Letter to the Editor, from Eric Beheim, 7; "Ringling Bros. and Barnum & Bailey Circus Musical Programs, 1969 to 1984: An Overview—Part 4 of 6," by Eric Beheim, circus music historian, 13.

11. Ibid., "The Sousa of the Circus Is Back," by Allan Keller, 21. The most famous circus fire occurred at a Ringling tent performance in Hartford, Connecticut, on 6 July 1944. When Evans saw the fire, the first to do so, he was leading a soft waltz but immediately switched to "The Stars and Stripes Forever."

12. See About the Association of Concert Bands of America (ACB) at www.acbands.org/Our-History.html. Gustave Hoehn, an E-flat clarinetist on the Community Band of America journey to Rome, October 2000, kindly gave me a copy of the tour's personnel and works from which the concert program would be taken. Besides the *Nabucco* overture, already mentioned, the other operatic possibilities were the overture to *Orpheus in the Underworld,* Offenbach, arr. L. Odom; galop from *Geneviève de Brabant,* Offenbach, arr. John R. Bourgeois; *Raymond (The Queen's Secret),* Thomas, arr. V. F. Sofranek; and *Cavalleria Rusticana,* intermezzo sinfonico, Mascagni, arr. Von O. Brinkmann.

13. From an interview on 14 June 2010 and subsequent correspondence with Gustave Hoehn, a clarinetist in the band.

14. The Sudler Silver Scroll interview with Delbert Eisch, in *The Journal of the Association of Concert Bands* 27, no. 3 (October 2008): 13. Eisch, emeritus conductor of the Racine Concert Band, is also a past president of ACB as well as having served as its historian.

Chapter Nine

Edward Franko Goldman and the Goldman Band

The Goldman Band, initially under the name the New York Military Band, played its first season in New York in 1911 and soon, aided by radio broadcasts, won national attention. Ultimately, after Sousa's death in 1932 and Clarke's retirement in 1943, it would become one of the country's most important civilian concert bands not only for skill in performance but also for number of performances and trends noticeable in its programs. Founded by Edwin Franko Goldman, a respected trumpet and cornet soloist in the Metropolitan Opera orchestra, the New York Military Band, despite its name, had no tie to any military organization, but from the start was a civilian group, sustaining itself, at least at first, entirely on donations. Its founder, conductor, and chief in all respects, musical and administrative, was Goldman, who in 1920 reorganized it as the Goldman Band, its name until the death of Goldman's son in 1980, after which it continued first as the Guggenheim Concerts Band and then as the Goldman Memorial Band.[1]

Though the elder Goldman had been born in Louisville, Kentucky, on New Year's Day 1878, his time in the South was short, for the next year the family moved across the Ohio River to Indiana, where his father died in 1886. His widow and their four children, with Edwin at eight the second oldest, moved to New York, where Eddy, as friends and family called him, enrolled in the Hebrew Orphan Asylum and began to study the cornet. To those who knew his mother, a former professional pianist and member of the Franko family (which claimed many musicians), the boy's skill in music was promising, and in 1892, having won a scholarship, he continued with the cornet and trumpet at New York's National Conservatory of Music. The following year, at age fifteen, with occasional employment he began his professional career. Then in 1901, or possibly two or three years earlier, as an accomplished soloist he joined the Metropolitan Opera orchestra where his uncle Nahan Franko was concertmaster and assistant conductor. Though playing with bands in the summer (his uncle led one), he stayed with the opera orchestra through its spring tour of 1909, and so played under three of its great conductors, Mancinelli, Mahler, and Toscanini. Asked by Toscanini why he was resigning, he spoke of his eagerness to create a professional concert band, and was wished success. Thus more important than his southern birth, which some journalists liked to emphasize—"he is eminently a product of the South"—he grew up a New Yorker, seemingly acquainted with everyone in the city's musical community and through it with many rich and potential patrons. By all reports, in addition to his remarkable musical and executive skills he had an exceptionally genial personality. In 1911 when still only thirty-three, he could recruit a concert band of professional musicians, dominate it, and persuade others to fund it.[2]

The New York Military Band, initially numbering fifty with most of the men from the New York Philharmonic or Metropolitan Opera orchestras, began slowly, with just a few summer concerts and the musicians dressed in a mixture of white suits, which reportedly caused one disappointed lady to remark that the band couldn't be much good if it couldn't afford uniforms. But by the summer of 1918 and 1919, and presumably more uniformly attired, it was offering as many as thirty evening concerts "on the Green" at Columbia University, a large, open space at 120th Street and Amsterdam Avenue. In the case of rain, the concert moved to the university's nearby gymnasium. Not surprisingly, considering Goldman's skills, on the organizing committee were several members of the Guggenheim family, who had a fortune in mining and smelting; several of city's leading lawyers; as well as Mrs. John Purroy Mitchel, the wife of its recently deceased mayor; and Mrs. Nicholas Murray Butler, the wife of the university's president. As much as a good conductor, any large, public musical event needs a good impresario, and in both roles Goldman excelled.[3]

In the reorganization of his band in 1920 Goldman slightly enlarged it, changed its name to the Goldman Band, which many people already called it, but kept its instrumentation roughly as before and similar to the bands of Sousa and Clarke. Now numbering fifty-five (including the conductor), it was without strings except for two basses, had nineteen B-flat clarinets, one also in E-flat as well as an alto and a bass, and in all counted thirty-one woodwinds, seventeen brass, two strings, and four percussion, The musicians, unlike those in contemporary dance bands, sat in a semicircle around the conductor, and at side stage a large placard announced each work. Besides the scheduled program, there usually were one or two unannounced encores during the performance as well as an equal number at its close.[4]

He continued with summer concerts on Columbia's "Green," and in July 1920 the *Musical Messenger* noted with approval three programs as typical. The first of these, on 5 July, was moved to the university's gymnasium because of rain, but even so it reportedly gathered an audience of several thousand with a few hundred or more listening from the grounds outside. For the second and third concerts, both outdoors, audiences numbered upward of twenty thousand, and in all respects the concerts won praise: the musicians were skilled and well rehearsed, the conductor was "free from irritating mannerisms," and the programs were interesting.[5]

The 5 July program was devoted entirely to American composers, ranging from a song by the oldest, Francis Hopkinson (1737–1791), to a "romance" by the youngest, A. Walter Kramer, (b. 1890). Yet the ratio of living to dead, the latter being Hopkinson, MacDowell, and Nevin, was seven to three, clearly favoring contemporaries, a trait which, though shared with others, became associated with Goldman.

Program, 5 July 1920

1. Festival March .... Henry K. Hadley
2a. "To a Wild Rose" .... Edward A. MacDowell
2b. "Romance" .... A. Walter Kramer
3. "A Chant from the Great Plains" .... Carl Busch

A Prize Composition. A prize of $250 was offered in November 1919, by Edwin Franko Goldman for the best original work for band. Numerous new and interesting manuscripts were submitted, but the "Chant from the Great Plains" was considered the most worthy. Mr. Busch is the conductor of the Kansas City Symphony Orchestra.

4a. "On the Green Intermezzo" .... Edwin Franko Goldman
4b. "Sagamore" March .... Edwin Franko Goldman
4c. "A Bit of Syncopation" .... Edwin Franko Goldman

Songs:

5a. "My Days Have Been So Wondrous Free," .... Francis Hopkinson
5b. "A Birthday," .... R. Huntington Woodman

(Miss Margaret Ringo, soprano)

6a. "Narcissus" .... Ethelbert Nevin
6b. "The Lady Picking Mulberries" .... Edgar Stillman Kelley

(A Chinese Episode)

7. American Fantasie .... Victor Herbert

The prize, offered to an American composer and awarded to Carl Busch by the judges, Victor Herbert and Percy Grainger, was an early example of Goldman's burgeoning interest in expanding the repertory of works composed specifically for band. By 1934 he passionately believed that with an enlarged repertory of its own "the real Concert Band in the comparatively near future will reach a position of musical respectability and artistic excellence, at least equal to the Symphony Orchestra, and perhaps superior to it." To that end he commissioned works from composers of all nationalities, among the more famous foreigners were Roussel, Milhaud, Shostakovich, and Schoenberg, and among the Americans, Henry Hadley, George Perle, and Virgil Thomson. The Busch work was not one of the more successful. Sousa played it in his 1922 season, though not again, and Grainger, at Interlochen in 1937. Not every prize or commissioned work was a masterpiece.[6]

Notably, on this all-American program there is no work by Sousa, although perhaps some march appeared as an unannounced encore. And the work representing Victor Herbert was not taken from one of his operettas, although these were considered his best work. In fact, no work from American musical theater was chosen, and the program as a whole, led by Hadley, MacDowell, and Nevin, leaned to the "classical" wing of American composers. In this, Goldman seems to differ from Sousa, perhaps in part because of personality but perhaps also in part because of early experience: ten or so years of playing a settled repertory in the Metropolitan Opera orchestra versus a like period in the more rough-and-tumble of theater bands.[7]

Moreover, three of the composers chosen, Kramer, Woodman, and Kelley, were as much critics, teachers, and journalists as composers. Kramer, for one, worked for twelve years on the staff of *Musical America*, and served 1929–1936 as its chief editor. Woodman, primarily a church organist, taught music at several schools and edited a page on church music for the New York *Evangelist*. Kelley's experience was more varied, but it also included years of teaching at the Yale Music School and the Cincinnati Conservatory of Music, along with considerable critical writing. All that these men did was no doubt honorable and valuable to their students, but—if the example of Charles Ives is considered—a composer wishing to develop an individual voice perhaps does better to earn his daily bread, if such he must, in a nonmusical field, such as insurance, rather than on the fringes, literary or academic, of music performance. In sum, Goldman, who composed many stirring marches—his "On the Mall" (1924) is sometimes said to rank second in popularity only to "The Stars and Stripes Forever"—tended early to look to the academic and critical world for the composers he wished to feature. And possibly another sign of that tendency, though perhaps merely a part of the price for the use of Columbia's gymnasium and its Green, was his undertaking in this same year, 1920, to lead the Columbia University Band.[8]

Yet the second July concert noted by the *Musical Messenger* would seem to deny any lack of interest in theatrical music, for, though devoted entirely to French works, its program was almost exclusively operatic and theatrical—indicating also an interest in certain French composers.

Program, 14 July 1920

1. March, Sambre et Meuse ...."Turlet" (Josef F. Rauski)
2. Overture, *Phèdre* .... J. Massenet
3. Le Cygne (The Swan) .... Saint-Saëns
4. Excerpts from *Carmen* .... Bizet
5. Reminiscences of Offenbach .... W. Winterbottom
6. Aria for Contralto from *Samson and Dalila* .... Saint-Saëns
7. Meditation from *Thaïs* .... J. Massenet
8. Excerpts from *Chimes of Normandy* .... R. Planquette

Though he continued to schedule such unabashedly operatic programs in the years ahead—in the summer of 1932, for example, he had programs devoted specifically to "grand" opera, "comic" opera, Gilbert and Sullivan, Wagner, and Verdi—these gradually become rarer. Meanwhile, in the summer of 1920, *The Musical Messenger* would describe as "unusually interesting" the third July program, which it defined as "an invasion into the realms of what has heretofore been considered orchestra music." Yet it was also, in 1920, a conventional program, for despite the suggestion that it was a new departure, Sousa in his concerts had played every number on it, except the waltz by Josef Strauss.[9]

Program, 21 July 1920

1. Rakoczy March .... Hector Berlioz
2. Beautiful Galathea Overture .... F. von Suppé
3. Wedding Sounds Waltz .... Josef Strauss

(First time ever performed with band)

4. *Finlandia,* Tone Poem .... Jean Sibelius
5. Prelude .... Serge Rachmaninoff
6. Fantasie Brillante for Cornet .... J. B. Arban

(Performed by Ernest S. Williams)

7. Polish Dance .... Xavier Scharwenka
8. Excerpts from *The Bohemian Girl* .... M. W. Balfe

Until 1923 the summer concerts were held at Columbia, but in that year, because of new buildings rising on the Green, Goldman moved them to the mall in New York's Central Park and to the Music Grove in Prospect Park, Brooklyn. Soon, with additional support from the Guggenheim family, the band was giving as many as sixty concerts a summer, with audiences continuing to number in the tens of thousands. In the 1924 season, as a salute to Central Park, Goldman introduced his march "On the Mall" for which a tradition soon developed that band members and the audience would hum, whistle, or sing the main theme (even sometimes so recorded), and performances of it soon became a feature of a Goldman Band concert, often by demand of the audience.[10] (See photospread.)

He also had a popular success with a number of other marches—he composed more than seventy-five—and among the more frequently played are "Cheerio," which, like "On the Mall," has a tuneful trio for the audience to hum or whistle, as well as "Onward-Upward," "Illinois March," "Interlochen Bowl," and "Kentucky March." The last, based on Stephen Foster's "My Old Kentucky Home," Virgil Thomson judged to be one of Goldman's "stronger works."[11]

Besides audience singing and whistling to "On the Mall" and "Cheerio," Goldman fostered other traditions. Like Sousa's men, Goldman's musicians now wore simple dark uniforms and caps, but for himself, unlike Sousa, whose uniform, except for additional braid, usually mirrored those of his men, Goldman appeared in vivid contrasting colors: white trousers and dark blazer, topped by a shock of uncapped white hair. As he strode to the podium, brisk and jaunty, to the farthest row of the audience he was unmistakable, and at the final concert of any season—in 1953, for example, after the unusually large number of five encores, with the first "On the Mall"—he would close with "Auld Lang Syne," during which he would take out his white pocket handkerchief, turn to the audience, and with a smile wave farewell, a gesture the audience in its thousands delighted to return.[12]

Annually, too, toward the end of each summer season, he would conduct a Memory Contest in the first half of a program, during which the band would play unannounced snippets of twenty-five pieces played earlier in the current concert series. Any nonprofessional musician in the audience was invited to identify the works, adding name and address to the questionnaire that had been distributed. Answers, often numbering in the thousands, then were collected, and at the end of the second half of the concert, or perhaps, if necessary, at the next concert, the winner would be announced and a medal along with a certificate of honor issued. (For answers to the contest's twenty-five questions in July 1938, see appendix 15.)[13]

In other ways, too, Goldman worked to advance the cause of band music. In 1929 he founded the American Bandmasters Association, with headquarters in New York and the now elderly Sousa named as honorary life president. A photograph of the nine charter members, all a generation younger than Sousa, shows a group of men, most of them pudgy, balding, and badly tailored, while in the front row a trim, seated Goldman, with luxuriant white hair, spats, cane, and white handkerchief peeping from his breast pocket, outshines them. One of the association's purposes, aimed at a long-standing obstacle, was to persuade bandmasters everywhere to agree on a basic instrumentation for all wind bands—say, sixteen clarinets, two oboes, four horns, and so forth—so that music publishers would have a greater incentive to publish arrangements and parts for instruments. For as long as every band kept to its own idea of basic instrumentation, and relied on its own handwritten parts, the publishers found arrangements and parts unprofitable to print. On this point, in part because of the increasing number of high school and college bands entering the market, the association in time achieved its aim.[14]

The association grew swiftly, and by April 1932, for its Third Annual Convention, held in Washington, D.C., it had eighty members and drew many interested observers. On the convention's fourth day, as its concluding program, it presented a concert in memory of Sousa, who had died the previous month. In the course of the seventeen numbers, the army, navy, and marine bands all played individually and then, toward the end, as a single, massed band. For the five numbers specifically designated "In Memory of John Philip Sousa," the U.S. Marine Band led off with an arrangement of Chopin's "Funeral March," after which the massed bands played Sousa's "U.S. Field Artillery March," "Washington Post March," *El Capitan* March, and "The Stars and Stripes Forever." The concert closed with Goldman conducting the massed bands in his own University Grand March, perhaps chosen because, besides several brilliant fanfare passages, it introduces in its trio as a counter melody in the bass, "Auld Lang Syne."[15]

Moreover, among the concert's seventeen numbers were ten listed as "New," presumably U.S. if not world premieres, achieving another of the association's aims: to commission new works for band. Presumably many of the association's members believed, like Goldman, that concert bands were not second best to orchestras, and through the association they invited composers to exploit that difference.[16]

Goldman also had a part in two other memorials to Sousa, as well as sharing in a poll shadowed by Sousa's death. First, on the day Sousa died, 6 March 1932, he shared in a radio program eulogizing the conductor, composer, and man—to Goldman "a gentleman of the old school"—interspersed with performances of the composer's works. Then in August, in Central Park, he scheduled a "Sousa Memorial Program," with Mrs. Sousa present. The band played many Sousa marches, including the two said to be the widow's favorites, "Semper Fidelis" and "King Cotton." In return, in a midconcert ceremony, she presented Goldman with her husband's baton, but neither Goldman nor any other bandleader ever claimed to be Sousa's successor.[17]

Lastly, he was among the distinguished conductors and bandleaders polled on the then topical question: "Should radio audiences stand when *The Star Spangled Banner* is broadcast?" With results published in early April, the poll clearly had been planned and started before Sousa's death, and was haunted by the absence of his opinion. Still, among conductors questioned by the *New York Times* were Sir Thomas Beecham, Leopold Stokowski, and Ernest Schelling of the New York Philharmonic; and among bandmasters, Arthur Pryor, Goldman, and Capt. William J. Stannard of the U.S. Army Band.

Beecham's answer was an unequivocal yes. Schelling agreed, but added: "I am opposed to the use of flags on visual advertising—hence, to the use of the national anthem in commercial radio presentations." Stokowski, using yes to say no, was less blunt: "If the words had any relation to life today, and if the music were good and one could sing it, then I would say, yes." Among the bandmasters, Pryor stood squarely with Beecham: "If the listeners are alone at home . . . all the more reason why they should stand. It is a matter of respect." Goldman started strong: "The same reverence is due the national anthem at all times," but then qualified, "It should not be played by ten or more orchestras in one night on the radio." Capt. Stannard of the army band was pragmatic: "Yes, if it seems natural . . . [but not] if eating at table, lying in bed, or working in the kitchen." The paper's readers doubtless wondered what Sousa might have said.[18]

As the country's economic depression continued, however, the number of professional concert bands dwindled. In some towns they were succeeded by amateur high school and college bands, which, though important for education, played less often and less well. But many professional bands died without replacement, and by 1934 Goldman was lamenting, "There are so very few of them left."[19]

One problem for all bands was an emerging dark side to the advances in radio. Its programs increasingly favored popular songs, and among them not only the current top ten but also many of the older standards. By 1946 this practice had become so pervasive that one critic remarked, "The radio feeds its audience a constant diet of 'favorites,' a diet so unvaried that many of the old favorites are finally becoming indigestible." In 1934 Goldman had regretfully observed that radio was making audiences "musically lazy." Instead of going to a park or hall to hear music or, better still, learning to play an instrument at home, listeners now simply "pushed a button." Much was being lost. As he stressed, "*After all, the greatest joy in music is in being able to make it yourself.*[20]

Though Goldman and his band were less neglected than most by radio, enjoying steady sponsorship from the Cities Service and Puroil companies, bands of less renown found themselves increasingly shut out from broadcasts. As early as 1932 several articles in the *New York Times* summarized the problem: "Commercialism came along and pushed the bands off the ethereal streets in the evening or else gave them only a short period compared to the days when the entire concert was broadcast. Those were happy days for listeners. . . . The music was not interrupted by commercial words." And a week later: "Reports from members of the radio audience indicate that they want to hear more of the Goldman Band concerts this Summer than they did last year." Radio now threatened to cut the size of live audiences, and for most bands the job of raising money to fund their concerts was job enough without adding the costs incurred in finding a sponsor for radio. Thus, at least in New York and on the East Coast, radio, for more than a decade an important outlet for concert bands, began to abandon them. Goldman, pleading for the less renowned, said: "Radio is a great blessing—so is the phonograph. They have brought music to places it would never have reached otherwise. But give a thought to living music."[21]

In 1934 Goldman published, not his first book but perhaps his best known, *Band Betterment: Suggestions and Advice to Bands, Bandmasters, and Band-players*. Besides offering chapters on specific instruments, how to play and how to care for them, he discussed the making of a good program for an out-door summer concert, stressing that the conductor should always strive "for plenty of contrast." Moreover, "under no circumstances" should the concert run longer than two hours. "An hour and a half to an hour and three-quarters is the ideal time, and even then there should be an intermission of about ten minutes, and a little breathing spell between the program numbers." The wind instrument players, he said, needed time between numbers to rest their lips. Otherwise to his ear most bands by intermission are "completely played out" and the second half of the program suffers.[22]

He warned against playing too many "encores" or "extras," preserving "encore" to mean a repeat of the work just played and "extra" the rendition of an unscheduled piece. His rule was to play an "extra" only when "actually demanded by the audience." For any extra he favored a march, "but it is not wise to perform too many of them at any single concert, for they are tiring to the lips of the players." Hence, at a Goldman concert the extras usually came at the end of the program, and those chosen "should never be long." His "On the Mall," for example, runs three minutes. Another frequent extra, introduced in the opening concert of 1932, was an arrangement of Ravel's *Boléro,* shortened by roughly two-thirds to run approximately five minutes. A critic for the *New York Times* complained: "[The work] was so effective instrumentally that one wished it had not been presented in an abridged ver-sion which lessened noticeably its greatest virtue—namely, the cumulative piling up of volume over the same oft-repeated rhythmic pattern." Yet, even so, "it was enthusiastically applauded, and had to be repeated." Soon it ranked close to "On the Mall" as an audience favorite.[23]

Goldman suggested opening a program with "a Grand March, for this gives the players a chance to 'warm up.'" But after any major piece, say, an over-ture or operatic selection, "the band is entitled to at least two or three minutes rest in order to be fit to do justice to the next number." Those bandmasters who, in imitation perhaps of Sousa, turned swiftly to the next piece made "a grave mistake. Music should not be hurled or forced on an audience in such a manner." And about operatic selections he voiced some doubt: "Many of the so-called Operatic Fantasies (or Selections), and Comic Opera Selections are too long. They can generally be cut so that the more important and pleasing parts are retained. This seems to be an age of speed."[24]

Finally, and with increasing strength over the years, he insisted that bands needed their own repertory. "The band is *not* inferior to the orchestra. It is simply *different.* Each can achieve certain effects which the other cannot. . . . There are those who feel that a band is a mere 'noise-maker.' There have been such bands and some of them are in existence today, but a good band is a fine medium for artistic expression of the best that the art of music has to offer."[25]

His concerts reflected that belief and were a reflection of himself: they were jaunty, brisk, artistic, and, as the large audiences proved, popular. Like Sousa, but in his own way, Goldman became, at least for his New York audiences, a beloved figure. In forty-four seasons of summer concerts he never missed a performance by his own band. He died, aged 78, on 21 February 1956; his son, Richard Franko Goldman, who had been the band's associate conductor since 1937, took his place, and the concerts continued without a break.

As might be expected, in the elder Goldman's later years, roughly 1936 to 1956, as the number of original compositions for band increased, the number of transcribed operatic selections declined (see appendix 16). The band soon became famous for its premieres of original works, such as in the summer of 1937 the first complete performance of Grainger's *Lincolnshire Posy,* in 1945 the world premiere of Milhaud's *Suite française*, Op. 248, in 1946 the world premiere of Schoenberg's Theme and Variations, Op. 43a, and in 1947 the U.S. premiere of Berlioz's *Symphonie funèbre et triomphale.*

The program to open his thirty-third season on the mall, in June 1950, is listed below, with an asterisk indicating a premiere conducted by its composer.

Program, 15 June 1950

1. March, Orient and Occident .... Saint-Saëns
2. Overture in F .... Mehul
3. Intermezzo for Symphonic Band* .... W. Piston
   [Commonly known as "Tunbridge Fair"]
4. Prayer from Tannhäuser .... Wagner (34)
   (Helen Phillips, soprano)
5. Suite No. 1 in E-flat .... Holst
6. Concert Waltz* .... Goldman
   (cornet solo, James F. Burke)

7. Divertimento for Band* .... V. Persichetti
8. The Spinning Top .... Villa-Lobos
9. March, Kentucky* .... Goldman

A review of the concert in the *New York Herald Tribune* reported two extras: "The Carnival of Venice," with J. F. Burke as soloist, and Sousa's "The Stars and Stripes Forever." As usual, Goldman offered something for everyone. The paper's critic, Virgil Thomson, however, was somewhat cool in his praise of the new works by Piston and Persichetti while noticeably warmer in speaking of those by Gustav Holst and Sousa, and calling "The Carnival of Venice," "ever the perfect work of its kind, charming, comical and utterly brilliant." He closed by recommending the concerts as "calm, cultured, unhurried, thoroughly musical."[26]

At a later concert in 1955, devoted entirely to "original band music," Goldman offered three more commissioned works, *Triumphal March* by Albert Chiafferelli, *Celebration Overture* by Paul Creston, and *Pageant for Band* by Persichetti. Of these Chiafferelli's work seems to have died at birth, while Creston's overture achieved at least a brief life, being played in 1955, 1960, and 1962 by the Eastman Wind Ensemble, and then dropped. Persichetti's *Pageant,* on the other hand, is still played, though perhaps not as often as his *Divertimento* or *Psalm.*[27]

The three composers, Piston, Creston, and Persichetti are sufficiently well established to stand as whipping boys for the many others whom Goldman commissioned but whose works and names have largely disappeared. The problem was that the music of the three, when compared to that of their theatrical contemporaries who worked in ballet, musical comedy, or opera, impressed most audiences as boring, lacking in melody and drama (action, passion, and portrayal of character).

As journalists then constantly declared, the twentieth century was the Century of the Common Man, and in 1943 Copland composed "Fanfare for the Common Man," much played by orchestras, bands, rock bands, and pop groups, as well as on radio and television—the sort of success that Piston, Creston, and Persichetti never achieved. In a phrase then popular, the common man might have said of their music, "Nothing came out and grabbed me." To succeed with the common man, it seems, even on first hearing something somewhere in the music must instantly appeal.[28]

In June 1941, Virgil Thomson, writing for the *New York Herald Tribune,* scolded Goldman for the trend in his programs. Thomson had attended the opening concert in Central Park on 18 June and found it "excessive to have to sit through so much frankly non-essential repertory in order to hear two short works from the band's essential repertory." Among the nonessential works were Tchaikovsky's *Romeo and Juliet* and Sibelius's *Finlandia,* and Thomson left no doubt about what he considered essential: "Everything is trimming and filling at a band concert except the military marches." He liked the arrangements of Wagner, however, for "the absence of violins removes that juicy-fruit quality that is so monotonous in the orchestral versions." And while sympathetic to Goldman's desire to increase the number of works composed originally for bands, he tackled directly Goldman's apparent disdain of popular songs and theatrical works because they had to be played in arrangements: "Such music," he said, "must naturally be performed in 'arrangements'; but since it is never played anywhere except in arrangements, it is legitimate to consider all arrangements of it as equally appropriate to the instruments for which they are made. Such compositions frequently contain, indeed, writing for wind ensemble that is in every way idiomatic, sonorous, and satisfactory."[29]

He might have added, in defense of arrangements from operas, for example, that Wagner reorchestrated several of his early operas for use by smaller orchestras in the smaller German houses, and Verdi, in the finale of act 2 in *Otello* suggested by an asterisk in the score that the trumpets and trombones remain silent in smaller houses. On this point, at least, Thomson surely was right. In any music for theater, popular song, or opera, arrangements are expected and, when good, approved.

A year later Thomson's article was republished by *The Etude* and prompted a response by the bandleader in the next month's issue. Politely, E. F. Goldman reiterated many of his usual points, such as, "The band is not inferior to the orchestra. It is simply different"; "I feel that in each concert several marches should be included"; and "Our bands are different to-day—different in size—and different in instrumentation. We have oboes and bassoons—and French horns, and other instruments, and we insist that they have 'individual' parts, and not merely 'double' with some other instruments." In passing he mentioned an interesting figure: "To-day we have over 75,000 bands in the United States (mostly school organizations) that are devoting their time to concert music." Finally, he reached the crucial question: "As to what we should play."[30]

He agreed that Wagner was effective in arrangements for band, "but so is much of Tchaikovsky, Beethoven, Bach." He thought *Finlandia,* however, sounds "better for band than for orchestra." Moreover, he remarked, "the orchestra can play arrangements of operatic or chamber music, of far-fetched arrangements of Bach, Handel and other old masters, but the band is criticized for it. What the band needs is considerably more attention and sympathetic treatment." He concluded, "We do not aim to be 'highbrow.' We feel that unless we give some music of the masters our concerts would be in vain. . . . We try to please all 'musical' tastes."

In the way of the world, neither man won the exchange; rather, for a time the issue sank from the press, except that Thomson included his review in his 1947 book *The Musical Scene.* Meanwhile each continued to pursue his likes and dislikes. Goldman, despite Thomson's praise of it, all but ignored Gershwin's *Rhapsody in Blue*, along with Gershwin's other orchestral works and much of contemporary American theatrical music, though living through an age which ran from the operettas of Herbert and Romberg to the musical comedies of Kern, Berlin, Rodgers, and Loewe—all of whom had composed music appealing greatly to the general public and hence likely to please summer, outdoor audiences.[31]

Similarly, Goldman seems oddly deaf to the best of what was happening in opera. American composers in this genre were not strong, but elsewhere others were. It seems remarkable, for example, that neither Goldman nor any other bandleader, so far as is known, picked up any music from Benjamin Britten's opera *Peter Grimes,* which had its world premiere in London in 1945, and the following year an American premiere at Tanglewood, Massachusetts. A success in both countries, the opera, about a fisherman, offered to bands (and still does) not only sea chanteys, rounds, and choruses (including one for a town posse determined to "strike and kill"), but a passacaglia that reflected the gathering tension in Grimes's mind, portrayed by a bass figure, repeated over and over beneath a theme introduced by a solo viola and followed by nine short variations with much work for horns. Its tone is increasingly ominous, a presentation (five mins.), easily understood and strongly felt, of trouble to come. In addition, the opera offered four interludes about the sea: the sea at dawn, on Sunday morning, at night, and then a storm.

Some may complain that the passacaglia and the interludes, being purely orchestral, are more pictorial than operatic, but good theatrical music often is pictorial, setting the scene emotionally—happy, sad, or promising conflict. Consider the waltzes in Strauss's *Der Rosenkavalier,* which its characters seldom sing or dance and which yet provide the opera's tone. For many years these were continually played by bands, which makes it all the more remarkable that in later years bands did not pick up on the waltzes from Prokofiev's *War and Peace;* or on a piece that seemed ideally suited to them, the gorgeous moonlit interlude from Richard Strauss's *Capriccio,* a four-minute serenade for horn.

But this was not the direction in which serious music was headed then. In the 1950s, especially in the works of some leading composers and as taught in most music schools, music was becoming ever more complicated and intellectual. Structure, not melody or even rhythm, was becoming the chief source of interest. So-called twelve-tone or dodecaphonic music offers an extreme example: first the tone row is displayed in prime, then by inverse (upside-down), retrograde (backward) and by retrograde-inverse. And then the same progression can be applied to rhythms. Pleasure in such music for many listeners, perhaps for most, lies in being able to hear and follow the intricacies of that structure, a feat often best achieved alone at home, score in hand, and quite beyond the ability of most in any large live audience. As early as 1925, H. L. Mencken, an experienced listener, was beginning to complain: "The so-called moderns interest me very much, for I am fond of experiments in the arts. But I'd rather read their music than hear it. It always fails to come off: it is *Augenmusik*" (eye music).[32]

Creston, Piston, and Persichetti were not blinkered disciples of the new style, but none of them primarily composed music for theater or opera, indoors or out. They were not skilled in it, and they tended in their music to downplay melody, emotion, and obvious drama. And so, perforce, did Goldman in favoring them and others like them in the works he commissioned, while ignoring the opera composers of his day. Yet he wanted to give free outdoor concerts to audiences in the thousands.

Curiously, he seems to have been unaware of the tension between what he liked to commission and what his summer audiences wanted to hear. Significantly, in 1948 when the country's League of Composers wanted to honor him on his seventieth birthday, it played "A Program of Contemporary Music Written for Symphonic Band," which included many of the works he had commissioned. It happened, perhaps by chance, that of the ten composers represented only one, Henry Cowell, was an American. And perhaps also only because Goldman's birthday fell in January, the league chose to play the program not in Central Park but in Carnegie Hall. Yet that indoor venue, seating a limited and perhaps on average a more sophisticated audience, better suited the works.[33]

Cowell anticipated the concert by a week, with an article in the *Herald-Tribune,* "Goldman's Influence," in which he described Goldman's "permanent niche in musical history."

> He has kept the Goldman Band in active relationship with the living music of his time. It is now possible, for the first time, to offer a program of fine art music of great variety and interest, all written expressly for the band by famous living composers. That this is true is very largely due to the efforts and influence of Dr. Goldman and his son Richard.[34]

Cowell noted that the achievement had not come easily. In his park concerts Goldman had started a policy of playing the "fine art music" in the concert's first half, and then following in the second half, "more popular works, including marches." This had not always been accepted by his audiences. In fact, according to Cowell, it had been "met with a resistance difficult to imagine for those who live in the indoor concert world. The omission of the marches in the first part which the outdoor audience expected to hear was several times noisily and persistently resented."

While Goldman lived, his summer audiences could count on at least half a concert devoted to "popular works." If one piece didn't please, then soon another would. But what if Goldman's successor and other younger leaders pushed his tendencies further, what if the influence on band music of the academic educators and musicians featured by Goldman continued to grow, what then was the future of the indoor or outdoor band concert to entertain and educate the general public?

NOTES

1. The public's distress at the likely demise of the Goldman Band, following the death of Goldman's son Richard (10 January 1980), stirred a movement to have the band continue, which it did, first under the name Guggenheim Concerts Band and then, in 1984, as the Goldman Memorial Band.

2. Nahan Franko, more important to the orchestra as concertmaster than occasional conductor, yet was noted as "the first native-born American to lead an opera in the Metropolitan." See Irving Kolodin, *The Metropolitan Opera, 1883–1966: A Candid History* (New York: Knopf, 1966), 172, and obituary, *Times*, 8 June 1930, 26. When not at the Metropolitan, Nahan Franko led his own orchestra, in which Goldman played and had a part in management, see Herbert N. Johnston, "Edwin Franko Goldman: A Brief Biographical Sketch," *Journal of Band Research* 14, no. 1 (Fall 1978): 3. Toscanini and EFG, see Johnston, "Edwin Franko Goldman," 5. "Product of the South," see Walter Lewis, "Edwin Franko Goldman: An Appreciation," *Musical Messenger*, vol. 16, no. 12, December 1920, 3.

3. Disappointed lady, see R. F. Goldman, *The Concert Band,* 5. The committee appears on programs for the 1919 season. See the Edwin Frank Goldman Collection, Special Collections, University of Maryland Libraries.

4. On the use of a string bass in a concert band, R. F. Goldman, *The Concert Band,* 51; according to Goldman its earliest appearance occurred in 1867. On 106 he quotes Sousa, who in 1900 argued against it and insisted that "the bass tuba does all and more." Sousa added, if a band admits a cello, then why not the other strings, and so lose its wind individuality. But, adds Goldman, writing in 1946, "Sousa's view is apparently not held by the majority of bandmasters today." Both Goldmans employed string basses. Those bandmasters in favor of going further, adding cellos, argue that these can take "the edge off the tuba tones and the baritones." But opinion in 1946 was "still strongly divided," as seems the case today.

5. See *Musical Messenger,* vol. 16, no. 12, December 1920, 3.

6. See Edwin Franko Goldman, *Band Betterment: Suggestions and Advice to Bands, Bandmasters, and Band-players* (New York: Carl Fischer, 1934), 24–25. Sousa's repertory, Bierley, *The Incredible Band,* 335.

7. On Herbert's operettas, for example, *The International Cyclopedia of Music and Musicians*, 9th ed. (New York: Dodd, Mead, 1964), 936–37.

8. "On the Mall," Schwartz, *Bands of America,* 310.

9. Operatic programs, *Times,* 8 May 1932, sec. VIII, 6.

10. For example, *Hands Across the Sea,* by the Eastman Wind Ensemble, cond. Frederick Fennell, Mercury Records, 434 334–2.

11. *Herald Tribune*, 17 June 1950, 7, Thomson on "Kentucky March."

12. *Herald Tribune*, 17 August 1953, 5, on the previous night's concert, which closed the 1953 season with an audience estimated at 16,000. Ibid., 12 August 1946, 13, for closing the season.

13. Answers to Memory Contest, *Times*, 4 August 1938, 14. Contest winners, *Herald Tribune*, 3 August 1950, 15: first place, Aaron Gold, of the Bronx, with a perfect score, repeating his win in eighteen previous contests; second place, Albert E. Koontz, of the Bronx, who had been in the top three in twenty-two previous summers.

14. See E. F. Goldman, *Band Betterment,* 29–31, 38–39, 42–43, 60–61.

15. The Sousa Memorial Concert, 17 April 1932, at Constitution Hall, Washington, D.C. I thank the staff at the Performing Arts Library, University of Maryland, College Park, for providing me with a copy of the program and other information concerning this concert and convention.

16. E. F. Goldman, *Band Betterment,* 42–43.

17. Eulogizing Sousa, *Times*, 7 March 1932, 17. Sousa's successor, *Times*, 16 August 1932, 20. Goldman's publisher, Carl Fischer, however, in the foreword to *Band Betterment,* declared, "No one can seriously contest his right to be known as the successor to John Philip Sousa."

18. *Times*, 10 April 1932, sec. IX, 8, 1.

19. E. F. Goldman, *Band Betterment,* 29.

20. R. F. Goldman, *The Concert Band,* 13. E. F. Goldman, *Band Betterment*, 9.

21. For the Goldman Band and radio in the late 1920s, see Johnston, "Edwin Franko Goldman," 9. *Times*, 10 April 1932, sec. IX, 8, "Listening In," by Orrin E. Dunlap Jr.; *Times*, 17 April 1932, sec. VIII, 8, "Listening In," by Orrin E. Dunlap Jr.; E. F. Goldman, *Band Betterment,* 10.

22. He first published *The Amateur Band Guide and Aid to Leader: A Reference Book for All Wind Instrument Players Describing the Construction and Maintenance of Bands, Their Organization, Instrumentation, and All Other Complete Information That Is Necessary or Desirable* (New York: Carl Fischer, 1916). And later, *The Goldman Band System for Developing Tone, Intonation and Phrasing* (New York: Carl Fischer, 1935). E. F. Goldman, *Band Betterment,* 55, 56.

23. E. F. Goldman, *Band Betterment*, 56, 58. *Bolero*, presumably the arrangement Goldman describes in ibid., 39–40. Commissioned by the Goldman Band, it was arranged by Mayhew Lester Lake, approved by Ravel, and published in Paris by Durand.

24. Ibid., 56, 57.

25. Ibid., 37.

26. "Carnival of Venice," probably the work by the French cornetist Joseph Jean B. L. Arban, associated in the United States chiefly with Herbert L. Clarke but played,

or at least attempted, by many soloists. Virgil Thomson review, *Herald Tribune*, 17 June 1950, 7.

27. Concert on 1 July 1955. For Creston, see *The Wind Ensemble and Its Repertoire: Essays on the Fortieth Anniversary of the Eastman Wind Ensemble,* eds. Frank J. Cipolla and Donald Hunsberger (New York: University of Rochester Press, 1994), 276.

28. Copland's "Fanfare for the Common Man" was commissioned by Eugene Gossens for the Cincinnati Symphony Orchestra and premiered on 12 March 1943. It runs two minutes and is scored for brass and percussion: four French horns, three trumpets, three trombones, tuba, timpani, gong, and bass drum. It has frequently been rearranged for other instruments. Curiously, the Goldman Band seems never to have played it.

29. Thomson, *Herald Tribune*, 22 June 1941, sec. 6, 6; republished in *The Etude,* July 1942, and in Thomson, *The Musical Scene* (New York: Knopf, 1947).

30. Thomson, *The Etude,* July 1942, 453ff. E. F. Goldman, ibid., August 1942, 525ff.

31. Thomson, *The Musical Scene* (New York: Knopf, 1947). Thomson on Gershwin, *A Virgil Thomson Reader* (Boston: Houghton Mifflin, 1981), 23–27, from *Modern Music,* November 1935.

32. *H. L. Mencken on Music,* "From a Letter to Isaac Goldberg," 200–201.

33. Concert on 3 January 1948. The conductors were Walter Hendl and Percy Grainger, with works by Vaughan Williams, Mihaud, Schoenberg, Grainger, Pedro San Juan, Honegger, Roussel, Auric, and Miaskovsky. Henry Cowell's piece was *Shoonthree,* composed in 1939 and premiered by the Goldman Band in 1941.

34. Henry Cowell, "Goldman's Influence," *Herald Tribune,* 28 December 1947, sec. 5, 7.

Chapter Ten

The Decline of the Goldman Band, Frederick Fennell, and the Rise of the Wind Ensemble

On the death of Edwin Franko Goldman in February 1956, his son, Richard Franko, who since 1937 had assisted his father with the band as an arranger, assistant manager, and associate conductor, was prepared to take command, and the free summer concerts, funded by the Guggenheim family, continued without break. Aged fifty-five, "Dick" was well known in musical circles, not only in connection with the band, but also as chairman of the Music and Literature Department at the Juilliard School of Music, a visiting professor at Princeton, and founder and editor of the *Juilliard Review*, for which, as well as for other journals, he wrote many incisive articles and critical reviews. On the podium at his opening concert, however, as the *New York Times* observed, he presented a personality quite different from his "jaunty, high-spirited father. . . . Instead, the man who came to the microphone was a slim, rather romantic-looking young man with thick black hair, who, when he took the microphone, had a trace of Harvard in his speech." More modest and retiring, and perhaps more intense, he was less of a natural showman.[1]

His educational background was more academic than his father's. Whereas the elder Goldman instead of college had played his cornet, the younger graduated in 1930 from Columbia College, did some postgraduate work in the study of music, and then, like many American composers such as Piston, Copland, Cowell, and Thomson, went to Paris to study composition with Nadia Boulanger. He also studied privately with the highly individualistic American composer Wallingford Riegger. Thus, when in 1937 he joined the Goldman Band as associate conductor, he was more steeped in contemporary "serious" or "art" music than his father, and as the evidence bears out, after 1937 many such selections played by the band were initiated and conducted by the younger Goldman.[2] (See photospread.)

Initially, he was unimpressive as a conductor, but he practiced and improved, and in reviewing the opening summer concert in 1941 the critics for both the *Times* and *Herald Tribune* praised him. Ross Parmenter for the *Times* liked "his sensitivity which contrasted with the more rough-and-ready style of his father," and for the other paper Francis Perkins declared, "The interpretations under his direction were among the most expressive of the evening."[3]

He also had a notable success with some of his arrangements for band, among them one of the excerpts from Stravinsky's ballet, *The Firebird.* Gradually his influence on the band's repertory, moving it more into the "serious" side of American music, was recognized. Carl Buchanan in 1942 wrote in *Modern Music*: "Major tribute must go to Richard Goldman, who conceived the idea of presenting the series of new works and conducted the greater part of them with characteristic insight into their content." As if to anticipate criticism of the direction he was taking the repertory, that same year Goldman wrote an article, "New Band Repertory," for the *Herald Tribune,* in which he declared that the band was not intending to go "highbrow," his word, but merely to reflect the greater interest that many composers were taking in writing music specifically for bands. The band thus was merely keeping abreast of musical trends and opportunities, while keeping its audiences up to date.[4]

A month before the start of the band's 1960 summer season and four years after succeeding his father as bandmaster, Goldman gave an interview to a reporter for the *Herald Tribune,* the "Business of Being a Bandmaster." The band, as he then described it, had a summer season of eight and a half weeks, four concerts a week in Central Park and two a week in Prospect Park for a total of some fifty concerts. As each concert offered an average of ten works, in order to provide variety and contrast, some five hundred had to be scheduled and rehearsed. Planning the programs therefore went on all winter, but the musicians could not be hired until after the Guggenheim Family foundations had guaranteed the funds for the coming season. This did not occur without the foundations making sure they had the money in hand and so required an annual reassessment and resolution. As Goldman stressed, the Guggenheim support "over the years represents, I think, the largest gift ever given to one musical group by any single donor. There is not a dime of taxpayer money involved in the Goldman concerts, except for the upkeep of Central and Prospect Parks."

As for the band's repertory, the reporter put Goldman's statement in his lead paragraph: "The function of a band concert is to entertain, not educate. . . . In the winter I'll go out and hear Elliott Carter's Second Quartet and other kinds of advanced music that pleases me. But the summer is a time for Suppé and Sousa. That, at any rate, is what our audience wants. That's what it gets."[5]

Though perhaps unconsciously, he precisely stated what seemed to be an increasing division in the band's repertory. With Elliott Carter "and other kinds of advanced music that pleases me," Goldman was keeping abreast of all the best in contemporary serious music; but with Suppé and Sousa he was falling behind in the popular. In his very first concert as bandmaster, in 1956, he had scheduled—unusual for the band at that time—three songs from Richard Rodgers's *The King and I,* but such dips into contemporary American theatrical music were still rare, and further, like his father, he seemed prepared to ignore all modern operatic music, whether American or foreign, on the ground that the music had not been originally written for bands.[6]

He was not unaware of the direction he was heading. For example, he had introduced in 1946 a work for band by Arnold Schoenberg, Theme and Variations for Wind Band, which he declared in his book *The Concert Band* (1946) "is nothing if not highly serious, undoubtedly too much so for most band audiences. An extremely complex work, rich in invention and rewarding in the quality of its ideas, it represents a landmark in the history of band literature." And though in 1962, in *The Wind Band,* he still ranked it as standing "alone in this field," he now questioned its place "among the best of Schoenberg's works," and restated that "it is not a work that is ever likely to be widely popular with band audiences." So it proved, and because of it and other works somewhat like it, there finally came a public reproof.[7]

Harold Schonberg of the *New York Times* in the Sunday paper on 15 July 1962 accused the band of going "highbrow" in its attempts to present more and more original band music. In a long article titled "Summer Time: Outdoor Band Concerts Are Just the Thing" he declared that "summer music" had a "place in the scheme of things."

> Summer music is a specific kind of music that is light, that arouses nostalgia and that does not demand fierce concentration. It is nearly always band music. The big out-door symphonic series in Boston, New York, Philadelphia, Chicago, and elsewhere really have little to do with "summer music." They are welcome enough, and it is wonderful to have the chance to hear Beethoven and Brahms in the summer. Indeed that is the growing pattern—the summer symphony. As it grows, the old-fashioned band concert tends to disappear. . . . Even the Goldman Band, though, has gone highbrow. It tries more and more to present original band music—Wagner, Berlioz, Catel and what have you—and when it approaches Sousa it is with a certain amount of prim bashfulness. . . . Television is already making inroads on the tradition of outdoor band concerts. . . . It may be that the outdoor band concert has outlived itself. It belongs to a more innocent and more leisurely generation. . . . The band tradition itself is a long way from being defunct. Every high school and college has its band. But the free band concert, played by professional musicians in park and plaza—this is the

> institution that is getting less and less support. . . . And as American civilization grows more and more urban, as the pace gets more and more neurotic, the band concert and its particular repertory will probably eventually disappear.[8]

Two Sundays later the *Times* published Goldman's reply: "I am shattered by his suggestion that the Goldman Band has gone highbrow! What a sad accolade for a conductor who performs more Suppé Overtures and Sousa marches, and more music of this genre than perhaps all the other conductors in the country laid end to end." Always Suppé and Sousa! As if Sousa in his programming had not attempted to keep abreast of popular music, which as much as the serious could change its style. By the mid-1960s, in this Century of the Common Man, much of the general public, especially those of it under thirty, were chanting with Chuck Berry or the Beatles "Roll over Beethoven, and tell Tchaikovsky the news!"[9]

Certainly Suppé's overtures, such as "Light Cavalry" and "Poet and Peasant," have a place in any band's repertory, but by the time of the Beatles, or even earlier, surely repertories could have made a little room for some of Gershwin's. His were composed for theater bands, usually eighteen or twenty players, but could easily be expanded for larger groups; in fact, six of them have been arranged for symphony orchestra. Of these, perhaps the best is the overture to *Of Thee I Sing,* followed closely by those to *Strike Up the Band* and *Let 'Em Eat Cake.* And just as one need not entirely dismiss Beethoven and Tchaikovsky to let in Schoenberg and Hindemith, one need not altogether dismiss Suppé to let in Gershwin; or, from a later generation, such works as the "Carousel Waltz" (Rodgers), "Aquarius" from *Hair* (MacDermot), or "Fugue for Tinhorns" from *Guys and Dolls* (Loesser). But try them, and see which, if any, survive.[10]

As if in response, or perhaps in repugnance, to the trends overtaking popular music in the 1950s, a new movement started in music schools and university departments around the country. One of its leaders was a professor at the University of Rochester's Eastman School of Music, Frederick Fennell, who in 1952 founded the Eastman Wind Ensemble. A man of exceptional energy and talent, he had a long association with the University of Rochester, for as an undergraduate he had organized its first marching band for the stadium and continued for ten years thereafter to give indoor concerts with it. Though even shorter than Sousa, standing only five foot one inch, he became an outstanding conductor, band leader, and organizer, and his willingness to share his talent and to work with students at the Interlochen, Tally-Ho, and other music band camps, as well as with concert bands of all skills and sizes, led some to call him the "Godfather" of concert bands.[11]

He had an even longer tie, however, to the Interlochen Center for the Arts, lasting from 1931, when he was a high school student, to 2004, when he died at aged ninety. In 1931 at Interlochen (then the National Music Camp), he had studied percussion and played the bass drum in the National High School Band, which on 26 July of that year had been conducted by Sousa. Later, in 1935, he served as a librarian for the camp, an experience which perhaps stimulated his lifelong penchant for studying, editing, annotating, and sometimes publishing his editions of scores and parts. Later still, as a graduate of the Eastman School and as a professor of music he returned often to Interlochen to teach and conduct, so that for at least fifty years he was a figure at the camp. Upon death, at his request, his ashes were scattered in the Interlochen woods, and later the lower level of the center's new Bonisteel Library was named the Fennell Music Library to honor Fennel and his wife, whose generous gift led to the library's construction. The Fennell Music Library, along with music and recordings of all kinds, houses a unique collection of wind ensemble works.[12] (See photospread.)

While a young professor of conducting at the Eastman School in Rochester he returned to Interlochen in 1940 and 1941 to conduct the National High School Band in thirteen concerts, in which of the seventy-four works performed twenty-five (not including nine excerpts from ballets) were operatic in origin. These included six of Wagner, and fewer each chiefly of Rossini, Verdi, Bizet, Humperdinck, Smetana, R. Strauss, and Prokofiev. But in Fennell's last thirty-one years, when he came to Interlochen each summer and conducted performances with bands of different types and skills, perhaps the one band most comparable to the National High School Band was the Interlochen High School Symphonic Band, with which he conducted at least one concert every year during 1974–2004. But the number of operatic excerpts dropped, while he substituted works mostly by Schoenberg, Holst, Persichetti, Grainger, and Milhaud. In that period, out of a total of 163 works scheduled only 12 were arrangements from opera, of which five were Wagnerian and the only composer of twentieth-century opera represented was Leonard Bernstein, with a "*Candide* suite." Like the Goldmans, father and son, Fennell soon was replacing arrangements from operas with works originally scored for band. In this he no doubt was partly influenced by his success with the wind ensemble group he had founded in 1952 at the Eastman School.[13]

He had introduced his ideas in a number of journals, such as *The American Music Teacher*, and the *New York Times,* with manifestos which, in their blunt, unapologetic tone, set high goals for what he described as "a discriminating audience."[14]

> I sent a mimeographed letter to approximately four hundred composers in all parts of the world telling them of our plan to establish an ensemble of the following instrumentation: [roughly twenty-two reed instruments, seventeen brass, percussion, harp, celeste] and other solo instruments and choral forces as

desired. . . . My correspondents were informed that the Eastman School would have one annual symposium for the reading of all new music written for the Wind Ensemble, and that there would be no "commissions" save those of a performance that was prepared with skill and devotion.[15]

Then, having founded the Eastman Wind Ensemble on this basis, he later described its instrumentation to the critic for the *Times:* "[It] consists of the reed-brass-percussion combination of the orchestra which Wagner assembled for Bayreuth plus a section of saxophones. All of the perhaps less pleasant reactions one customarily associates with a band I do not think you will find present here. From the standpoint of texture it is not bloated, is clear and at the same time intense, in tune, flexible, virtuosic—contains a magnificent range of dynamics plus a beautiful tone quality."[16]

Clearly, Fennell, like Sousa and other bandmasters, liked the special tone of a wind band, but whereas his predecessors and to a greater extent the two Goldmans had gone a short way to increase the quality and quantity of original works for bands and to substitute them for arrangements from other sources, Fennell intended, if possible, to go the whole way. Moreover, in a gesture then unusual, he promised the composers not to "double" the instruments on any part just because he had players available (as often happened in school and university bands) but to assign to each part only the number specified by the composer. For his opening concert with the ensemble, on 8 February 1953, he chose three works: Mozart's 10th Serenade in B-flat for Thirteen Winds, Wallingford Riegger's Nonet for Brass, and Paul Hindemith's Symphony in B-flat for Concert Band.

The program certainly was different from those traditionally offered by concert bands. It consisted of only three works: the Mozart, running for forty-seven minutes, with seven movements for only thirteen instruments; the Riegger nonet for nine brass lasting nine minutes, and finally the three-movement Hindemith symphony for the full wind, brass, and percussion group. The setting, too, was quite different: in the university's Kilbourn Hall, seating only 455.[17]

The common man, however, likely would have asked: Why play a lengthy, minor work by Mozart in place of a shorter, greater work or an excerpt arranged from a symphony, concerto, or opera? Even Richard Franko Goldman, in reviewing a recording of the Hindemith symphony by Fennell, while praising the ensemble's execution, questioned the music's worth. "It is undeniably true that 'original' band music is in principle better than the old repertory of transcribed chestnuts; but, alas, because a work is 'original for band' doesn't always make it a happy experience. . . . [Hindemith's] intentions are noble . . . [but the work] falls . . . between the effort to be popular and obvious, and the intention to remain unsmiling and uncorrupted." And though played by the Eastman Wind Ensemble in nineteen of its forty seasons, 1952–1992, and often by other ensemble groups less renowned, it seems likely that a sizeable number of any audience (excluding the students who receive a course credit for attendance) would declare with Goldman that the work is "singularly dead."[18]

Fennell's wind ensemble concept soon spread from Eastman to other college and university music schools and departments. A university band typically might have a roster of a hundred players for the football season, but for the rest of the school year a wind ensemble group of fifty, recruited chiefly from the more skilled and zealous of the student musicians. In part because of limitations of time and expense, these ensemble groups gave only a small number of concerts and almost none away from home. At Rochester for one, the Eastman group in the 1980s typically offered a concert a month, October through May, eight performances, using as sites either the Eastman Theatre (capacity about 3,000) or tiny Kilbourn Hall. Compared to the Sousa or Goldman Bands, the schedule was short, the venues small, and the repertory, at least according to some, overrefined.

Against that opinion, however, the Eastman group could point out that in the years 1952–1992 the composer most often played was Sousa, with performances of fifty-seven of his works, twenty-eight of them in more than one season. In addition, chiefly under Fennell, it had made a splendid series of twenty-two recordings with the Mercury Label. Eleven of these offered chiefly wind and percussion music; four, historical surveys, such as "The Spirit of '76: Music for Fifes and Drums"; and seven, all marches. With the march albums the Eastman Wind Ensemble reached a large audience across the country and was much admired. Thus Fennell, an outstanding conductor, seemed to have two personas, one for a small "discriminating audience," the other for the general public which wanted a more traditional repertory. Unhappily, most of the publicity, and scholarly interest (Fennell excepted), accrued to the wind ensemble groups, depriving the country's concert bands of attention and musical leaders, and while some of the latter continued with traditional programs largely unchanged and perhaps growing stale, others began to imitate the ensemble concept and its style of programs.[19] (See photospread.)

Then one day in 1981 Gunther Schuller, a composer for the Eastman group, in a speech to the College Band Directors National Association (an audience predominantly academic) began by saying softly: "It bothers me enormously that the wind ensemble and band medium is not yet perceived by our culture, by our musical establishment and by our tastemakers and cultural leaders as an important, viable, *and integral* [sic] part of the country's musical life." But then he went on to say:

> I think you must get partially or to some extent out of academia. You are too much like the preacher preaching only to the converted in that you play for each other most of the time. You are safe in your academic cocoon—with your tenure

and security, your relatively safe budgets and your calm avoidance of the need to test what you do at the box office. . . . The next step must be the establishment of professional wind ensembles and bands . . . [which now don't] exist for the professional musician. . . . You will say: How do we do that? Where do we get the money? The answer to that is leadership, enterprise, vision, and courage. . . . Sure it's risky. Nothing of value is undertaken without risks. But I say to you: you cannot have your cake and eat it too; you cannot remain only in your safe academic cocoon. . . . My next point may be of some surprise to some of you. . . . It concerns the matter of classical or symphonic repertory and transcriptions. I think you all do far too little of that. . . . I think you, as a field, have arrived at a juncture where, by virtue of your already considerable accomplishments, you can relax a little. Perhaps this relaxation could take the form of being even more selective in your choice of new music. It is also time to leave some room for the best music that is not indigenous to your field.[20]

Six years later another composer, Warren Benson, in an address to a conference of the World Association for Symphonic Bands and Ensembles, returned to the point: "We are so inbred. . . . I'm sick of reading hardly literate, badly written articles by band conductors about band music. We talk to each other in a kind of code, never stepping on anyone's toes. The reviews of new music that we read in the journals are designed not to offend anybody. . . . We need the other guy to look on us and say, 'You're not cutting it folks.'"[21]

As early as 1961 the younger Goldman in an article for the *Musical Quarterly* had fretted over the trend in musical criticism: "Discussion is taking precedence over listening." Critical analysis and the composer's explanation of his piece, set out in the program and often at length, were becoming the test of any work. Six months later, he wrote: "It is a commonplace now that the prose accompanying new music is often more interesting not to say more 'artistic,' than the music itself. It is also harder to understand." And he quoted an annotator's long note that seemed to mean nothing. In the same article he made fun of the increasing practice of taking far-fetched texts, fragments from various languages and books, and pretending that, as one composer wrote: "The fragment again consists of fragments, and the totality of the fragmental universe results in its negation, that is, totality." Goldman's comment: "What price macaroni?"[22]

Many years later, in 1994 and in partial answer, Donald Hunsberger, the conductor of the Eastman Wind Ensemble since 1965, summarized the situation as he then saw it in an article titled "The Wind Ensemble Concept."

During the past forty-two years, the music world has witnessed the development of a new approach to the wind band, an approach that has drawn attention to an emerging original repertoire and to new performance possibilities for concerted wind music. An increasing number of conductors, composers and performers

> have moved away from the popular-culture aspects of the traditional concert or military band toward a classical performance medium. . . . As a result, the wind band moved far ahead of other types of performing ensembles in contemporary repertoire. In doing this, it has sometimes surpassed its audiences' ability to comprehend contemporary music trends. . . . Today, each conductor must decide upon a course of activity that is conducive to forward thinking and leadership. One must not be merely a bystander, willing to stand by and reject the movement of time and effort, confident that the successes of the past will return to regain their former, self-proclaimed statue. The pendulum swings slowly, but it continues to swing, and it is better to be on the cutting edge of the swath than to be dragging behind it.[23]

He could point to the Eastman Wind Ensemble's many achievements, recordings of historical and contemporary musical interest, performances at academic conferences, tours to Japan funded by the Sony corporation, and a remarkable series of publications on the subject of wind ensembles and their repertory. Academics excel in recording the history of their affairs, footnoting and publishing their accomplishments and in this case, to their credit, also critics like Schuller and Benson. Yet as Hunsberger admitted, in moving "away from the popular-culture aspects of the traditional concert or military band toward a classical performance medium," many composers, conductors, and performers had abandoned the greater part of their audience. And with his metaphor of the pendulum and the "cutting edge" he dashed any hopes that those enamored of the wind ensemble concept might help the cause of those who wanted professional civilian concert bands to survive and prosper. Just like the dance bands in the 1920s and 1930s and the Beatles and their offspring in the 1960s and 1970s, the wind ensemble movement in the 1980s had become a genre unto itself and actively competed for attention with the traditional civilian concert bands. Further, most of the ensemble leaders, far more than Fennell himself, seemed quite happy to ignore any calls to engage with the outside world.

In trying to keep a foot in both worlds, the Goldman Band, like others, faced many conditions in the real world over which it had no control. As early as 1962 Schonberg in his *Times* article "Summer Time" had noted that the Central Park audience was predominantly old. Young people, if they came on bicycles or roller skates, soon pedaled or rolled away. In Brooklyn, at Prospect Park, the problem was not only one of age but also of demographic change. In an interview with a critic for the *Times* in May 1971 Goldman explained: "People in Brooklyn have not been coming out in great numbers. . . . The best crowd last summer was about 8,500, and the average was around 2,000." Goldman felt a change in the racial makeup of the neighborhoods around the park explained the decrease in audience:

INTERLOCHEN ARTS CAMP
Interlochen, Michigan
240th Program of the 78th Season

A TRIBUTE TO FREDERICK FENNELL

The Interlochen Symphony Band
The World Youth Wind Symphony

Saturday, August 6, 2005   7:00 p.m. Interlochen Bowl

*

Interlochen Symphony Band
Michael Kaufman, conducting

Second Suite in F for Military Band	Gustav Holst (1874-1934)
Al Fresco	Karl Husa (b. 1921)
Elegy for a Young American	Ronald Lo Presti (1933-1985)
The Klaxon – March	Henry Fillmore (1881-1956)

* * *

Remarks, Memories and Traditions	President Jeffrey Kimpton

* * *

World Youth Wind Symphony
Jerry Junkin, conducting

Selections from "The Danserye"	Tylman Susato (c. 1510-1570) arr. by Patrick Dunnigan
Lincolnshire Posy	Percy Aldridge Grainger (1882-1961) ed. Frederick Fennell
A Jazz Funeral	Christopher Coleman (b. 1958) ed. Frederick Fennell
His Honor	Henry Fillmore (1881-1956) ed. Frederick Fennell
National Emblem	**Edwin Eugene Bagley (1857-1922) ed. Frederick Fennell**

The audience is requested to remain seated during the playing of the Interlochen Theme and to refrain from applause upon its completion.

Figure 10.1. Interlochen Center for the Arts, A Tribute to Frederick Fennell.

> Flatbush used to be largely middle-class. Jewish, Russian, Italian Nights were great successes at the Park, and Music of Eastern Europe, that sort of thing. Now that area is largely black. We do get a good sprinkling, but they do not represent a large percentage of the audience. The repertory does not seem to lend itself to programs keyed to black audiences. However, our repertory is certainly more varied than it used to be. We still do all the Sousa marches and my father's marches. . . . But we have Schoenberg and Hindemith, little marches of Rossini and Donizetti, and since Ainslee Cox became our associate conductor (in 1968), we've been reviving the old band music of the 18th and 19th centuries—things like Raff's *Macbeth* Overture and Berlioz's *Waverly* Overture.[24]

Cox also greatly increased the number of old and new Broadway show tunes, even opening the season in 1978 with a program titled "Regards to Broadway" that included works by Cohan, Herbert, Berlin, Kern, Loewe, Rodgers, and Gershwin. Ultimately, in Brooklyn, however, the band shifted its concerts from Prospect to Seaside Park, where a band shell was built for it.[25]

In the same year, 1971, that Goldman spoke of his difficulty drawing the blacks in Brooklyn to the free concerts in Prospect Park, the New York Public Library gave a concert devoted entirely to the black composer Scott Joplin, "King of Ragtime" (see Figure 10.2.). Among other works there were performances of selections from his opera *Treemonisha*, which previously had never been performed and existed only in a piano-vocal score.

The next year Morehouse College in Atlanta staged the opera *Treemonisha* in full, as did the Wolf Trap Festival in Virginia, close to Washington, D.C., and in 1975 the Houston Grand Opera mounted a production, with "Orchestration and Music Supervision by Gunther Schuller," which later came to New York. In short, in the early 1970s, as in the years 1898–1917, Scott Joplin was again everywhere, on the air, in the theaters, on recordings and home pianos.

His opera is not perfect, but it does have some remarkable numbers. Schonberg reviewing the Morehouse College production for the *New York Times* wrote: "There are moments when *Treemonisha* comes unforgettably to life, as in some of the choruses that reflect the tradition of the spiritual, or above all the slow drag—'A Real Slow Drag,' as Joplin called it—that ends the opera. This slow drag is amazing. Harmonically enchanting, full of the tensions of an entire race, rhythmically catching, it refuses to leave the mind. Talk about soul music! The audience tonight went out of its mind after hearing 'A Real Slow Drag.'"

Two weeks later, still excited, Schonberg delivered to the *Times* another major article on *Treemonisha,* this time extolling "Aunt Dinah Blowed de Horn," the second act's finale. It "is one of the great curtains of American musical theater. It hits the listener like an explosion—exultant, swinging, wonderfully spiced harmonically. This is the real thing."[26]

With Joplin so popular in the mid-1970s, a question rises: did the Goldman Band in Brooklyn ever play "Aunt Dinah" or "A Real Slow Drag"? I

Concert of Music by Scott Joplin

Program

Paragon Rag (1909)
Solace — A Mexican Serenade (1909)
The Ragtime Dance (1906)

William Bolcom, piano

Elite Syncopations (1902)
Pleasant Moments — Ragtime Waltz (1909)
Pine Apple Rag (1908)

Mary Lou Williams, piano

The Entertainer — A Ragtime Two Step (1902)
Bethena — A Concert Waltz (1905)
Magnetic Rag (1914)

Joshua Rifkin, piano

Four Excerpts from the Opera, *Treemonisha* (1911)

The Corn-Huskers — "We're Goin' Around": A Ring Play
Miss Christopher and Chorus

The Sacred Tree
Miss Christopher

Good Advice
Mr. Mosley and Chorus

A Real Slow Drag
Miss Christopher, Miss Dale, and Chorus

Barbara Christopher, soprano
Clamma Dale, mezzo soprano
Robert Mosley, baritone
Dennis Moorman, accompanist
Chorus

John Motley, conductor

This program has been made possible by the Margaret Fisher Fund.

Auditorium
Library & Museum of the Performing Arts
Friday, October 22, 1971
8:45 p.m.

Figure 10.2.

cannot claim to have seen every Brooklyn program in all their years, but with the assistance of the librarian for the Goldman Collection at the University of Maryland we have searched a great many, and in only one, for a Seaside Park concert in July 1974, did we find any Joplin work: an arrangement of his piano rag, "The Entertainer." Nothing ever, in Manhattan or Brooklyn, from *Treemonisha.* Yet when ragtime first appeared, in 1898, Sousa, always anxious to play at least some of what his audiences wanted, had picked it up as early as 1899 and successfully introduced it the following year to Europe. The most likely explanation for Goldman's failure to seize on the success of *Treemonisha* seems to confirm Schuller's charge against the academics, a reluctance to break out of their "cocoon." Though Goldman as a critic saw the danger in too much minor Schoenberg, Hindemith, Persichetti, and Creston, as a conductor or programmer he seemed unable to break with academic fashion and replace them with arrangements of the best in popular song and contemporary opera.[27]

After the death in 1980 of younger Goldman, the band continued for another twenty-five years but in gradual decline, though more in number of performances than skill. In part because Central Park at night had become increasingly dangerous, another trend over which the band had no control, the concerts had moved in 1970 to Damrosch Park, alongside the Metropolitan Opera House in Lincoln Center. There was an adequate band shell and a seating area before it with benches for 2,500, and several thousand more could stand or sit among the trees or in niches in the Metropolitan's serrated wall. The acoustics, however, were not as good as in Central Park. The huge opera house on one side and the State Theatre at the back enclosed the area, and immediately behind the shell was Amsterdam Avenue and its roar of traffic. Certainly, too, the perfection of television and of air conditioning in homes and theaters diminished the audience, but for whatever balance of reasons, musical and otherwise, gradually the number of performances each summer dwindled.

Another problem of the real world that increasingly plagued the free concerts was money. After Goldman in 1979 retired in ill health, leaving the band in charge of Cox, the Guggenheim Foundation indicated that it no longer could be the band's sole support. It willingly would sponsor the band in part, but other donors would be needed. After a scramble against time as spring came and went, three other foundations and two corporations contributed enough to rescue the summer season. The list of donors thereafter frequently changed, but soliciting from many was harder than collecting from one, and by 1992 the number of free concerts in Damrosch Park had diminished to eight.[28]

Ultimately, in the spring of 2005, the band, by then named the Goldman Memorial Band, ceased to exist. Its board of directors had offered the fifty-three musicians a guarantee of four concerts a summer along with the reduction over three years of the band in size from fifty-three to forty-eight. The musicians rejected the offer, and the board, deciding not to negotiate further, ended the band's existence. Despite the continual threats of changing conditions, which Schonberg had noted as early as 1962, the Goldman Band had enjoyed a longer run, ninety-four years, than either those of Gilmore or Sousa. But the rise of the two extremes, dance bands and wind ensembles, had desiccated the middle.[29]

NOTES

1. *Times*, 21 June 1956, 34, and Noel Lester, "Richard Franko Goldman and the Goldman Band, *Journal of Band Research* 24, no.1 (Fall 1988): 1, 4, 7.

2. Students of Boulanger, *Virgil Thomson Reader,* 390. Studied with Riegger, *New Grove Dictionary of Music and Musicians,* 2nd ed. (London: Macmillan, 2001). Evidence, Lester, "Richard Franko Goldman," 3–4.

3. *Times*, 19 June 1941, 24, and *Herald Tribune*, 19 June 1941, 16.

4. *Firebird* excerpt, the ballet's berceuse and finale, which "lent themselves to the band treatment surprisingly well," *Times*, 19 June 1941, 24. Buchanan, *Modern Music* 20 (1942–43), 46–48, quoted by Lester, "Richard Franko Goldman," 4. *Herald Tribune*, 9 August 1942, sec. 4, 6.

5. *Herald Tribune*, 29 May 1960, sec. 4, 5.

6. First concert, *Herald Tribune*, 21 June 1956, 11.

7. R. F. Goldman, *The Concert Band,* 201–202, and *The Wind Band,* 235.

8. Schonberg, "Summer Time," *Times*, 15 July 1962, sec. 2, 7.

9. R. F. Goldman, *Times*, 29 July 1962, sec. 2, 7

10. The Gershwin overtures, arranged by Don Rose and played by the Buffalo Philharmonic on CBS MK 42240. The three not mentioned in the text are to *Oh, Kay!, Funny Face,* and *Girl Crazy,* the last with "I Got Rhythm" as its main theme.

11. "Godfather," Dallas Wind Symphony program, 8 October 2011, on page titled "Frederick Fennell." The Tally-Ho Music Camp, Richmond Hills, New York, was the camp "of the finger lakes," with ties to Rochester and the Eastman School of Music it operated from 1948 to 1965. Fennell not only conducted and taught there, but for its directors, Mr. and Mrs. Fred L. Bradley, in 1951 composed the "Tally-Ho March," which became the camp's signature piece.

12. Program titled "A Tribute to Frederick Fennell, Interlochen Symphony Band and World Youth Wind Symphony, Interlochen Center for the Arts, Saturday, August 6, 2005." I thank Byron Hanson, archivist at Interlochen, for a copy of the program.

13. Ibid.

14. "Discriminating audience," Donald Hunsberger, "The Wind Ensemble Concept." *The Wind Ensemble and Its Repertoire: Essays on the Fortieth Anniversary of the Eastman Wind Ensemble,"* eds. Frank J. Cipolla and Donald Hunsberger (Rochester, NY: University of Rochester Press, 1994), 6, quoting Frederick Fennell, "The Wind Ensemble," *American Music Teacher*, March/April 1953, 12ff.

15. Ibid., 6–7.

16. Ibid., and *Times*, 26 July 1953, sec. 2, 5.

17. Hunsberger, *The Wind Ensemble,* 9, quoting Fennell in the *American Music Teacher.* See also R. F. Goldman, *The Concert Band,* 165–68.

18. "Intentions noble," but the work is "Dead," R. F. Goldman, *Selected Essays and Reviews, 1948–1968,* ed. Dorothy Klotzman (Brooklyn: Institute for Studies in American Music, School of Performing Arts, Brooklyn College, 1980), 167–69, from the *Musical Quarterly* 44, no. 1 (January 1958).

19. Importance of the recording contract with Mercury Label, Hunsberger, *The Wind Ensemble,* 15–17. Appendix A2c of *The Wind Ensemble,* 287–97, offers the "Complete Discography of the Eastman Wind Ensemble, 1952–1993."

20. Gunther Schuller, "An Address to the CBDNA National Conference, 13 February 1981," *The Wind Band and Its Repertoire,* ed. Michael Votta, Jr. (Miami: Warner Bros. Publications, 2003), 1–2.

21. Warren Benson, "An Address to the Third International Conference of the World Association of Symphonic Bands and Ensembles, 23 July 1987," *The Wind Band and Its Repertoire,* 5.

22. R. F. Goldman, *Selected Essays and Reviews,* "discussion," 179, from *Musical Quarterly* 47, no. 4 (October 1961); "prose accompanying the music," 180, from *Musical Quarterly* 48, no. 3 (July 1962); "far-fetched texts," 181, ibid. Here is a more recent example from a wind ensemble concert in a southeastern Pennsylvania music school on 5 December 2010. The composer, to explain his composition, offered six paragraphs of prose with the first describing the work as "music of dialectical tension—a juxtaposition of contradictory or opposing musical and extra-musical elements and an attempt to resolve them. The five connected movements hint at a narrative that touches upon naiveté, divination, fanaticism, post-human possibilities, anarchy, order, and the Jungian collective unconscious. Or, as I have described it more colloquially: W. B. Yeats meets Ray Kurzweil in the Matrix."

23. Hunsberger, "The Wind Ensemble Concept," 6; "As a result," 34; "cutting edge," 35.

24. *Times*, 2 May 1971, 87.

25. Cox's program, *Times*, 7 July 1978, sec. 3, 13, included George M. Cohan's "Give My Regards to Broadway," from *Little Johnny Jones*; Irving Berlin's "Alexander's Ragtime Band; Victor Herbert's "March of the Toys," from *Babes in Toyland*—as well as excerpts from Herbert's *Naughty Marietta*; from A. J. Lerner and F. Loewe's *Camelot* and *My Fair Lady*; from Jerome Kern's *Roberta* and *Show Boat*; from Richard Rodgers's *The King and I*; and from George Gershwin's *Funny Face.*

26. Rudi Blesh, "Scott Joplin: Black-American Classicist," *The Collected Works of Scott Joplin,* in 2 vols., ed. Vera Brodsky Lawrence (New York: New York Public Library, 1971), vol. 2, xxxvii. Schonberg, *Times*, 30 January 1972, 51, and ibid., 13 February 1972, sec. II, 15; also R. Ericson, *Times*, 9 April 1972, sec. II, 17. Equally enthusiastic, *Washington Post*, 9 April 1972, sec. E, 1; 6 August 1972, sec. F, 1; and 13 August 1972, Books, 11. See also Southern, *The Music of Black Americans,* 321–323.

27. I thank the librarians at the Performing Arts Library, University of Maryland, College Park, for an exhaustive search of the Goldman Collection for Joplin ragtime

numbers played in both Manhattan and Brooklyn in the years 1971 through 1977. In Damrosch Park, Manhattan, "The Entertainer," was played 19 June 1974; 4, 6, 18 July 1974; 29 June and 3 August 1975. The "Rag-Time Dance" (a piano rag, not the opera's "A Real Slow Drag") was played 18 July 1974; and at Seaside Park, Brooklyn, "The Entertainer," 6 July 1974. In sum: a brief nod, only two years and two samples, with neither from the newly unveiled opera. Sousa and ragtime, Bierley, *The Incredible Band,* 13; and Bierley, *American Phenomenon,* 136. In the former, Bierley does not list any work of Joplin (though some by others) among Sousa's programs; but Rudi Blesch, "Scott Joplin: Black-American Classicist," xiii, suggests that in 1900 he played "The Maple Leaf Rag" in Paris.

28. Guggenheim, *Times*, 16 December 1979, 84. Eight concerts, *Times*, 30 June 1992, sec. C, 12. The program for the first, which reportedly was well attended, included the opening movement of Beethoven's Fifth Symphony, Wagner's overture to *Rienzi,* Bach's *Fantasia in G* (likely in the arrangement by R. F. Goldman and Robert Leist), Dukas's overture to (the *Fanfare pour precédé) La Péri,* Valenti's *March Pasha,* works by Roy Harris, William Schuman, and Richard Rodgers, and "On the Mall" by E. F. Goldman. During this last march, the audience, as always, sang and hummed along.

29. The band's demise, *Times*, 27 May 2005, sec. E, 5.

Conclusion

Certainly opera suffered as concert bands, starting in the mid-twentieth century, ceased to play arrangements of opera overtures, arias, and choruses and, despite the occasional exception, ignored all operas composed after Puccini's last, *Turandot,* premiered in 1926. The aging Sousa, as was his custom, had started playing selections from *Turandot* as soon as 1928, but after his death no American bandleader seems to have played any music from, say, Britten's *Peter Grimes* (1945) or Joplin's *Treemonisha* (1972), both highly successful onstage. Thus their music failed to reach the wider audience that over the years had enjoyed excerpts from Rossini, Verdi, Wagner, and Puccini. Unexposed by bands to the new music, much of the public knew nothing of it, and so came to conceive, ever more strongly, that opera was a foreign sport, of interest only to the rich and few. Yet, despite the success in recent years of taped and live performances relayed into movie theaters at popular prices, bands of all kinds today still play few or no arrangements taken from contemporary opera. A misfortune for opera.[1]

In the preceding chapters I touched on many of the nonmusical reasons for the demise of the operatic repertory, but I also suggested two musical developments that I believe shortened the life of professional concert bands, the turn toward dance bands and current popular song, and the turn toward original compositions for band. This latter turn, taken to an extreme in academic communities, favored chiefly composers of serious or fine art music with a strong focus on structure rather than on melody or rhythm, and, I believe, had more to do with the decline of the leading concert bands than generally acknowledged. Today, when only a few professional concert bands still perform, we have many conductors of amateur bands of all kinds imitating their more famous colleagues who lead the best-known wind ensemble groups. Many of these lesser known conductors seem to believe that band music must feature not arrangements of excerpts but works originally scored for bands; that true band music begins with works by Percy Grainger or Gustav Holst; and that for their programs to be respectable these must include something by Schoenberg or Hindemith. With that turn bands as well as opera suffered.

On this point consider a statement made in 2008 by Del Eisch, a former conductor of the Racine Band and presently the historian of the Association of Concert Bands: "It behooves conductors now to keep in proper perspective a programming balance between entertainment and education. Our audiences still want to be entertained. As conductors we need to suppress our desires to be always on the 'cutting edge' with the newest publication. Keep the programming in balance and our audiences will continue to come."[2]

The merit of his advice can be seen in the history of one of the newer professional civilian concert bands, the Dallas Wind Symphony, founded in 1985 and which came into being only because two men, indulging their hopes, took sudden action. One day in the summer of 1985 into the office of Howard Dunn, a professor of music at Southern Methodist University, came a young man with a trombone, Kim Campbell. Introducing himself, he requested a moment's interview. Invited to sit, he declared: "I would like to start a reading band of the finest wind and percussion players in the city, and I want you to conduct it." Without hesitation the professor replied: "I've been waiting for you all my life." Within two weeks they had recruited musicians, many of them long out of practice, had begun reading through a variety of works, and, amid mounting excitement, before the year was out had evolved into something more: they had given their first public performance.

Today the band numbers fifty-six, is led by Jerry Junkin, schedules annually a series of monthly concerts at the Meyerson Symphony Center, and for occasional summer concerts uses the band shell in Fair Park. National Public Radio broadcasts its performances, and the band has issued many recordings, one of which is unique. For many years the band's principal guest conductor, until his death in 2004, was the distinguished and always helpful, Frederick Fennell, and the band's recording *Fennell Favorites!* is said to be the only live recording of the conductor ever issued. It includes Fennell's arrangement of Halvorsen's "Entry March of the Boyars," from the orchestral suite *Dance Scenes from Queen Tamara,* as well as the scherzo and march from Prokofiev's *The Love for Three Oranges*. The band often closes its concerts with a Sousa march, and for its programs often schedules excerpts from opera (though mostly from the nineteenth century). In the October 2011 concert, for example, the two operatic excerpts were both from Wagner, the overture to *Rienzi,* and from *Lohengrin,* "Elsa's Procession to the Cathedral" (arr. by Bourgeois), for which the Texas A&M University-Commerce Wind Ensemble Brass provided the antiphonal trumpets. By all reports, it was grand.[3]

Dallas Wind Symphony

Jerry Junkin, Artistic Director and Conductor

Hymn to a Blue Hour

October 18, 2011 8:00 PM

Morton H. Meyerson Symphony Center

Fanfare

Singularity...Mark Scott

The Texas A&M University-Commerce Wind Ensemble Brass

Phillip L. Clements, Conductor

Program

Overture in C Major for Winds..Felix Mendelssohn-Bartholdy

Hymn to a Blue Hour...John Mackey

Bells for Stokowski...Michael Daugherty

Intermission

Rienzi Overture...Richard Wagner

Second Suite in F for Military Band...Gustav Holst

1. March
2. Song Without Words "I'll Love My Love"
3. Song of the Blacksmith
4. Fantasia on the "Dargason"

Elsa's Procession to the Cathedral...Richard Wagner

From *Lohengrin*

Antiphonal Trumpets by members of

Texas A&M University-Commerce Wind Ensemble Brass

Name That Tune!

gifts for tonight's program:

Elsa's Procession to the Cathedral - Robert Froehner

This concert is dedicated to the memory of George Hunter Engman, Director of Finance and Information Technology at TACA, and friend of the Dallas Wind Symphony.

Supported in part by the City of Dallas - Office of Cultural Affairs, the Texas Commission on the Arts, TACA, The 500, Inc., and The National Endowment for the Arts.

Pianos for the Meyerson Symphony Center are provided through the courtesy of Yamaha Music Corporation of America and Grand Staff Piano Centers.

Figure C.1. The New York Public Library concert that started the Joplin revival. G. Hoehn Collection.

The band's declared aim is to perform "an eclectic blend of musical styles ranging from Bach to Bernstein and Sousa to Strauss," and it seeks "to combine the tradition of the British brass band with the musical heritage of the American town band and the pioneering spirit of the 20th century wind ensemble." So a model exists; and maybe others could follow it and perhaps make even greater use of excerpts from twentieth-century opera.[4]

Earlier in the book, I suggested that this might be one way to keep the programs more interesting to the common man, and I offered examples of what I think concert bands might well have played: in some detail the music from Britten's *Peter Grimes* and Joplin's *Treemonisha,* and more briefly the waltzes from Prokofiev's *War and Peace* and the horn interlude from R. Strauss's *Capriccio.* These, being without need for singers, would be easy to arrange for band, and if there were any problem about copyright, the example of Goldman getting Ravel's approval for an arrangement of *Boléro* gives room for hope. Composers want their works to be heard.[5]

Here I offer two more examples in some detail, each more complicated to arrange and perhaps needing singers. And finally, I offer in appendix 17 a list of other operatic excerpts that I think might have made the repertory more appealing to the common man. Here at the book's close it seems only fair to allow those who wish to disagree with me a chance to shake their heads in disapproval.

Poulenc's 1947 opéra-bouffe *Les Mamelles de Tirésias (The Breasts of Tiresias)* provides my first suggestion for excerpts. The opera's two acts are joined by an Entr'acte (2.43 min.) which is melodic, rhythmic, and delightfully orchestrated and to it could be joined the next act's opening number, which, with the vocal lines rearranged for band, could extend the piece to 3.54 minutes. The whole would need no explanation; the music's appeal is instant.

A slightly more complicated excerpt from the opera might need a note in the program, but it could be a single sentence, needing to say only an early feminist named Thérèse wished to change her sex to become Tiresias, and to that end she released her breasts to fly away and promptly grew a beard and moustache. The scene, which includes a delicious waltz, "Envolez-vous, oiseaux de ma faiblesse" (Fly Away, Birds of My Weakness), requires a singer. In the past, however, concert bands frequently had one. The music would take some rearranging (I would plead for a slight extension of the waltz), but then Virgil Thomson, quoted earlier, has approved of arrangements of theatrical music.[6]

The singer and band at first would portray Thérèse in a state of dissatisfaction with her life, but then as she releases her breasts, one red, one blue balloon, both bobbing overhead but attached to her dress by their strings, she becomes calm (the waltz), and soon thereafter explodes the balloons with her cigarette lighter (or a pin), grows her beard and moustache, and stamps the ground in bold Spanish rhythms. The music's variety, contrast, and climax are plain, and likely Sousa, with his interest in theatrical music would have seized on the scene. During Prohibition, remember, he composed two comments on it, "Follow the Swallow" and "The Mingling of the Wets and Drys," and he reputedly said more than once, "The man who does not practice showmanship is dead." If still alive when the feminist movement strengthened, he might have remarked on it, perhaps with an excerpt from Poulenc.[7]

I would like to digress for a paragraph. Humor in music has always pleased the public—"Pop, Goes the Weasel!"—and in those band concerts today in which the music is to be pondered intellectually, humor, even in an elevated form, is notably lacking. Sousa, to cite him for the last time, composed humoresques, and one, on Kern's song "Look for the Silver Lining," ends by repeating the chorus but now with every note of the melody assigned to a different instrument, and in its sequence of boop, bop, beep, and purr, could serve as an early parody of much of today's "advanced" music.[8]

Lastly, to end with a spoof on opera, the Pyramus and Thisbe scene from Britten's *A Midsummer Night's Dream.* Pyramus and Thisbe, lovers separated by a wall, agree to meet at Ninny's Tomb. Thisbe arrives first and is killed by a lion, and Pyramus, finding her body, kills himself, sighing multitudinously "die, die." Pyramus, a bass, sings in an exaggerated Verdian style of *Trovatore,* and Thisbe trips in and out to a flute mocking Donizetti's *Lucia.* The piece could be performed without singers: Pyramus, a trombone; Thisbe, a flute, and the band having a grand time as the growling, chomping lion. A note on the program, if needed, could be two sentences.

Of course, times have changed, and today no professional concert band can reproduce the sort of touring schedule that financed many bands before World War I. Nor can any, it seems, rely on a single private subsidy such as the Guggenheim family for more than fifty years gave the Goldman Band. Moreover, it seems, no civilian concert band can depend with confidence on any municipal, state, or federal grant, and perhaps, too, at least in the bigger cities, urban sprawl and noise have made outdoor summer concerts, whether free or at low prices, unfeasible. Thus it is easy to say, and no doubt true to say, that no return to the days of Sousa is possible.

On the other hand, the perfection of air conditioning has made summer indoor concerts pleasant, and perhaps a slight imitation of Gilmore's indoor garden concerts could be achieved. And today there are families far richer even than the Guggenheims. As Gunther Schuller declared and the Dallas Wind Symphony demonstrates, the answer to "Where do we get the money?" lies in "leadership, enterprise, vision, and courage."[9]

No one can fault those who, pursuing the music they love, have developed the wind ensembles which chiefly proliferate in an academic setting. And no one can fault those amateur bands scattered about the country which, lacking national leaders to show the way, stick to a traditional and now dated repertory. But the common man might ask of all bands and wind ensembles: "What of me? Are there not musicians in the United States who want to play what appeals to me?" If asked to state what he liked, he would reply: "Melody, rhythm, color, humor—music that stirs feelings." In the past such music often came from opera—action, passion, portrayal of character—and today can be heard in contemporary operas. Why ignore it? Moreover, even if instructed in the intricacies of much modern music, the common man might add—and he would be right—"Life isn't structural or logical; it's emotional."

NOTES

1. Sousa played "Selections" from *Turandot* in 1928, Bierley, *The Incredible Band,* 391.
2. "Sudler Silver Scroll Interview," *Journal of the Association of Concert Bands* 27, no. 3 (October 2008): 16.
3. Dallas Wind Symphony, *Fennell Favorites!,* Reference Recordings, RR43-CD. The concert was on 8 January 1991. The accompanying pamphlet has remarks by Fennell on the works played. The arranger of the Prokofiev selections was W. J. Dutholt.
4. Program for concert on 18 October 2011, interview with Gustave Hoehn on 20 October 2011; see also About the Dallas Wind Symphony at http://dws.org/about.
5. E. F. Goldman, *Band Betterment,* 39–40.
6. Thomson, "Band Music," *Herald Tribune,* 22 June 1941, sec. 6, 6. Republished in *The Etude,* July 1942 and in Thomson, *The Musical Scene* (New York: Knopf, 1947).
7. "Showmanship," Bierley, *American Phenomenon,* 138, citing "Keeping Time" (part 5), *Saturday Evening Post,* 5 December 1925.
8. "Look for the Silver Lining," on the recording *John Philip Sousa "At the Symphony,"* Naxos, 8.559013, Keith Brion conducting the Razumovsky Symphony Orchestra.
9. Schuller, Address to the CBDNA National Conference, 13 February 1981, *The Wind Band and Its Repertoire,* 2.

Appendix One

Operatic Repertory of the Dodworth Band, July–August 1859

Titles of works for the first seven concerts were taken from announcements of the program in the New York *Tribune,* and for the eighth, for which the *Tribune* offered no announcement, from a review of the concert published in the *Herald* the following day. The latter may not have listed all the numbers played, although it named six operatic numbers, which, according to the *Tribune,* would have been half the usual number of works performed. As the appendix shows, of that usual number slightly more than half (forty-nine of an estimated ninety-six) were operatic in origin. The balance of the programs were made up of songs, waltzes, galops, marches, polkas, and medleys. Thus, on any afternoon the weightier numbers were apt to be operatic, opening and closing the programs. The concerts were held on 9, 16, 23, 30 July, and 6, 13, 20, 27 August; the conductor was Harvey B. Dodworth. The series was underwritten by a group of private music lovers, see *Albion*, 16 July 1859, 343.

Composer	Opera	Title of Work	No. of Perfs.
Auber	*La Sirène*	Overture	2
	Fra Diavolo	Overture	1
	Crown Diamonds	Overture	1
Beethoven	*Egmont*	Overture	1
Bishop	*Clari*	"Home, Sweet Home"	1
Donizetti	*Gemma di Vergy*	March	1
	La Fille du régiment	Selections	2
	Poliuto	Cavatina	1
	Don Pasquale	Selections	1
Flotow	*Alessandro Stradella*	Overture	2

(continued)

Composer	Opera	Title of Work	No. of Perfs.
	Martha	Selections	2
Hérold	*Zampa*	Overture	1
Lortzing	*Zar und Zimmermann*	Song	1
Mendelssohn	*Midsummer Night's Dream*	Wedding March	1
Meyerbeer	*Robert le diable*	Selections	2
	L'Étoile du Nord	Potpourri	2
	Le Prophète	March	2
		Mazurka	1
	Les Huguenots	Selections	2
Rossini	*Guillaume Tell*	Overture	2
		Selections	1
	Moses in Egypt	Selections	2
	Tancredi	Overture	2
	Semiramide	March	1
Verdi	*La traviata*	Potpourri	1
	Ernani	Sextet	2
	Rigoletto	Quartet	1
	Il trovatore	Selections	1
		"Anvil Chorus"	2
	Nabucco	Cavatina	1
	Luisa Miller	Quintet "Fra mortali . . ."	2
Wagner	*Tannhäuser*	Festival March	3
Weber	*Freischütz*	Overture	1

Appendix Two

Advertisement for the First of Jullien's Farewell Concerts, June 1854

In the *New York Times,* 15 June 1854, p. 5, col. 5, the paid announcement of the series' opening concert ran for an unprecedented full column and two inches. After promising 1,500 performers, it listed as among those already engaged:

The Germania Society
The Philharmonic Society of Philadelphia
Dodworth's Cornet Band
The United States Military Band
The Italian Opera Orchestra
M. Jullien's full concert orchestra
And many orchestral artists and amateurs from Boston,
Philadelphia, Baltimore, Cincinnati, New Orleans and New York.

[It then listed twenty more groups likely to be present, before continuing with the program.]

THE PROGRAMME
Which will be selected from the sacred and classical chef d'oeuvres of
the Grand Masters, will include selections from the following works.
HANDEL'S MESSIAH
HAYDN'S CREATION
MOZART'S REQUIEM
MENDELSSOHN'S MISDUMMER NIGHT'S DREAM
SEBASTIAN BACH'S CRUCIFIXION
SPOHR'S LAST JUDGEMENT
BEETHOVEN'S CHORAL SYMPHONY
FĖLICIEN DAVID'S LE DĖSERT

MENDELSSOHN'S FUGUE IN E MINOR
MEYERBEER'S OPERA OF LE PROPHÈT
and
LES HUGUENOTS
ROSSINI'S GUILLAUME TELL
and
MOSÈ IN EGITO
WAGNER'S TANNHÄUSER
HECTOR BERLIOZ'S ROMEO E GIULETTA
And for the first time in America
MEYERBEER'S INCIDENTAL MUSIC
To
THE TRAGEDY OF STRUENSEE
(the complete work)
FOR THIS OCCASION THE DISTINGUISHED AMERICAN COMPOSERS
MR. W. M. H. FRY and MR. G. E. BRISTOW
WILL CONTRIBUTE SOME OF THEIR LATEST WORKS
and
M. JULLIEN
Has composed, as a companion to "The American Quadrille,"
A GRAND DESCRIPTIVE PIECE
entitled
THE FIREMAN'S QUADRILLE

The last was repeated at every performance, and as the concerts proceeded, there were many selections from opera composers not included in the advertisement's list, such as Auber, Balfe, Bellini, Hérold, Ricci, and Weber.

Appendix Three

Operatic Repertory for the First Four Days of Gilmore's International Peace Jubilee, Boston, 1872

The first four days of the festival, which opened on 17 June and closed on 4 July 1872, were designated "American," "English," "German," and "French," and on the named day featured the band of that nation. The term "operatic repertory" has been stretched to include such works as Rossini's *Stabat Mater,* any overture (because usually theatrical in style), whether or not written to precede an opera, and all of the works of Johann Strauss Jr., some of which include themes heard before or later in one of his operettas. A statement at the end of each "day" compares the number of operatic numbers to the program's full number.

"AMERICAN" DAY, 17 JUNE

Featuring the United States Marine Band, led by Henry Fries, director:

Composer	Opera	Work's Title	Description
Wagner	*Rienzi*	Overture	Orchestra of 1,000
Meyerbeer	*Le Prophète*	Skating Ballet	Piano solo
Rossini	*Stabat Mater*	Inflamatus	Vocal soloist with full chorus, organ, and orchestra
Donizetti	*Lucia di Lammermoor*	Sextet	Sung by "a bouquet" of sextets of artists (about 150 soloists), full chorus, and orchestra
Gantes		Overture Triomphale	U.S. Marine Band
Strauss		*Blue Danube*	Small select orchestra
Verdi	*Trovatore*	"Anvil Chorus"	Full chorus, organ, orchestra, military bands, bells, anvils, cannon

In all, seven of fourteen numbers. The festival opened with a chorale, "Old Hundred," employing the full chorus, organ, orchestra, and closed, using the same forces, with the hymn "Nearer My God to Thee." The U.S. Marine Band played a selection of national airs of America, England, Austria, France, and other countries as well as the Overture Triomphale by the little known composer Gantes.

"ENGLISH" DAY, 18 JUNE

Featuring the Grenadier Guards Band of London, led by Dan Godfrey:

Composer	Opera	Work's Title	Description
Beethoven	*Leonore*	Overture No. 3	Large orchestra
Verdi	*Ernani*	Finale to Act 3	Bouquet, see above
Macfarren	*Robin Hood*	Overture	English band
Weber	*Freischütz*	Overture	English band
Strauss		"Wine, Women, and Song"	Select orchestra
Verdi	*Trovatore*	"Anvil Chorus"	As previously
Halévy	*L'Éclair*	Romanza	Sopranos, tenors, and full orchestra

In all, seven of sixteen numbers. The concert opened with Bach's chorale, "Now May the Will of God Be Done," and closed with the hymn, "From Greenland's Icy Mountains."

"GERMAN" DAY, 19 JUNE

Featuring the Kaiser Franz Grenadier Regiment Band of Prussia, led by Heinrich Saro:

Composer	Opera	Work's Title	Description
Wagner	*Tannhäuser*	Overture	Orchestra
Strauss		*Morgenblätter*	Select orchestra
		Pizzicato Polka	Select orchestra
Meyerbeer	*Le Prophète*	Fantasia on Themes	Prussian band
	L'Africaine	Selections	Prussian band
	Les Huguenots	"Benediction of the Swords"	Prussian band
Weber	*Oberon*	Overture	Prussian band
Verdi	*Trovatore*	"Anvil Chorus"	As previously

In all, eight of twenty numbers. The concert opened with the Luther chorale, "A Mighty Fortress Is Our God," and closed with the hymn, "Kingdoms and Thrones."

"FRENCH" DAY, 20 JUNE

Featuring the Garde Républicaine Band of Paris, led by MM. Paulus and Maury:

Composer	Opera	Work's Title	Description
Leutner		Festival Overture	Orchestra
Verdi	*Trovatore*	"Anvil Chorus"	As previously
Strauss		*1001 Nights*	Select orchestra
		Pizzicato Polka	Select orchestra
Rossini	*Guillaume Tell*	Overture	French band
Meyerbeer		Marche aux flambeaux	French band
Mozart	*Zauberflöte*	Recitation and aria	Vocal solo with orchestra
Gounod	*Faust*	"Soldiers' Chorus"	Full chorus, orchestra, and cannon

In all, eight of sixteen numbers. The concert opened with the "Gloria" from Mozart's Twelfth Mass, and closed with the hymn, "Watchman, Tell Us of the Night."

As can be seen, the number of works of operatic origin in each program usually totaled between a third and a half, a slight decrease from the Dodworth Band's Central Park concerts in 1859 (appendix 1), when slightly more than a half.

Appendix Four

Gilmore's Repertory in San Francisco, 17–29 April 1876

What follows is a partial list of the repertory of the band's fifteen concerts in the Mechanics' Pavilion (it played at least two more elsewhere), compiled from the announcements of programs and reviews found in the *San Francisco Chronicle* and the *San Francisco Evening Bulletin.* It is not complete, for on some nights, such as the last when the announcement merely stated "the best programme of the Series," the works scheduled were not listed, and works played not reviewed. Still, as nine of the fifteen programs are covered, the appendix may give a sample of the kind of symphonic, sacred, and operatic music scheduled. The announcements usually list ten works to a program, but neither they nor the reviews specify encores. On at least some nights, such as the fourth in the series, 20 April, the operatic arrangements were six of the ten announced, with the balance "arias varie" for solo saxophone, solo cornet, and two for the soprano vocalist. As in previous appendixes, overtures, whether or not composed to precede an opera, are listed in the operatic repertory because they are usually theatrical in style.

Of other essentially orchestral works arranged for band, Gilmore scheduled one performance of Gungl's Concert Waltz from *Immortellen,* and four of Liszt's Hungarian Rhapsody No. 2. The latter evidently was one of the hits of the series, scheduled once as "by request" and once as "for the gratification of lovers of Classical Music." As stated in chapter 3, for his choral night, Gilmore scheduled the "Hallelujah Chorus" from Handel's *Messiah* and from Haydn's *The Creation* "The Heavens Are Telling" and "The Marvelous Work."

As a work composed specially for the country's centennial year and premiered in San Francisco, the band played at least twice a "Grand Centennial Quadrille, introducing the Airs of all nations, with variations for the principal soloists."

In the operatic repertory, note that Wagner, even in 1876, is still limited to arrangements from *Rienzi* and *Tannhäuser*, though by then *Lohengrin, Rheingold, Walküre, Tristan,* and *Meistersinger* had all premiered at least eight years earlier. By 1892 his position would be much stronger, see appendix 5. Compared to Sousa, Gilmore was slower to take up new works.

Composer	Opera	Title of Work	No. of Perfs.
Beethoven		Egmont Overture	1
		Prometheus Overture	1
Bellini	*Norma*	Fantasie	1
	?	Air and variations (solo trombone)	1
Flotow	*Stradella*	Overture	1
	Martha	Selections	1
Litolff		Robespierre Overture	1
Meyerbeer	Reminiscences of *Huguenots*, *L'Étoile du Nord*, *Dinorah*, and *L'Africaine*		1
	Robert le Diable	Aria for solo cornet	1
	Dinorah	"Shadow Song" (sung by E. Thursby)	1
		Fackeltänz No. 3	1
		Schiller Festival March	1
		Fackeltänz No. 1, Marche aux flambeaux	1
Rossini	*Semiramide*	Overture	1
	William Tell	Overture	1
	Il Barbiere	"Una voce poco fa" (sung by E. Thursby)	1
Thomas	*Mignon*	"Polonaise" (sung by E. Thursby)	2
Verdi	*Attila*	Fantasie for cornet	2
	Rigoletto	Quartet (played by full band)	1
	Macbeth	Selections	1
Wagner	*Tannhäuser*	Overture	1
	Tannhäuser	Festival March	1
	Rienzi	Overture	1
Weber	*Oberon*	Selections	1
	Oberon	Overture	2
Westmeyer		Overture on Austrian Airs	2

Appendix Five

Repertory of Twelve Summer Band Concerts in New York City's Central Park, 1892

This list of works played by Cappa's 7th Regiment Band in the first twelve Saturday and Sunday free afternoon concerts in New York's Central Park in early summer 1892 is taken from a report in the *Musical Courier*, 20 July 1892, by one who attended the concerts. The report, however, is not complete, sometimes saying merely "mosaics" from the operas of Rossini, Donizetti, Verdi, and Meyerbeer, and ending a list of minor composers played with an "&c." Inasmuch as the newspapers did not publish announcements of the programs, they cannot be filled out. Still, though incomplete, the list gives a sense of the band's educational impact on audiences that reportedly numbered usually between ten and twenty thousand. Note, by comparison to programs for Central Park in 1859 (appendix 1), the increase in such composers as Bach, Beethoven, Liszt, and Mendelssohn, though operatic composers still are well represented. Note also the addition to Wagner of excerpts from two of his later operas, *Die Walküre and Die Meistersinger.*

Composer	Opera	Work	Description
Bach		Air and Gavotte	
		Chorale and Fugue	
Beethoven	*Leonore*	Overture	
		2nd Symphony	Larghetto
		3rd Symphony	Allegro con brio
		5th Symphony	Andante
		6th Symphony	Two Movements
		7th Symphony	Allegro e presto
		8th Symphony	Scherzo
Berlioz		Overture	Roman Carnival
Bizet	*L'Arlesienne*	Fantasy	

Composer	Opera	Work	Description
	Carmen	Fantasy	
	Pearl Fishers	Fantasy	
Donizetti		Mosaic from operas	
Gottschalk		Pasquinade	
		"Last Hope"	
Gounod	*Faust*	Selections	
		"Ave Maria"	
Liszt		Hungarian Rhapsody No. 2	
		Hungarian Rhapsody No. 14	
Masacagni	*Cavalleria*	Interlude	
	Cavalleria	Potpourri	
Massenet	*Le Cid*	Ballet music	
		Scenès Pittoresque	
		Scenès Napolitaines	
Mendelssohn	*Midsummer Night's Dream*	Incidental music	
		Symphony No. 3 (Scotch)	
Meyerbeer		Mosaic from operas	
Ponchielli	*La Gioconda*	"Dance of the Hours"	
Rossini	*William Tell*	Overture	
		Mosaic of operas	
Schubert		Overture in the Italian Style	
Verdi		Mosaic of operas	
Wagner	*Rienzi*	Overture	
	Tannhäuser	Overture	
	Holländer	Selections	
	Meistersinger	Selections	
	Walküre	Scene	

And in its closing list the *Musical Courier* names only "Bellini, Litolff, Suppé, Strauss, Waldteufel, Gurza, d'Aman, Wilson, Braham, &c.," for a total of 118 "different pieces in twelve concerts in forty-five days."

To this list, Leon Mead, "The Military Bands of the United States," *Harper's Weekly,* 28 September 1899, 785, would add, as included in a "typical program" (but not mentioned by the *Courier* reporter): "Verdi, overture to *Sicilian Vespers*; Auber, overture to *Crown Diamonds*; Donizetti, sextet and Grand March from *Lucia di Lammermoor;* Wagner, Selections from the *Flying Dutchman*; and *Reminiscence of Veteran Firemen,*" with "the fire alarm, the start, the run, and the falling of the wall."

Appendix Six

Repertory of the U.S. Marine Band under Francis Scala, 1855–1871

The year in which Scala became the band's leader is uncertain. David M. Ingalls, in his master's thesis, "Francis Scala: Leader of the Marine Band from 1855 to 1871," follows the U.S. Marine Corps in opting for 1855, but as he notes, a letter written in 1859 by the officer in charge of the band sets the date at "about eight years ago." On this point, and others, this appendix follows Ingalls.

Working with the Scala Collection in the Library of Congress, Ingalls broke down the 596 selections for band into three groups: music for concerts, music for military formations, and music for White House functions. And "although there is much overlapping, these groups each contain roughly about one-third of the band selections." Taking the three together, works of operatic origin comprise nearly 33 percent. As might be expected, in "music for military formations" marches predominate, and in "music for White House functions," dances. The startling figure, according to Ingalls, is that for "music for concerts" works of operatic origin total 88 percent.

Scala, a Neapolitan by birth, liked Italian opera, and his favorite among its composers was Verdi. In all, at least in the Scala Collection, he seems to have made at least twenty-nine arrangements of music from thirteen of Verdi's twenty operas preceding *La forza del destino* (1867). The collection also has arrangements by others from many of these same operas, as well as from two more, *Macbeth* and *Luisa Miller*. Nine of Scala's arrangements are taken from *Ernani,* which considering the opera's popularity in the United States is not surprising. More so, is to see two arrangements from *Giovanna d'Arco,* which had its U.S. premiere only in 1966, and one each from *I due Foscari* and *Attila,* both of which, after U.S. premieres in the late 1840s, disappeared, though of *Attila* some of the music remained popular. In addition, and least surprising, were arrangements from *Rigoletto, Trovatore,* and *Traviata.*

From *Trovatore*, Scala arranged a funeral march, a "dirge" based on the Miserere, which he played at Washington's tomb when the Prince of Wales visited Mount Vernon in 1860. The prince was impressed, had a copy of the arrangement sent to the queen, and, according to Scala, the work soon became popular in England. The U.S. Marine Band played it for Scala's funeral in April 1903.

Other operatic composers in Scala's repertory were Auber, Bellini, Boieldieu, Donizetti, Flotow, Gounod, Meyerbeer, Offenbach, Rossini, and Weber. But an important person complained of too much opera. Gideon Welles, Lincoln's secretary of the navy, protested that during the Civil War the marine band should play more patriotic music. Yet Lincoln, reports Elise K. Kirk in *Music at the White House,* 88, defended Scala's choices. Though Lincoln himself played no instrument, he was our most opera-loving president, and besides enjoying the concerts on the White House grounds, he also while president attended nineteen performances of opera (Kirk, 80), with a favorite excerpt the "Soldiers' Chorus" from *Faust*. Plainly for him, as for many others, opera then was a large part of popular music, and as such Scala and the U.S. Marine Band played it at concerts.

One who greatly enjoyed the Scala concerts in the years 1866–1872 was Walt Whitman. Reportedly (see article by Hans Nathan), he frequently attended and often wrote reviews published in the Washington *Sunday Herald.*

Appendix Seven

Sousa's Repertory for Seven Summer Concerts, August 1882

Sousa and the U.S. Marine Band, in one of their rare trips from Washington, played a series of seven concerts on Congress Hall Lawn, Cape May, New Jersey, every evening 20–26 August 1882. The town, located on New Jersey's southern tip overlooking the juncture of the Delaware River and the Atlantic Ocean, was a stylish resort with hotels, beaches on both the ocean and large Delaware Bay, and with the added lure for ornithologists, both professional and amateur, of being a spot to sight migratory birds. Each of the seven printed programs (on file in the U.S. Marine Band Library) scheduled in some detail nine numbers; and though no encores were listed, surely some were played.

On five nights a "Mr." W. M. Jaeger offered a cornet solo, and one night played a duet with a soloist named simply "Petrola." It seems that marine custom at this time did not include rank in referring to the musicians or even sometimes their first names. Sousa, though granted his three names in large type, also lacked rank and appeared merely as "Conductor," whereas at a marine band concert fifteen years earlier, Francis Scala, also without his first name, had been described as "Leader" (indicating perhaps that he led with clarinet in hand) and was graced with the rank of "Prof." Evidently, with the passage of time and the growth of the band from thirty to roughly fifty, custom and nomenclature had changed.

Moreover, because Sousa was always rather free with his titles, what the difference may be between a "Fantasie," a "Mosaic," and a "Selection" is not always clear. It seems likely, however, that a "Collocation" of *Trovatore,* on 20 August, was a different piece from the "Potpourri" of *Trovatore,* on 23 August, if only because it seems *un*likely that Sousa would offer an exact repeat within four days to an audience that had changed very little if at all. Also, though the programs designated some pieces as "Song," because the band had no vocal soloist, these were band arrangements.

Of the sixty-three pieces scheduled, roughly a third are operatic or theatrical in origin, and all those which do not appear in Scala's catalogue of 1871 bear an asterisk. To these, as new to the band's repertory, could be added six works by Sousa and five waltzes and a polka by Waldteufel; also the four excerpts from operettas by Edmond Audran and Arthur Sullivan. For the first piece on opening night Sousa scheduled a new march, "Congress Hall," dedicated to Messrs. H. J. and G. R. Crump, who presumably had provided the building upon whose lawn the concerts were held. Where pertinent, to show Sousa keeping up to date with French, English, and Austrian operettas I have added their premiere years. Also note that excerpts from both Rossini and Verdi are fewer. Roughly speaking, about 1875, as Wagner became better known, Verdi began to go out of fashion.

Composer	**Title**	**Opera or Origin**	**Date**
Audran	Collocation	*Mascotte** (1880)	21 August
	Fantasia	*Olivette** (1879)	22 August
	Grand Selection	*Olivette** (1879)	26 August
Bizet	Mosaic	*Carmen** (1875)	21 August
Boito	Potpourri	*Mefistofele**	25 August
Glinka	Mosaic	*Life for the Tsar**	23 August
Mendelssohn	Reminiscences	Including the Overture* and Wedding March from *Midsummer Night's Dream*, and marches from *Cornelius** and *Athalia**	20 August
Meyerbeer	Grand Fantasie	Selections from *L'Africaine,* Huguenots,** *Star of the North,* Robert,* and *Le Prophète*	22 August
Offenbach	Fantasia	*La Grande Duchesse**	21 August
	Mosaic	*Orphée**	22 August
	Collocation	*La Belle Hélène*	22 August
	Collocation	*Madame Favart** (1878)	23 August
	Fantasia	*La Fille de Tambour Major** (1879)	23 August
	Fantasie	*Barbe Bleu**	24 August
Rossini	"Inflammatus" (cornet solo)	*Stabat Mater**	20 August
Sullivan	Song	*St. Agnes Eve**	20 August
	Collocation	*Patience** (1880)	21 August
	Song	*The Lost Chord**	24 August
Suppé	Overture	*Light Cavalry*	24 August
	Mosaic	*Fatinitza** (1876)	24 August
Verdi	Collocation	*Trovatore*	20 August
	Potpourri	*Trovatore*	23 August
Wagner	Mosaic	*Lohengrin**	20 August
	Potpourri	*Rienzi**	25 August

Appendix Eight

U.S. Marine Band Catalogue, 1885—Compared to Scala's Library List, circa 1871

When Francis Scala resigned from the U.S. Marine Corps in December 1871, after thirty years of improving the quality, size, and reputation of its band, he took with him much of the band's music. As then was custom, he considered his arrangements and compositions, including the band parts, as well as any works by others that he had obtained for the band, to be his personal library. And he continued to add to the collection until his death in 1903. Thereafter, his family gave it to the Library of Congress, where David M. Ingalls, in preparing his 1957 master's thesis on Scala, made a catalogue of it. Because some of the works are dated or are known to have been played before 1871, he was able to show, though speculatively, what Scala had taken with him on retirement. Thus it is possible to compare, again speculatively, the band's repertory under Scala, circa 1871, and under Sousa in 1885 as shown by the band's *Catalogue of Music* published that year.

As the band's director, Scala was succeeded by Henry Fries, who served only briefly, and who was followed in September 1873 by Louis Schneider. Both Fries and Schneider reputedly accomplished little, Fries perhaps because his term was short and the band's library depleted, and Schneider, perhaps because of illness, his inability to speak English, or other problems. His discharge in October 1880, for instance, declared him "unfit for service," and he was succeeded by Sousa, who gave his first concert with the band at a White House reception on New Year's Day 1881.

Ingall's catalogue of Scala's music library lists 608 items of which 342 are compositions or arrangements for band, either parts or score; whereas the band's 1885 *Catalogue of Music* lists 476 such works. Direct comparison, however, is difficult because the two lists differ in format and only the earlier offers any detailed descriptions of the works.

Those descriptions, however, make clear that many of the works listed in the Scala collection were not yet arrangements in the band's library and repertory. Ingall's numbered the works straight through, listing them by composers taken in alphabetical order, and under Rossini, for example, items 295 and 296 are not arrangements for band but piano-vocal scores of *Il barbiere di Siviglia* and *La gazza ladra*; and item 304, the overture to *Tancredi,* is an arrangement for piano, not band. On the other hand, for *L'Italiana in Algeri* and *William Tell,* both overtures show arrangements for band by Scala, dated by him 1856 and 1864 and with parts available. Ingalls lists six such overtures and five more with arrangements for band by persons not identified.

The 1885 catalogue on the other hand lists works by genre, such as overtures, selections, waltzes, songs, and so on, and within each genre, though numbered, in haphazard order and without any description other than title and composer, as in the section "Overtures," "item 1: Poet and Peasant, Suppé." To limit the discussion to overtures, which being unsuited to marching were a specialty of concerts, compare the numbers listed: eleven in 1871, and fifty-three in 1885, of which forty-seven are new. Thus Sousa evidently dropped some of Scala's repertory as well as greatly expanding it. Of course, as in the earlier list, some of Sousa's forty-seven may not be arrangements for band, but as Bierley in *The Incredible Band* (see bibliography) shows, Sousa in his first four years with his independent band, 1892–1995, played with considerable regularity at least twenty-six of the listed overtures, a record which suggests he had worked hard to make or, at least, to collect arrangements.

Moreover, another reason for the differences in the two lists concerns a change in band instruments which needs a specialist's knowledge to explain. According to the U.S. Marine Band's current historian, MGySgt D. Michael Ressler, "During the Scala years, 1855–1871, the band was using over-the-shoulder brass instruments that were popular during the Civil War era and had been specifically designed to be used on the march (the bells of the brass instruments pointed backwards so the troops could hear the music). Therefore, Scala's arrangements were tailor made for this instrumentation. When Sousa became director I suspect that many of these instruments had disappeared. Sousa continued to modernize the band's instrumentation so most or all of Scala's arrangements would not have worked for the new instrumentation which Sousa used. This would help to explain why there was such a dramatic change in the two lists."

In general, in Scala's repertory for his more formal concerts the overtures, or pieces operatic in origin, if played complete or even nearly complete, would have been the longest and weightiest pieces. For example, at a concert in Boston in 1867 (program in the U.S. Marine Band Library) Scala opened with the overture to *William Tell*, closed the program's first half with a potpourri from Auber's *Fra Diavolo,* opened the second half with the Grand March from *Tannhäuser,* played Scala's arrangement of the Miserere from Verdi's *Trovatore,* and closed with "American Quadrilles" by Jullien. In between he played smaller works, a waltz, a polka, and three based on operatic arias by Petrella, Meyerbeer, and Verdi. For the most part he limited his own compositions to simpler works, operatic numbers slightly embellished, or songs turned into dances or quicksteps. According to Ingalls, 133, Scala composed "about thirty quicksteps on themes borrowed from popular songs and opera." To which Ingalls adds, "It is not clear how these quicksteps were used but judging from the number they would seem to have been very popular."

By 1885, as Sousa was increasing the band's number of musicians from thirty to forty, among overtures he had added to Scala's repertory were two by Wagner, *Rienzi* and *Tannhäuser*; five by Suppé of which *Morning, Noon, and Night* and *Pique Dame* were the most frequently played; and three by Rossini, *Tancredi, Semiramide,* and *Gazza ladra,* of which *Semiramide* was the leader. Also, Hérold's *Zampa,* Weber's *Oberon,* and Schubert's *Overture in the Italian Style.* What he repeated from Scala's catalogue, but likely in his own arrangements, were Flotow's overture to *Martha,* Verdi's to *Giovanna d'Arco,* Suppé's *Poet and Peasant* and *Light Cavalry,* as well as, of course, Rossini's *William Tell.*

In short, upon taking up his position with the U.S. Marine Band at age twenty-five, Sousa at once started on the course he followed thereafter, to raise the quality of the band in all respects, and to introduce his concert audiences to a wider range of "serious" music, much of it operatic in origin.

Appendix Nine

Sousa and the U.S. Marine Band: Six Concerts in Philadelphia, 1889–1891

These six concerts in Philadelphia's Academy of Music, as far from Washington as the marine commandant seemingly wanted his band to travel, are among the last that Sousa conducted before the short spring tours of 1891 and 1892 after which he resigned to create his own, independent organization. The concerts took place, three in each season, on 19 October and 17 December 1889, and 19 April 1890; and the next year on 18 October and 13 December 1890, and 14 March 1891. Printed programs for each can be found in the U.S. Marine Band Library, Washington, D.C., and though these do not record the encores played, they do reveal what Sousa in these years believed a good concert program should include. As befits a concert in the Academy of Music, the selections are more sumptuous than those he offered outdoors at Cape May in 1882 (see appendix 7); and, of course, after seven years under Sousa's baton, the band was more skilled.

Four of the programs list twelve works and two of them, eleven, and of those seventy pieces at least twenty-nine are operatic or theatrical in origin, a percentage slightly higher than at Cape May. Moreover, instead of a single soloist on the cornet, he offered a more varied roster on violin, flute, clarinet, cornet, trombone, as well as both male and female vocalists. Band members, though not individually listed, presumably numbered about fifty, with Sousa now granted an "assistant," Salvadore Petrola, and himself now designated as "Director."

As usual with Sousa, there is no clear distinction between mosaic, potpourri, and collocation, but note that a mosaic though sounding small may be large. In the first concert, for example, the program states that the mosiac of *La Gioconda* will comprise "The Sailor's Chorus," "Thanks Unto the Angelic Voice," "Marenesca, Barcarole and Furlana," "Romance," "Him I Love as the Light of Creation," and "The Dance of the Hours." The last alone, if played complete, runs nine minutes.

Though Rossini is the composer most often played, five times, that was partly because the *William Tell* overture was repeated "by request." But if with Rossini, Sousa may be said to look backward in the repertory, with Saint-Saëns and Massenet he looked forward. And though for the soprano solo at the concert on 17 December 1889 he titled the selection from Saint-Saëns's *Samson et Dalila* as merely "Song," because the opera has but one solo soprano role, it was most likely her aria "My Heart at Thy Sweet Voice," which in two later concerts he scheduled and so described. Because the aria then had been sung apparently in only two symphony concerts (New York and Boston), in Philadelphia it likely was being heard for the first time. The opera itself, though in concert form, was first heard in the United States in New York on 25 March 1892. Similarly with Massenet's *Esclarmonde*; it had premiered in Paris at the Opéra-Comique on 15 May 1889 and reached its one hundredth performance there the following February. When Sousa played his selection from it, on 13 December 1890, he possibly was introducing the work to the United States. Not until 10 February 1893 did the opera have its U.S. premiere, at the French Opera House in New Orleans. The following were programs at the Academy of Music, 1889–1891:

Date	Composer	Title	Opera or Origin
19 October 1889	Mendelssohn	Overture	"Son and Stranger"
	Boito	Collocation	*Mefistofele*
	Thomas	"Connais tu le pays" (vocal)	*Mignon*
	Ponchielli	Mosaic	*Gioconda*
	Sullivan	Song (cornet)	"The Lost Chord"
	Delibes	Valse lento	*Sylvia*
	Weber	Invitation to the Dance (originally piano solo)	
	Hérold	Overture	*Zampa*
17 December 1889	Mendelssohn	Overture	"Fingal's Cave"
	Massenet	Excerpts	*Herodiade*
	Wagner	Fantasia	*Tannhäuser*
	Saint-Saëns	Song (vocal)	*Samson et Dalila*
	Gounod	Marionette's Funeral March (originally piano solo)	
	Nicolai	Overture	*Merry Wives of Windsor*
19 April 1890	Rossini	Overture	*Semiramide*

Date	Composer	Title	Opera or Origin
	Verdi	Duet for cornet and trombone	*Ernani*
	Berlioz	Fantasia (Reveille, Easter Hymn, Ballet of the Sylphs, Hungarian March)	*Damnation of Faust*
	Mozart	"Gli angui d'Inferno"	*Il Flauto Magico*
18 October 1890	Mendelssohn	Overture	"Son and Stranger"
	Rossini	"Cujus Animam" (trombone)	*Stabat Mater*
	Saint-Saëns	"My Heart at Thy Sweet Voice" (vocal)	*Samson et Dalila*
	Bellini	Polonaise (vocal)	*I Puritani*
	Rossini	Overture	*William Tell*
	Delibes	Ballet music	*Sylvia*
	Verdi	Romanza (vocal)	*Aida*
13 December 1890	Massenet	Grand Scene	*Esclarmonde*
	Berlioz	Invocation of Nature (vocal)	*Damnation of Faust*
	Delibes	Ballet	*Coppelia*
14 March 1891	Rossini	Overture	*William Tell*
	Sullivan	Incidental Music	*Henry VIII*
	Meyerbeer	"Blessing of the Daggers" (featuring four trombones)	*Huguenots*
	Weber	Scene and Prayer (vocal)	*Der Freischütz*
	Chopin	Funeral March from Sonata, Op. 35 (originally piano solo)	
	Rossini	"Una voce poco fa"	*Il barbiere*
	Saint-Saëns	"My Heart at Thy Sweet Voice" (vocal)	*Samson et Dalila*
	Sousa	*The Chariot Race* (with a synopsis by Ben-Hur), symphonic poem	

Because of encores, however, the final concert, as reported by the *Philadelphia Public Ledger,* 17 March 1890, p. 8, col. 4, lasted "nearly three hours" and included many encores. The unsigned critic found some nit to pick with almost every piece: clarinets could not fully replace strings in Rossini and Meyerbeer; the *Chariot Race* should close "with something else than a dozen rallentando bars"; and a march that included a section "whistled" by a large contingent of the band "had little snap to it." Yet he bothered also to state that the house was sold out, the audience demanded frequent encores, including one of the *Chariot Race*, and "on the whole the concert was an unusually successful one."

The *Philadelphia Inquirer,* 15 March 1891, concluded: "The concert was a delightful one and was received enthusiastically by the audience. This closes the season of Marine Band concerts, which has been successful beyond all anticipations. The Marine Band fills an entirely distinct place in music and it is yearly becoming more appreciated." Under Scala the band had become a good local group; under Sousa, it became a national asset, in the opinion of many occupying "an entirely distinct place in music."

Appendix Ten

Sousa's Programs for the Columbian Exposition, Boston, 4–7 May 1893

The information is taken chiefly from reviews, which also announce programs, in the *Boston Herald* and *Boston News.* The seven concerts were held in Mechanics Hall, an auditorium seating some four thousand and with standing room for as many more, and which had been decorated in "an elegant manner" with "draperies and streamers" employing "the national colors." The constituent musical groups were Sousa's Band, an orchestra of seventy young women led by Arthur W. Thayer, vocal soloists, a chorus, and for one concert a chorus of school children. Sousa and his manager David Blakely had recruited the forces, and Sousa, as the exposition's musical director, planned the programs. Among his important soloists were sopranos Emma Fursch-Madi and Marie Van Cauteren; contralto, Harriet Minnie Behnee; tenors Albert Guille and Italo Campanini; baritone William Mertins, and bass Ludovico Viviani; also the violinist Leonora Von Stosch and the cornetist Herbert L. Clarke. It is not possible to be sure how frequently the orchestra played, either alone or with the band. With regard to the band, however, nothing is ascribed to it that is not also listed in Paul E. Bierley's appendix V, *The Incredible Band of John Philip Sousa,* as in Sousa's repertory in 1893.

OPENING CONCERT, THURSDAY NIGHT, 4 MAY

Composer	Title of Work	Performers
Gilmore	"Columbia"	Band, orchestra, chorus
Tobani, Theo. M.	Hungarian Fantasy	Orchestra
Nicolai	*Merry Wives of Windsor* Overture	Orchestra

(continued)

Composer	Title of Work	Performers
Rubinstein, A.	Ballet Suite from the opera *Feramors*	Band
Liszt	Hungarian Rhapsody No. 6	Band
Sousa	"Salute to the Nations"	Band, orchestra, chorus

The salute, according to the *Herald,* opened with a "group of trumpeters and drummers proclaiming the 400th anniversary of the discovery of America. The flourish is answered in return by two other groups of trumpeters and drummers, and finally taken up by the band, orchestra and chorus [which] merge into *Hail Columbia*. Then comes a short fugue on *Yankee Doodle*, while Brother Jonathan is supposed to busy himself receiving the guests as they land. The Spanish hymn is played by the band and followed by a concerted number by Spanish students of characteristic national music of Spain. At the end of that, the fanfares sound the flourish to the royal march, followed by the band playing the Italian national air. The oboe is then heard in plaintive Swiss Ranz des vaches, which is in turn followed by a company of Swiss warblers in folk songs. Then the drums are heard in the distance, gradually growing louder. Enter the band of the Prussian guards playing *Wacht am Rhine*. After a short prelude by the orchestra the Russian hymn is played. The trumpets announce the approach of the French legions, and *La Marseillaise* is heard. This is followed by the entrance of the Irish drum and fife corps playing *The Wearing of the Green* during which enter the British Grenadiers. They are followed by *Scots, Wha Hae Wi Wallace Bled* which is the signal for the entrance of the band of Scotch pipers in the national costume playing *The Campbells Are Coming*. Then amid the roll of drums and the general acclaim is heard *The Star Spangled Banner* by the combined forces, and the tableaux vivant of Columbia triumphant."

SECOND CONCERT, FRIDAY AFTERNOON, 5 MAY

Composer	Title of Work	Performers
Wagner	Invocation to battle, *Rienzi*	Band, orchestra
	"Evening Star," *Tannhäuser*	Vocalist, band, orchestra?
	Overture, *Tannhäuser*	Band, orchestra?
	"Elsa's Dream," *Lohengrin*	Vocalist, band, orchestra?
	Prelude, *Meistersinger*	Band, orchestra?
	Love song, *Walküre*	Vocalist, band, orchestra?
	Ride of the *Walküre*	Band, orchestra?
	Prayer and finale, *Lohengrin*	Vocal quintet, band, orchestra?
Sousa	"Salute to the Nations"	Band, orchestra, chorus

As the question marks indicate, the extent of the orchestra's participation in the selections, other than the first, is not clear. Nor is it certain that the band played in every number. Yet all the Wagner was in the band's repertory, which most likely was not true of the orchestra.

THIRD CONCERT, FRIDAY EVENING, 5 MAY

Composer	Title of Work	Performers
Sousa	"Presidential Polonaise"	Band, orchestra
Tchaikovsky	Suite from *The Nutcracker*	Band
Trepak	Children's Dance	The Mirlitons (the music was not yet a year old. The ballet had its premiere in St. Petersburg in December 1892)
Verdi	Tenor solo from *I Lombardi*	Vocalist, band, orchestra?
Wagner	"Hail, Bright Abode," *Tannhäuser*	Chorus, band? orchestra?
Sousa	Scene historical, *Sheridan's Ride*	Band
Rossini	Trio, *William Tell*	Male vocalists, band
Gounod	Entr'acte and Dance of Bacchantes from *Philémon et Baucis*	Band
Verdi	"Caro nome," *Rigoletto*	Soprano, band
(Georges?) Gillet	Gavotte	Orchestra
Sarasate	Gypsy Dances	Violin solo, band
Sousa	"Salute to the Nations"	Band, orchestra, chorus

The orchestra for this concert consisted only of strings. And either in addition or substitution for the unidentified solo from *I Lombardi,* the tenor sang "Celeste Aida" from Verdi's *Aida* and as an encore "M'appari" from Flotow's *Martha.* The women's string ensemble had such success with Gillet's Gavotte that they had to repeat the final movement, which led the *Herald* to declare, "Boston has approved of women as orchestral players. The rest of the country will probably follow this sensible example."

FOURTH CONCERT, SATURDAY AFTERNOON, 6 MAY

Composer	Title of Work	Performers
Meyerbeer	Torch Dance No. 3	Band, orchestra?
Mozart	Bass solo, *Magic Flute*	Vocalist, band

(continued)

Composer	Title of Work	Performers
Tufts, J. W.	Sanctus	Chorus of Boston Public School children
Wagner	Overture, *Flying Dutchman*	Band, orchestra?
Thomas	Polonaise, *Mignon*	Soprano, band
Lacombe	Suite, "Gitanilla"	Band
Flotow	"M'appari," *Martha*	Tenor, band
Edith Swepstone	Gavotte	Orchestra?
Hauser	Rhapsodie Hongroise	Violin solo, band
Sousa	*Last Days of Pompei*	Band
Beethoven	Quartet, *Fidelio*	Band, orchestra?
Sousa	"Salute to the Nations"	Band, orchestra, chorus

FIFTH CONCERT, SATURDAY EVENING, 6 MAY

Composer	Title of Work	Performers
Sousa	March militaire, *The Thunderer* (new this year)	Band, orchestra?
Thomas	Ballet suite, *Hamlet*	Band, orchestra?
Wallace	"Yes, Let Me Like a Soldier Fall," from *Maritana*	Tenor solo, band
Massenet	Grand aria, *Herodiade*	Soprano solo, band
Arban	Fantasie Brillant, cornet solo	H. L. Clarke, band
Bizet	Toreador song, *Carmen*	Baritone solo, band
Wagner	Quartet, *Meistersinger*	Vocalists, band, orchestra?
Berlioz	Selections, *Damnation of Faust*	Band, orchestra?
Mascagni	Church Scene, *Cavalleria* (The opera had its world premiere in 1890 and its U.S. premiere in 1891; the Metropolitan company had brought it to Boston in March 1892.)	Band, orchestra? chorus?
Sousa	"Salute to the Nations"	Band, orchestra, chorus

SIXTH CONCERT, SUNDAY AFTERNOON, 7 MAY

Composer	Title of Work	Performers
Meyerbeer	Marche du Sacre, *Le Prophète*	Band, orchestra
Wagner	An Album Leaf	Band, orchestra?
Flegier, A,	"Stances," tenor solo	Band
Verdi	"Miserere," *Trovatore*	Band, cornet and euphonium soloists

Composer	Title of Work	Performers
Orth, C. J.	"In a Clock Store" (descriptive piece)	Band
Meyerbeer	"Nobil Signor," *Huguenots*	Band, contralto solo
Grieg	Two numbers from Peer Gynt Suite No. 1	Women's orchestra
Donizetti	Mad Scene, *Lucia*	Band, soprano solo
Vieuxtemps	Reverie	Violin solo, band?
Wieniawski	Russian mazurka	Violin solo, orchestra?
Sousa (arranger)	"Songs of Grace and Glory"	Band

According to the Boston *Herald,* 7 May, p. 15, these would include "the prelude to Verdi's *Requiem, Rock of Ages*, Chant of the Greek Church, *Steal Away*, *Mary and Martha*, Gloria Laudamus from Giorza's mass; New Year's hymn of the Hebrew church, *The Palms* and *Nearer, My God, to Thee*, with cathedral chimes."

Composer	Title of Work	Performers
Wagner	Prayer and finale, *Lohengrin*	Band, vocal soloists
Sousa	"Salute to the Nations"	Band, orchestra, chorus

SEVENTH CONCERT, SUNDAY EVENING, 7 MAY

Composer	Title of Work	Performers
Verdi	Grand March, *Aida*	Band, orchestra
Titl, A. E.	Overture, *King's Lieutenant*	Band
Balfe	"Then You'll Remember Me"	Band, tenor solo
Sousa	*The Chariot Race*	Band
Gounod	"Unfold Ye Portals," *Rédemption*	Band, chorus
Tobani	Fantasia upon Hungarian Airs	Women's orchestra
Gounod	"Le Soix"	Band
Sarasate	Gypsy Dances	Band, violin soloist
Sousa (arranger)	"Songs of Grace and Glory"	Band
Rossini	"Inflammatus," *Stabat Mater*	Band, orchestra, chorus, soprano soloist
Sousa	"Salute to the Nations"	Band, orchestra, chorus

Appendix Eleven

Sousa's Operatic Repertory in Rochester, New York, 1894–1901

This appendix, with data extrapolated from the programs published in Paul Edmund Bierley's *The Incredible Band of John Philip Sousa,* lists the operatic repertory Sousa scheduled for sixteen concerts in the Lyceum Theatre in Rochester, with the term "operatic" here defined to include concert overtures composed independent of any dramatic work, such as Litolff's *Maximilian Robespierre,* or Anton Rubinstein's *Triumphal Overture*. Performances were in the evening (E) unless otherwise noted (there were some morning concerts). Each concert announced typically nine or ten numbers, to which were added as many encores, usually popular songs or marches. To indicate how Sousa was keeping up to date on new operatic music, I have included the premiere year for all those operas or operettas that were first staged after 1884. Other comments on the selections, along with some general remarks about his repertory in this period, may be found in the text of chapter 5 toward the close of the section on Manhattan Beach.

Composer	Opera	Selection	Dates
Bizet	*Carmen*	Dragoons	23 March 1895 (M)
		Excerpts	5 May 1901
Boito	*Mefistofele*	Prologue	5 May 1901
Donizetti	*Lucia*	Sextet (six brass soloists)	24 March 1895; 19 January 1896; 28 March 1901 (M) and (E)
	Linda	Aria (vocal)	3 March 1898
Flotow	*Stradella*	Overture	18 January 1896 (M)

Composer	**Opera**	**Selection**	**Dates**
Giordano	*A. Chenier*	Grand Scene and Ensemble	28 March 1901 (Prem. 1896)
Goldmark	*Cricket on the Hearth*	Entre-acte	28 March 1897 (Prem. 1896)
Gomez	*Il Guarany*	Overture	3 March 1898
Gounod	*Faust*	Scenes	19 January 1896 (M)
		Soldiers' Chorus	28 March 1901
	Romeo and Juliet	Waltz Song (vocal)	19 January 1896
Hérold	*Zampa*	Overture	24 March 1895; 5 May 1901
Humperdinck	*Hansel and Gretel*	Prelude	23 March 1895; 19 January 1896 (Prem. 1893)
Kistler	*Kunihild*	Overture	18 January 1896 (M) (Prem. 1884)
Lassen		Festival Overture	23 March 1895 (M)
Leoncavallo	*Pagliacci*	Bell Chorus	19 January 1896 (Prem. 1892)
Leutner		Grand Festival Overture	28 March 1897
Litolff	*Maximilian Robespierre*	Concert Overture	19 January 1896
Luders	*Burgomeister*	"Tale of the Kangaroo" (trombone soloist)	28 April 1901 (Prem. 1900)
Meyerbeer	*Huguenots*	"Blessing of the Swords" (four trombones)	19 January 1896
	Dinorah	"Shadow Song" (vocal)	3 March 1898
Ponchielli	*Promessi Sposi*	Overture	3 March 1898
Rameau	*Dardanus*	Rigadon	19 January 1896 (M)
A. Rubinstein		Triumphal Overture	18 January 1896
Suppé	*Agonies of Tantalus*	Overture	23 March 1895
	Schöne Galatea	Overture	23 March 1895
	Paragraph III	Overture	16 April 1899
	Isabella	Overture	28 April 1901
Verdi	*Traviata*	"Ah, fors' e lui" (vocal)	16 April 1899

(continued)

Composer	Opera	Selection	Dates
	Aida	Death Scene, "Oh, Fatal Stone" (cornet and trombone)	28 March 1901
	Aroldo	Overture	5 May 1901
Wagner	*Tannhäuser*	Overture	11 November 1894; 19 January 1896 (M)
		"Oh Hail, I Greet Thee" (vocal)	11 November 1894
		"Pilgrims Chorus" and "Evening Star"	3 March 1898 (band and saxophone solo)
	Lohengrin	Prelude, Act 1	11 January 1894; 28 March 1897
		Prelude, Act 3	24 March 1895; 16 April 1899
		Wedding Music	19 January 1896 (M); 31 May 1896
	Tristan	Night Scene	31 March 1898 (M)
	Walküre	"Ride of the Valkyries" and "Fire Music"	18 January 1896 (M)
	Siegfried	Fantasie	18 January 1896
	Gõtterdämmerung	Siegfried's Death	23 March 1895 (M)
	Parsifal	Prelude, Act 1	24 March 1895
		"Knights and Holy Grail"	16 April 1899

Appendix Twelve

Repertory of Sousa's Band, 1892–1932

This appendix lists the chief works of all kinds played by Sousa's Band in fifteen or more years of its forty-year span, as extracted from Paul Edmund Bierley's massive appendix V in his *The Incredible Band of John Philip Sousa.* In my appendix 12, however, Sousa's own works are not listed. As recounted, he played encores throughout his programs, not merely at their close, and because he often chose for an encore one of his own marches or waltzes even Bierley does not attempt to count their years of repetition, merely stating after the work's first appearance "in succeeding years." In forty years and 15,623 concerts such favorites as "The Stars and Stripes Forever," "El Capitan," or "Semper Fidelis" no doubt were played more than a thousand times. As Bierley notes: "People paid premium prices to see him and expected to hear his music." Although heard less frequently, some other works, such as Daniel Emmet's "Dixie," the Reminiscences of Scottish and Irish songs, and national airs such as "My Country 'Tis of Thee" and "The Star-Spangled Banner" also were played countless times.

Apart from highlighting such oft-repeated works, the aim of this appendix is to show the core of Sousa's repertory, with some indication of how it changed over the years as well as what part of it was operatic in origin, either taken from an opera, written by an opera composer, or merely inherently dramatic, as are many concert overtures. For these composers I have listed at the end of their entries their other operatic works from which Sousa played arrangements along with the number of years performed. There are, of course, composers not tied to opera, such as Grieg, Brahms, or Chopin, and for some of them, too, I have added a further note of works played. What the difference may be, if any, between arrangements with such titles as "Mosaic," "Suite," "Selections," or "Reminiscences" is not clear. Sousa sometimes played the same, or mostly the same work under different titles.

What the appendix does not show, for it would have opened the gate too wide, are composers who may have had a number of works played but none in more than the qualifying fifteen years. Among these are many contemporary composers whose popular works Sousa would program for a year or two and then replace with their next latest hit. Victor Herbert is an example. He does not qualify for this appendix, and yet Sousa over the years played thirty-eight arrangements of Herbert's works. As stated in chapter 4, one of the most enduring was the "Italian Street Song" (vocal solo) from *Naughty Marietta,* which lasted seven years and was four times taken on tour. Other popular contemporary composers who go unrecorded here are Rudolf Friml, fifteen arrangements, and to a lesser extent three at the start of their careers, Jerome Kern, Irving Berlin, and George Gershwin. Similarly some American composers of "serious" music, notably Cadman, Chadwick, Hadley, and Parker, though mentioned in chapter 4, are not listed here.

In all, a rough count shows that Sousa played works by at least 2,030 composers, not including another hundred or so listed by Bierley under entries such as traditional, undetermined, or various. Of Sousa's own works, which Bierley numbers at 324 original compositions and 322 arrangements, Sousa played, at one time or another, some 263.

Composer	Opera	Description	Years Played	On Tour
Auber	*Fra Diavolo*	Overture	22	1892, 1893
Balfe	*Bohemian Girl*	Selections	19	———
Berlioz	*Benvenuto Cellin i*	Roman Carnival Overture	21	1898, 1899, 1901–1903, 1914, 1915, 1930, 1931
Bizet	*L'Arlesienne*	Suite No. 1	25	1909, 1911
	Carmen	Second mosaic	19	1900, 1911
	Played in ten years or more: Selections, 14; Aria (unnamed; vocal), 11; *L'Arlesienne,* Suite No. 2, 11; and Suite No. 2, Agnus Dei, intermezzo, 11; *Carmen,* Suite, 10			
Boito	*Mefistofele*	"Night of the Classical Sabbath" (vocal solo; band)	16	1899, 1900, 1911, 1918
		Played in ten years: *Mefistofele,* Selections		
Bonnisseau	———	Reminiscences of Scotland	28	1911
Brahms	———	Hungarian Dances (violin solo, or band)	17	1903, 1908–1910
Chopin	———	Reminiscences	25	1900, 1911
Clarke, H. L.	———	Bride of the Waves (polka; cornet solo)	19	1900, 1901, 1906–1908, 1911
	———	Sounds from the Hudson (waltz; cornet or saxophone solo)	18	1904, 1907–1908, 1911, 1925, 1926
	———	From the Shores of the Mighty Pacific (rondo; cornet solo)	15	1909–1911, 1913–1915

(continued)

Composer	Opera	Description	Years Played	On Tour
	————	Reminiscences of Stephen Foster	23	1901–1902, 1911
DeKoven	*Robin Hood*	Selections	16	1892
Delibes	*Coppelia*	Ballet Suite	25	1907, 1911
	Sylvia	Ballet Suite	23	1911, 1929
	Lakmé	Bell Song (vocal or cornet solo)	13	1898, 1899, 1903, 1905, 1925
	Also: *Lakmé,* Selections, 5			
Donizetti	*Lucia*	Sextet (brass)	26	1893–95, 1897, 1898, 1900, 1901, 1905–1909, 1911, 1913, 1916, 1918, 1920, 1928
	Also: *Lucia,* “Mad Scene” (vocal solo), 10; Reminiscences of Donizetti, 12			
Dukas	*Sorcerer's Apprentice*	Scherzo	16	1911, 1924
Dvorak	New World Symphony	Largo	16	1903, 1905, 1911, 1912, 1917, 1918, 1925, 1926
	Also: Humoresque (violin or xylophone solo, or band), 11			
Elgar	Pomp and Circumstance No. 1	March	22	1904–06, 1911, 1925
	Also: the march played as a cornet solo, 7; *Salut d'Amour,* reverie, 10; and *Sevillana*, 7			
Flotow	*A. Stradella*	Overture	30	1895, 1911
	Martha	Selections	18	————

		Overture	15	1911
Ganne	*La Gypsy*	Mazurka	15	1905, 1907, 1908, 1911
German, E.	————	Welsh Rhapsody	15	1905–1907, 1911
Giordano	*Andrea Chenier*	Selections	24	1901–1903, 1911, 1924
Godfrey, F.	————	Reminiscences of Wales	26	1911
	————	Reminiscences of Scotland	15	————
		Also: Reminiscences of England, 14		
Goldmark	*Im Frühling*	Overture	16	1909, 1911, 1921, 1922
	Also: *Sakuntala,* overture, 12; and Rustic Wedding Symphony, Selections, 10			
Gomez	*Il Guarany*	Overture	16	1898–1900
Gottschalk	————	Pasquinade	22	1892–1994, 1898, 1900
	————	The Dying Poet	19	1902, 1911
Gounod	*Faust*	Selections	28	1897, 1900, 1911
		Ballet music	15	1892
	Roméo et Juilette	Aria (unnamed; vocal)	24	1924
		Waltz (vocal)	15	1896, 1897, 1908
	Reine de Saba	Aria (unnamed; vocal)	16	1893
	Also: *Roméo,* Selections, 14; "Ave Maria" (vocal or band), 13; *Faust,* "Soldiers' Chorus" as a trombone quintet, 12, and as a trombone sextet or band, 12;			
Grieg	*Peer Gynt*	Suite No. 1	23	1892, 1907–1908, 1910, 1911, 1915

(continued)

Composer	Opera	Description	Years Played	On Tour
	Also: Norwegian Dances, 12; Lyric Suite (from piano works), 9; and Reminiscences of Grieg, 9			
Gungl, J	————	*Immortelen Valse*	21	1900
Handel	*Serse*	Largo	18	1895, 1896, 1898, 1900, 1910, 1911
	Also: *Messiah,* "Hallelujah Chorus," 11			
Hatton, J. L.	*Macbeth*	Overture	15	1895, 1897
Hérold	*Zampa*	Overture	36	1895, 1897–1899, 1900, 1911, 1919, 1920, 1926
Koelling, K.	————	*The Lion's Chase* (descriptive galop)	23	1902, 1903, 1911
Lassen, E.	————	*Thuringian Festival Overture*	25	1895–97, 1911
Leoncavallo	*Pagliacci*	Selections	30	1900, 1901
	Also: *Pagliacci,* Prologue (vocal or euphonium solo, or band), 11			
Leutner, Albert	————	Festival Overture	15	1897, 1900, 1911, 1929
Liszt	————	Hungarian Rhapsody No. 2	29	1892–1895, 1897, 1898, 1903, 1911, 1914, 1929
		Les Préludes, symphonic poem	27	1897, 1902, 1905–1911
	————	Second Polonaise	20	1902, 1905, 1911, 1914

	————	Hungarian Rhapsody No. 14	19	1894, 1896, 1900, 1901, 1905, 1911, 1921, 1922, 1914
	————	Also: Hungarian Rhapsody No. 1, 14; and No. 6, 11		
Litolff, H. C.	————	*Robespierre,* Concert Overture	29	1896–1898, 1905, 1907, 1911, 1912, 1924, 1925
Mascagni	*Cavalleria*	Selections	18	1911, 1929
	Iris	Hymn to the Sun	16	1898, 1899, 1903, 1905, 1925
	Also: *Cavalleria*, Prelude and Siciliano, 13; and *Guglielmo Ratcliff*, Intermezzo, 6			
Massenet	————	Scènes Neapolitaine	23	1894–1897, 1901–1903, 1911, 1925, 1927
	————	Scènes Pittoresque (suite)	16	1892, 1900
	Played in more than ten years: *Phedre,* Overture, 14; Scènes Alsaciennes, suite, 14; Scènes Pittoresque, "The Angelus," 12; and *Szabadi,* the gypsy caprice, 12			
Mehul	*Le Jeune Henri*	Overture	15	1913, 1915
Mendelssohn	————	Reminiscences	23	1900, 1911
	————	Violin Concerto (one or two movts.)	16	1893, 1903, 1906, 1911
Messager	*Véronique*	Selections	18	————
Meyerbeer	*Huguenots*	Blessing of the Daggers (trombone trio, or band)	31	1898, 1899, 1900, 1911
	Dinorah	"Shadow Song" (vocal or cornet solo)	1923	1897, 1898, 1921, 1923, 1925, 1926

(continued)

Composer	Opera	Description	Years Played	On Tour
	Robert le Diable	"Robert, toi que j'aime" (vocal or cornet solo)	18	1907, 1911
	————	Fackeltanz No. 1	18	1911
	————	Reminiscences	26	1911
	Also: *Prophète,* Coronation March, 10, and Selections, 10; *Robert le Diable,* Selections, 8; Fackeltanz No. 3, 8; *Huguenots,* Selections, 7			
Meyer-Helmund, E.	————	Reminiscences	15	————
Moszkowski	————	Spanish Dances	22	————
	————	"From Foreign Lands"	18	1924
Nevin	————	"The Rosary" (vocal or cornet solo)	19	1905, 1907, 1910, 1911, 1914
	————	Fontainbleau	17	1902, 1903
	Also: *A Day in Venice*, 13; *Narcissus,* 9			
Nicolai	*Merry Wives*	Overture	21	1892, 1904, 1905
Offenbach	*Hoffman*	Selections	22	1911
	Orpheus	Selections	18	————
	Also: *Grand Duchess,* Selections, 13; *Orpheus,* Overture, 10			
Ponchielli	*Gioconda*	Selections	28	1911

		Dance of the Hours	20	1897, 1928, 1930
	Also: *Promessi Sposi,* Overture, 9			
Puccini	*Bohème*	Selections	31	1900, 1901, 1911, 1925
	Butterfly	Selections	23	1911
	Also: *Tosca,* "Vissi d'arte" (vocal), 14; *Bohème,* "Musetta's Waltz" (vocal), 9; *Butterfly,* Aria (unnamed, vocal), 8; *Manon Lescaut,* Finale to Act III, 7; Selections, 7; Aria (unnamed vocal), 6; Grand Scene, 5; and Aria (unnamed, vocal), 5			
Rossini	*William Tell*	Overture	35	1892–1899, 1901–1904, 1906, 1908, 1911, 1914, 1915, 1921, 1925
		Ballet music	16	1892
	Stabat Mater	"Inflammatus" (vocal or cornet solo)	26	1907
	Semiramide	Overture	18	1892, 1894
	Also: *Stabat Mater,* "Cuius animam" (vocal, cornet, or trombone solo), 14; and *Semiramide*, "Bel raggio" (vocal), 5			
Rubinstein, A.	———	*Kamenoi Ostrow*	20	1907, 1908, 1911

(continued)

Composer	Opera	Description	Years Played	On Tour
	Also: "Melody in F," 10			
Saint-Saëns	*Samson*	Selections	21	———
	———	Introduction and Rondo Capriccioso (violin or cornet solo)	21	1896, 1898, 1899, 1905, 1910, 1911, 1927
	Also: *Danse Macabre,* 12; and *Samson,* "Mon Coeur" (vocal, cornet, or flugelhorn solo), 11			
Sarasate	———	*Ziguenerweisen* (fantasie)	20	1896–1899, 1901–1907, 1911
Sibelius		*Finlandia*	15	1910, 1911, 1924, 1928
Strauss, J.	———	*Blue Danube Waltz*	28	1899, 1900, 1911, 1923–1926, 1928, 1930
	———	*Morning Papers Waltz*	26	1911, 1926, 1929
	———	*Village Swallows Waltz*	19	1907
	Also: *Artist's Life Waltz*, 13, and *Voices of Spring*, 12			
Sullivan	———	"The Lost Chord" (cornet solo)	34	1899, 1900, 1905, 1910, 1911, 1921, 1926, 1927, 1929, 1930
	Iolanthe	Selections	21	———
	Pinafore	Selections	18	1900
	Pirates	Selections	18	———
	Patience	Selections	17	———
	Mikado	Selections	16	———
	———	Reminiscences of Sullivan	18	1892, 1911

	Also more than ten seasons: *Henry VIII,* Incidental Music, 12; and *Golden Legend,* Selections, 11			
Suppé	*Light Cavalry*	Overture	28	1923, 1927
	Poet and Peasant	Overture	28	1894, 1904
	Galatea	Overture	18	1892, 1895, 1911
	Flotte Bursche	Overture	16	1897
Tchaikovsky	————	*1812* Overture	23	1910–1912
	————	Marche Slave	20	1903, 1911
	————	Symphony No. 4 (scherzo and finale)	15	1911, 1921–1923, 1925, 1929, 1931
	————	Reminiscences of Tchaikovsky	16	————
	Also, in more than ten seasons: *Nutcracker,* Selections, 12; and String Quartet in D, Andante Cantabile, 12			
Thomas	*Raymond*	Overture	20	1892, 1894, 1905, 1909
	Mignon	"Je suis Titania" (vocal or xylophone solo)	16	1905, 1919, 1924–1926
Tosti	————	"Good-Bye" (vocal solo)	16	1916, 1924
Verdi	*Aida*	Final scene (cornet and trombone solo/ duet, or band)	18	1901, 1911
		Selections	29	1911, 1925, 1930
	Don Carlos	Selections	22	————
	Rigoletto	"Caro nome" (vocal solo)	21	1893, 1913, 1914, 1918, 1920, 1922, 1923, 1926

(continued)

Composer	Opera	Description	Years Played	On Tour
	Traviata	"Ah, fors' è lui" (vocal solo)	21	1899, 1918, 1919, 1920, 1922, 1926, 1927
		Aria (unnamed; vocal solo)	16	1899, 1902
		Selections	30	1911
	Trovatore	Selections	24	1911
		Reminiscences of Verdi	26	1911
	Also, played in five or more years: *Aida,* Ballet music, 7; *Aroldo,* Overture, 9; *Attila,* Selections, 5; *Ernani,* Aria (unnamed; vocal solo), and "Ernani, involami," (vocal or euphonium solo), 7; *Falstaff,* Selections, 14; *Giovanna d'Arco,* Overture, 11; *Rigoletto,* Quartet (brass), 10; *Trovatore,* "Miserere," 10; "Anvil Chorus," 5, and "Il balen" (vocal solo), 5; *Vespri Siciliani,* Overture, 8. In addition, played in fewer than			

	five years, extracts from *Due Foscari, Forza, Hymn to the Nations, Lombardi, Luisa Miller, Macbeth, Oberto,* and the *Requiem Mass.* In all, besides the two nonoperatic works, Sousa at some time offered arrangements from nineteen of Verdi's twenty-six operas. Left untried were only *Giorno di regno, Nabucco, Alzira, Masnadieri, Corsaro,* and *Battaglia di Legno.*			
Wagner	*Götterdämmerung*	Siegfried's Death and Funeral March	20	1895, 1899, 1900
	Lohengrin	Bridal Procession	19	1896–1898, 1907, 1911
		Prelude, Act 3	31	1894–1895, 1897–1899, 1902–1905, 1911, 1929, 1930
		Selections	22	1893, 1894, 1911
	Meistersinger	Selections	22	1900
		"Prize Song" (vocal or violin solo)	18	1899, 1900, 1904, 1911, 1915
	Parsifal	Knights' March	23	1897–1899, 1900, 1901, 1904, 1907, 1911, 1930, 1931
	Rienzi	Overture	19	1911, 1930, 1931
	Siegfried	Selections	22	1896–1899, 1900, 1906, 1911
	Tannhäuser	"Evening Star" (vocal, euphonium, or cornet solo)	19	1892, 1907, 1911

(continued)

Composer	Opera	Description	Years Played	On Tour
		Overture	32	1893–1902, 1905, 1909, 1911, 1923–1926, 1929
		"Pilgrims' Chorus" and "Evening Star" (band, or saxophone)	15	1896, 1898, 1911, 1915
		Selections	27	1907, 1911
	Tristan	Prelude and Liebestod	17	1911, 1915, 1928, 1930
	Walküre	"Ride of the Valkyries"	15	1900, 1911
		Selections	19	1900, 1911
	————	Reminiscences of Wagner	27	1900, 1911

	Also played in five or more years: *Holländer,* Overture, 13; *Lohengrin,* Prelude, Act 1, 8; “Elsa’s Dream” (vocal), 7; *Götterdämmerung,* Selections, 5; *Meistersinger,* Prelude, Act 1, 7; Apprentice March, 6; *Parsifal,* Prelude, 11; *Rheingold,* Entrance of the Gods, 6; *Tannhäuser,* “Elizabeth’s Prayer” (vocal), 7; Festival March, 10; “Hail Bright Abode,” (no soloist stated), 5. *Tristan,* Liebestod, 8; Nachgesang, 12; Selections, 5; *Walküre,* Fire music, 11; *Kaisermarch,* 5. Wagner’s only operas unsampled are his first two, *Die Feen* and *Das Liebesverbot*			
Weber	*Oberon*	Overture	23	1906, 1911
	————	*Jubel* Overture	22	1897, 1898, 1907
	————	*Invitation to the Dance*	20	1900, 1901, 1905, 1911, 1930
	————	Also: Reminiscences of Weber, 14		
Westmeyer, W.	————	*Kaiser* Overture	19	1900, 1901, 1903, 1907, 1908, 1911

Appendix Thirteen

Six Programs by Clarke and the Long Beach Municipal Band, 1923–1943

The aim of this appendix is to suggest how, as the years passed, Clarke scheduled fewer of the longer theatrical works, from opera and ballet, and substituted simpler, popular songs and dances. The programs are those noted in the doctoral thesis by James Thomas Madeja (see bibliography). In this appendix, for those composers who today are less well known I have added to these programs first names and middle initials as well as birth and death years, if able to find them, and corrected occasional misspellings. I also have added brief descriptions to the works, such as "overture," or "ballet suite"; and sometimes, at the foot of the program, offered further details as well as comments. An asterisk before the work indicates that, according to Paul Edmund Bierley's *The Incredible Band,* the work was also played by Sousa. Encores, which most likely were marches, are not included.

30 NOVEMBER 1923, CLARKE'S FIRST CONCERT

Works	Composer
*Marche Russe, from *Russian Suite*	Alexandre Luigini, 1850–1906
**Il Guarany,* overture	Antonio Carlos Gomes, 1836–1896
**La Feria,* ballet suite	Paul J. J. Lacombe, 1837–1927
*Hungarian Dances Nos. 5 and 6	Brahms
**Gold and Silver*, waltz	Lehár
*"Bells of St. Mary's," popular song	A. Emmett Adams, 1890–1938
"Long Beach Is Calling," composed for the occasion	Clarke
Nereid, cornet solo by Clarke	Clarke
**Southern Rhapsody*	Lucius Hosmer, 1870–1935

Luigini, a Frenchman and conductor at the Opéra-Comique, had composed, among other works, two operas; and Lacombe, besides orchestral suites, had composed several operettas. Gomes, a Brazilian living much of his life in Milan, composed many operas, of which the best known and sometimes still performed are *Il Guarany* and *Lo Schiavo.* Adams, an Australian, published "The Bells of St. Mary's," in 1917, which refers to a church in Southampton, England. It became popular in the United States and was adopted as the home song of St. Mary's College, Notre Dame, Indiana. In 1945 it furnished the title and theme of a movie starring Bing Crosby and Ingrid Bergman, and because it played during a Christmas scene it became associated with Christmas for many viewers. Lucius Hosmer, son of a bandmaster, was born, educated, lived, and worked in Massachusetts, where he became a church organist in Boston. He studied music at Harvard with the composer George Chadwick, and ultimately composed three operettas and many works in other forms. Of these, his rhapsodies, *Southern* and *Northern* were perhaps the most frequently performed.

29 JANUARY 1924

Works	Composer
Naval Brigade March	Clarke
**Barber of Seville,* overture	Rossini
*Polish Dances, xylophone soloist	F. Xaver Scharwenka, 1850–1924
**The Two Pigeons*, ballet suite	André C. P. Messager, 1853–1929
**Gold and Silver*, waltz	Lehár
**Voice of the Bells*, reverie	Luigini (see above)
"Macushla," song, cornet solo by Clarke	Dermot MacMurrough, 1872–1943
**Jolly Robbers*, overture	Franz von Suppé, 1819–1895

The ballet, *The Two Pigeons*, based on a La Fontaine fable, premiered at the Paris Opéra in 1886 with choreography by Louis Mérante. In 1961, with the same music but new choreography by Frederick Ashton, it was produced by the Royal Ballet in London. The sentimental song "Macushla," appearing in 1910, was sung by every Irish tenor but most stylishly by the operatic tenor John McCormack, with whom it became closely associated.

16 MARCH 1927

Works	Composer
Symphony No. 6 (complete)	Tchaikovsky
**The Flying Dutchman,* overture	Wagner

(continued)

Works	Composer
Scheherazade, symphonic suite (complete)	Rimsky-Korsakov
I. The Sea and Sinbad's Ship	
*II. The Kalendar Prince	
III. The Young Prince and the Young Princess	
IV. Festival at Baghdad	

Of Tchaikovsky's symphony, Sousa had played various movements, or at least parts, but always in different years, never all together. Rimsky-Korsakov's exercise in imagined orientalism, beautifully scored and rhythmically vital, premiered in 1888. The Ballets Russes de Monte Carlo in 1910 presented a version of it with choreography by Michel Fokine. The composer's widow protested. The dancers, by making visible at best only a part of what the composer had wanted the listener to imagine, had impoverished the work. Nevertheless, over the years other ballet companies included in their repertories Fokine's dances, or parts of them. Whether danced or played, the work was for many years Rimsky-Korsakov's most popular.

29 DECEMBER 1932

Works	Composer
The Klaxon, march	Henry Fillmore, 1881–1956
**The Four Ages of Man*, overture	Franz Lachner, 1803–1890
*Allegretto, flute solo	Benjamin L. P. Godard, 1849–1895
*Hungarian Rhapsody No. 2	Liszt
**The Blue Danube*, waltz	Strauss
*Danse Orientale	G. Lubomirsky, ????
Cortège du Sardar, march	Mikhail M. Ippolitov-Ivanov, 1859–1935
My Regards, waltz	Edward B. Llewellyn, 1879–1936 Cornet solo by G. H. Tyler
Festival	Taylor ?

Fillmore, born in Cincinnati, played the piano, guitar, violin, and flute, but was best known for the slide trombone, for which he composed some fifteen rag tunes featuring "smears." For a time he served as a circus bandmaster, but his chief work as a conductor came in the 1920s in Cincinnati, where he developed the Shriners Temple Band into one of the country's best marching bands. Among his other works are "His Honor," "Americans We," "Men of Ohio," and "Lassus Trombone." Lachner, a Bavarian conductor and composer of the early romantic era, worked mostly in Munich where he composed six operas of which perhaps the most successful was *Caterina Cornaro* (1841). Godard's best known piece, usually familiar even to those with no knowledge of its source, is his Berceuse for tenor in his opera *Jocelyn.* The "Cortège du Sardar" is the last movement of four that make up Ippolitov-Ivanov's Caucasian Sketches, Suite No. 1 (1894), and for many years appeared on "Pops" programs. Llewellyn was principal trumpet with the Chicago Symphony Orchestra, 1912–1936, and the solo part of his popular waltz (1915) was arranged for other instruments besides trumpet. See "Edward B. Llewellyn, Master of the Cornet and Trumpet," *Jacobs' Band Monthly,* September 1925, 8.

29 JANUARY 1943

Works	**Composer**
"Wings of Victory"	Joseph Olivadoti, 1893–1977
Snow White, The Disney film, overture	Frank Churchill, 1901–1942
"Carnival of Venice," saxophone solo	arr. Joseph O. De Luca (see below)
**El Capitan,* scenes	Sousa
**Looking Upward*, suite (complete)	Sousa
I. By the Light of the Polar Star	
II. Beneath the Southern Cross	
III. Mars and Venus	
"Alexander's Ragtime Band"	Irving Berlin, 1888–1989
"Ciribiribin," waltz song	Alberto Pestallozza, 1878–1940
"Ghost Dance," ragtime dance	Cora Salisbury, 1868–1916
*"On, Wisconsin," march	William T. Purdy, 1882–1918

Frank Churchill also cowrote the film scores for *Bambi* and *Dumbo*, for both of which he received an Oscar award. Perhaps his most popular song, a huge commercial success, was the theme of Disney's *The Three Little Pigs*: "Who's Afraid of the Big, Bad Wolf." The original "Carnival in Venice" was composed by the French cornetist Jean-Baptiste Arban (1825–1889) as a display of his technique and recorded in 1909 by Clarke, who in 1922 recorded his own arrangement of the piece (see bibliography, recordings). But by 1943 Clarke, now in his seventies, no longer was playing such difficult works; hence this saxophone arrangement by De Luca. Cora Salisbury was a vaudeville pianist, with at least three popular rags published, "Poodles Parade," 1907; "Lemons and Limes: A Sour Rag," 1909; and "Ghost Dance" (Dance Descriptive), 1911. The next year she briefly joined with the young Jack Benny in a vaudeville act. Irving Berlin composed some 1,500 songs, 19 Broadway shows, and 18 Hollywood films. He is generally acknowledged to be America's greatest song writer, with simple direct melodies and equally direct simple lyrics. "Alexander's Ragtime Band," 1911, was his first great hit and started a dance craze on both sides of the Atlantic. Curiously, despite its title, it is as much, if not more, a march than a ragtime number. William T. Purdy in 1909, upon entering a competition for a song for the University of Minnesota, ended up composing "On, Wisconsin," which became the University of Wisconsin's "fight" song as well as, with slightly altered lyrics, the Wisconsin state song. At the time Purdy had never set foot in the state, but at the request of his lyricist, who was a graduate of the University of Wisconsin, he substituted Wisconsin for Minnesota. Today, regardless of state, it is played by college bands everywhere. Sousa reportedly thought it one of the best of college marches.

31 JANUARY 1943, CLARKE'S FINAL CONCERT (ALL WORKS BY CLARKE)

New England's Finest
Fraternity
Nymph Frolics
**Sounds from the Hudson*, waltz, cornetist F. L. Ray
Southern Air, piccolo solo
**Tiberius*, overture
Sweet Memories
Past Glad Hours
Valse Caprice, saxophone solo
Twilight Memories
Long Beach Is Calling

Skimpy though the sampling is, it does suggest that by the mid-1930s Clarke no longer scheduled arrangements of such "serious" composers, as Brahms, Hosmer, Liszt, and Tchaikovsky. In part perhaps because during the 1930s and 1940s, when the Depression required Clarke to reduce the band from roughly fifty to thirty-five, he felt that some needed instruments and weight of tone which were no longer available. At the same time, and perhaps in part for the same reason, he seems to have cut from his programs the longer, more theatrical works, chiefly the operatic and ballet numbers, overtures and suites of dances. These had been drawn largely from the works of Europeans, and in their place, perhaps acceding to the wishes of his audience, he increasingly substituted the shorter, simpler popular songs of American composers. A shift that, despite the regrets of those who liked the operatic numbers, nevertheless testifies to the increasing vitality of American music, now including some composed for films.

Appendix Fourteen

Repertory of the Staten Island Musicians Society Concert Band, 1972–1976

This appendix is based on interviews in 2010 with Victor DeRenzi, who conducted the band from July 1972 to September 1976. As a boy he had heard the band weekly in concerts near his home, and he recalled that for his audition piece for the post of conductor he chose the overture to Gomes's opera, *Il Guarany*.

The band's library in the early 1970s contained many of the traditional classical band pieces that were going out of fashion, but in DeRenzi's years his programs show the following pieces played, and also reveal that the band, though strong on arrangements of opera overtures, marches, and ballet music, unlike Sousa played no arrangements of operatic arias, for lack of a vocalist.

Bartok: Bear Dance
Bernstein: *Candide* Overture; Danzon (*Fancy Free*); Three Dance Episodes (*On the Town)*
Clarke, Herbert L.: "From the Shores of the Mighty Pacific," cornet solo
Copland: An Outdoor Overture, Variations on a Shaker Melody
Delibes: March and Procession of Bacchus
Dvorak: Slavonic Dances
Gomes: *Il Guarany* Overture
Grieg: Peer Gynt Suite
Hérold: *Zampa* Overture
Holst: First Suite in E-flat; Second Suite in F minor; Fantasia on the "Dargason" (seemingly fourth movement of the Second Suite); and from *The Planets,* Jupiter
Ives: Variations on "America"; "1776" March
Khachaturian: Galop, and from the ballet *Gayane,* Saber Dance
Mendelssohn: March from the incidental music to *Athalie;* Overture for Band

Meyerbeer: Coronation March
Milhaud: Suite Française
Nelhybel: Trittico (Slavonic Triptych)
Offenbach: *Orpheus in the Underworld* Overture
Persichetti: Divertimento for Band
Prokofiev: March, Op. 99; March from *The Love of Three Oranges*; "Athletic Festival March"
Ponchielli: from *La Gioconda,* "The Dance of the Hours"
Respighi: "Pines of Rome"
Rossini: Overtures to *Barber of Seville, La gazza ladra, The Italian in Algiers, The Silken Ladder, William Tell*
Strauss, R.: Waltzes from *Der Rosenkavalier*
Suppé: *Morning, Noon and Night in Vienna*
Tchaikovsky: *1812 Overture*; *Capriccio Italien*; *Marche Slave*; *Nutcracker Suite*; *Romeo and Juliet*
Telemann: Concerto for Oboe
Thomas, A.: *Raymond* Overture
Vaughan Williams: *English Folk Song Suite*; Sea Songs; "Seventeen Come Sunday" (first movement of the Folk Song Suite); "Toccata Marziale"
Verdi: Overtures to *La forza del destino, Nabucco*
Wagner: *Meistersinger* Prelude; *Rienzi* Overture; *Tannhäuser* March
Weber, C. M.: Concerto for Clarinet (possibly the concertino)

Appendix Fifteen

Answers to the Goldman Band's Memory Contest in Central Park, New York City, 3 August 1938

From the *New York Times*, 4 August 1938, 14: "The program attracted an audience of more than 30,000, the largest that has listened to a concert by the band this season. . . . Written answers were turned in by 3,000, which is a high average. . . . It was evident from the audience's reaction that Mr. Goldman had inserted several stickers in his list. In several instances there was silence when the band finished playing an excerpt, whereas there was tumultuous applause when the audience instantly recognized the music. . . . The papers will be checked immediately and the prize winners will be announced in a day or two." The correct answers were:

Works	Composer
1. Procession of Nobles, *Mlada*	Rimsky-Korsakoff
2. Overture, *Beatrice and Benedict*	Berlioz
3. Theme and Variations	Tchaikovsky
4. Overture, *Ruy Blas*	Mendelssohn
5. *Madame Butterfly*	Puccini
6. Gavotte and Rondo	Bach
7. Italian Polka	arranged by Rachmaninoff
8. Overture, *La gazza ladra*	Rossini
9. Overture, *Halka*	Moniuszko
10. Italian Caprice	Tchaikovsky
11. Perpetuum Mobile	Strauss
12. Spartan March	Prokofieff
13. Menuet, First Symphony	Beethoven
14. Overture, *In Bohemia*	Hadley
15. Introduction to Act 3, *Lohengrin*	Wagner
16. Choral Dance from Eight Russian Folk Songs	Liadoff

(continued)

Works	Composer
17. Prelude, *The Deluge*	Saint Saëns
18. Humoreske	Dvorák
19. Miserere, *Il trovatore*	Verdi
20. Excerpts, *Babes in Toyland*	Herbert
21. Barcarolle, *Tales of Hoffman*	Offenbach
22. March, *Our Flirtations*	Sousa
23. Dance Caprice	Grieg
24. "Kiss Me Again"	Herbert
25. March, *Happy Go Lucky*	Goldman

Appendix Sixteen

Excerpts from Verdi Played by the Goldman Band, 1936–1946

This appendix attempts to show how the Goldman Band, in the years when the younger Goldman, Richard Franko, as assistant conductor, began to influence the repertory, gradually shrinking its operatic excerpts (in the case of Verdi) from considerable and varied to fewer and less varied. This was the period in which Henry Cowell, for example, in his article on the influence of the band (see the close of chapter 9) mentioned audience disapproval of the trend in the band's programming. I thank the librarians at the Performing Arts Library, University of Maryland, for their work in checking the programs in each year for all the summer concerts in both Brooklyn and Manhattan.

The programs, however, are seldom clear on what part of an opera was played. They use, without specification, such terms as "Excerpts," "Selections," "Fantasie," or "Aria." Though such selections as Aria from *Aida* or "O Don fatale" from *Don Carlo* presumably were sung, that was not always so. In the case of "O Don fatale," for example, in the 1930s the aria was offered as a cornet solo, yet in the mid-1950s was sung.

Even greater uncertainty surrounds the simple term "Manzoni Requiem," which surely was not played entire, for it runs on average 75–80 minutes. A likely selection of it perhaps was the opening "Requiem," which Sousa had played and titled "Prelude." Or equally likely was the fuller arrangement by Emil Mollenhaur, which, though published only posthumously (1956), had circulated in manuscript to bands even before his death in 1927. It was drawn—and I thank Byron Hanson, archivist at Interlochen for the description—"solely from the *Dies Irae* section; it begins with the *Dies irae, Tuba mirum* & *Mors stupebit* sections, does the *Recordare* portion as a cornet duet, then the *Ingemisco* as a euphonium solo, modulates to C minor and jumps to *Rex tremendae* and *Salva me,* drawing to a close by Mollenhauer with a plagal cadence thereafter. So the duration is c. 16:00 mins. This was a popular work in my youth; I performed it both in high school and in the Eastman Symphony Band a couple of years later."

If the second five years of the period are compared to the first, the total number of excerpts played lessens by only eight, 89 to 81, but the variety of excerpts decreases markedly. For example, in 1936 the band played excerpts from what were then such rarities as *Don Carlos, Lombardi,* and *Giovanna d'Arco.* Whereas in 1942 through 1945, it was beginning to limit itself to *Aida, Rigoletto, Traviata, Trovatore*, and the overture to *La forza del destino.* Notably absent from all years is any excerpt from *Otello* or *Falstaff,* though *Otello* had been introduced to the United States by a band in March 1887 when the 7th Regiment Band in New York offered a vocal performance of "Ave Maria" (see chapter 3).

Lastly, Richard Franko Goldman listed in his 1936 book, *The Band's Music*, arrangements for band of selections from *Aroldo, Attila, Macbeth, Nabucco,* and *The Sicilian Vespers.*

Appendix Seventeen

Possible Excerpts from Operas, 1940–1980

In this appendix, limited to operas premiered between 1940 and 1980, I suggest some excerpts that might have given pleasure to many in band audiences. I have limited the span of years to a time when the Goldman Band was at its height but was dropping excerpts from operas in favor of original compositions for bands or wind ensembles. I have also included in the list an excerpt from Douglas Moore's opera *The Ballad of Baby Doe,* though Moore recomposed it on commission for the Goldman Band. Yet most bandmasters and wind ensemble conductors since 1940 have ignored opera altogether, though many of the composers thus dismissed seem more distinguished than those whose works were played.

The list is merely suggestive, and to some extent the excerpts listed were selected to give some representation to composers in England, France, and Germany, as well as the United States. Moreover, anyone browsing the list should remember that no bandleader or conductor would make up a program entirely of operatic excerpts; at most, if following Sousa's example, he might include three or four.

Those entries preceded by an asterisk are what Sousa would have titled a humoresque, a genre always popular with band audiences.

BENJAMIN BRITTEN

——— from *Peter Grimes,* any of the Four Sea Preludes: Dawn, Sunday Morning, Night, and Storm.

——— from *Peter Grimes,* the passacaglia, representing the gathering tension in Grimes's mind, as he realizes his behavior has turned the town irrevocably against him.

——— from *Peter Grimes,* the march to which the borough's posse forms with intent "to strike and kill" Grimes.

——— from *Albert Herring,* the Threnody, in which a group of nine, thinking Albert dead, lament. Each has a solo line while the other eight repeat the equivalent of a ground bass. At the end all repeat their solo lines and close with a majestic coda.
——— from *Billy Budd,* a collection of the sailors' chanteys.
——— from *Billy Budd,* Billy's song, "Billy in the Darbies."
——— from *A Midsummer Night's Dream,* the Pyramus and Thisbe playlet.

CARLISLE FLOYD

——— from *Susannah,* the song "Ain't It a Pretty Night."
——— from *Susannah,* the lament "Come Back, O Summer."

SCOTT JOPLIN

——— from *Treemonisha,* the finale to the opera, "A Real Slow Drag."
——— from *Treemonisha,* the ring play "We're Goin' Around."
——— from *Treemonisha,* the finale to act 2, "Aunt Dinah Has Blowed de Horn," ending the work day.

GIAN CARLO MENOTTI

——— from *The Medium,* toward the close of act 1, the gypsy song "O Black Swan" with which Monica attempts to calm her hysterical mother.
——— from *The Medium,* the opening of act 2 and Monica's Waltz, which follows.
——— from *Amahl and the Night Visitors,* the march to which the kings enter and the Dance of the Shepherds, which begins slowly but ends in joyous frenzy.

DOUGLAS MOORE

——— from *The Ballad of Baby Doe,* the opening scene in which Tabor and his cronies sing of their "panhandlin" days: "Pick and shovel in my hand."
——— from *The Ballad of Baby Doe,* the political rally for William Jennings Bryan. This is the excerpt recomposed by Moore on commission from the Goldman Band and premiered by it in Central Park on 17 June 1959 under the title "The People's Choice! A March for Election Eve, for band." The commission was in memory of Edwin Franko Goldman. With it the band, now led by Richard Franko Goldman, not only played an excerpt from opera (repeated four times that summer), but also, in accordance with its policy, increased the number of works originally scored for band. The program described the piece as "a gay and lively march suggesting the atmosphere of a torchlight parade."

—— from *The Ballad of Baby Doe,* the closing scene as Baby Doe starts her vigil for her now dead husband at the mouth of the Matchless Mine. Through love she will be with him always.

FRANCIS POULENC

——* from *Les Mamelles de Tirésias,* the scene in which Thérèse releases her breasts, grows a moustache and beard, and stomps to strong Spanish rhythms.

—— from *Les Mamelles,* the finale to act 1 followed (as in the opera) by the Entr'acte, which might be followed by the opening scene to act 2.

—— from *Dialogues des Carmélites,* the opera's closing scene: the execution, during the French Revolution, of the nuns, one by one, so that their singing of the "Salve Regina" grows weaker and weaker as the knife of the guillotine drops until only one nun is left, and she goes to her death singing the last four lines of the "Veni Creator." (This excerpt, however, might strike some listeners as a desecration of a powerful, religious scene.)

SERGEI PROKOFIEV

—— from *War and Peace,* the overture, based on military themes from the opera, ending with one associated with Marshal Kutúzov and the Russian people. This overture is sometimes not used in performances and is replaced by a choral epigraph intended to balance the final chorus of the opera.

—— from *War and Peace,* act 1, the duet for Natasha and her cousin Sonya (soprano and mezzo), as they look out of their bedroom window on a moonlit night.

—— from *War and Peace,* act 2, Kutúzov, after consulting his generals, has decided to abandon Moscow to Napoleon without a fight and sings an emotional hymn to the city. The music reappears continually during the rest of the act and closes the opera.

——* from *Betrothal in a Monastery,* act 3, scene 2, the chamber music scene in Don Jerome's house, in which, in a trio of his own composing, "Lover's Minuet," he plays the clarinet; a friend, the trumpet; and a servant, the bass drum.

—— from *The Fiery Angel,* the interlude in act 3, close of scene 1, during which a duel takes place and which gives the percussionists a chance to impress the audience.

STEPHEN SONDHEIM

—— from *Sweeney Todd, The Demon Barber of Fleet Street,* the Prologue, in which the refrain, "Swing your razor wide, Sweeney!" is set to the opening notes of the judgment day hymn, "Dies Irae."

—— from *Sweeney Todd,* the song "By the Sea," in which Mrs. Lovett, in a parody of English music hall songs, tells Todd of the life she wants for them.

RICHARD STRAUSS

——— from *Capriccio,* an interlude in which a horn serenade accompanies moonlight as it seeps from the terrace backstage into the salon of an eighteenth-century French chateau.

——— from *Die Liebe der Danae,* an interlude commonly titled "Jupiter's Resignation," in which the god recognizes that Danae loves not him but Midas. He may visit Danae again but as an acknowledged older man bringing serenity, not love, and warming his heart, if he can, from her love for another.

KURT WEILL

———* from *Street Scene,* the opening scene's lament for a hot summer night in New York: "Ain't it awful the heat, ain't it awful."

——— from *Street Scene,* act 1, song and chorus about high school graduation, "Wrapped in a Ribbon and Tied in a Bow."

——— from *Street Scene,* act 1, the song "Moon-Faced, Starry-Eyed," followed by the jitterbug dance.

——— from *Down in the Valley,* a medley of the folk songs: "Down in the Valley," "The Lonesome Dove," "The Little Black Train," "Hop Up, My Ladies," and "Sourwood Mountain."

Bibliography

Because full bibliographical information for any source appears in the notes at the work's first mention, sources used only once or twice are not repeated here. However, several books not cited in text but relevant to main points are included. Newspaper sources are listed in notes only. The exception to this rule is *Dwight's Journal of Music,* whose bibliographical information is unusual. A brief list of recordings, including one CD-ROM, follows the bibliography proper.

BOOKS, ARTICLES, AND THESES

Ahlquist, Karen. *Democracy at the Opera: Music Theater, and Culture in New York City, 1815–60.* Urbana: University of Illinois Press, 1997.

Austin, Terry. "Bands at the 1904 World's Fair," see *The Wind Band and Its Repertoire: Two Decades of Research.*

Barnouw, Erik. *A Tower in Babel: A History of Broadcasting in the United States to 1933.* New York: Oxford University Press, 1966.

Bierley, Paul Edmund. *The Incredible Band of John Philip Sousa.* Urbana: University of Illinois Press, 2006.

———. *John Philip Sousa: American Phenomenon.* Englewood Cliffs, NJ: Prentice-Hall, 1973.

———, ed. *Marching Along: Recollections of Men, Women and Music*, by John Philip Sousa, rev. ed. With notes, foreword, afterword, and revised list of works. Westerville, OH: Integrity Press, 1994.

Brion, Keith. "The Uneasy Silence of History." See Recordings: *Sousa Marches, Played by the Sousa Band, the Complete Commercial Recordings.*

Brooks, Tim. "James Reese Europe and African-American Bandleaders of the World War 1 Era." See *The Wind Band in and around New York ca. 1830–1950.*

Broyles, Michael. "Art Music from 1860 to 1920," in *Cambridge History of American Music.*

———. "Immigrant, Folk, and Regional Musics in the Nineteenth Century," in *Cambridge History of American Music.*

———. *"Music of the Highest Class": Elitism and Populism in Antebellum Boston.* New Haven: Yale University Press, 1992.

Byrne, Frank. "Headstone Honors 19th Century Marine Band Leader [Francis M. Scala]," *Fortitudine, Bulletin of the Marine Corps Historical Program*, Winter 1989–1990, pp-99–10.

———. "The Recorded Sousa Marches—Story and Sound." See Recordings: *Sousa Marches, Played by the Sousa Band, the Complete Commercial Recordings.*

———. "Sousa Marches: Principles for Historically Informed Performance." See *The Wind Ensemble and Its Repertoire: Essays on the Fortieth Anniversary.*

Cambridge History of American Music, ed. David Nicholls. Cambridge: University of Cambridge Press, 1998.

Camus, Raoul F. "Grafulla and Cappa: Bandmasters of New York's Famous Seventh Regiment." See *European Music and Musicians in New York City, 1840–1900.*

Charosh, Paul. "'Popular' and 'Classical' in the Mid-Nineteenth Century. *American Music* 10, no. 2 (Summer 1992).

Cipolla, Frank J. "Patrick S. Gilmore: The Boston Years." *American Music* 6, no. 3 (Fall 1988).

———. "Patrick S. Gilmore: The New York Years. See *European Music and Musicians in New York City, 1840–1900.*

Clappé, Arthur A. *The Wind-Band and Its Instruments: Their History, Construction, Acoustics, Technique and Combination.* New York: Holt, 1911.

Clarke, Herbert L. *How I Became a Cornetist.* St. Louis, MO: Joseph L. Huber, 1934 (repr.; Kenosha, WI: Leblanc Corporation, 1973).

Cockrell, Dale. "Nineteenth-Century Popular Music," in *Cambridge History of American Music.*

Complete Catalogue of Sheet Music and Musical Works, 1870. Board of Music Trade of the United States, 1870 (repr.; New York: Da Capo Press, 1973).

Cooke, George Willis. *John Sullivan Dwight: Brook-Farmer, Editor, and Critic of Music.* Boston: Small, Maynard and Company, 1898 (repr.; New York: Da Capo Press, 1969).

Crawford, Richard. *An Introduction to America's Music.* New York: W. W. Norton, 2001.

Darlington, Marwood. *Irish Orpheus: The Life of Patrick S. Gilmore, Bandmaster Extraordinary.* Philadelphia: Olivier Maney Klein Co., 1950.

Dodworth, Allen. *Dodworth's Brass Band School: Containing Instructions in the First Principles of Music: Together with a Number of Pieces of Music Arranged for a Full Brass Band.* New York: H. B. Dodworth, 1853. A copy is in the New York Public Library. See Recordings: Allen Dodworth.

Dwight, John Sullivan. *Dwight's Journal of Music.* Besides copies on microfilm in libraries, a selection may be found in Irving Sablosky, *What They Heard, Music in America, 1852–1881: From the Pages of* Dwight's Journal of Music. Baton Rouge: Louisiana State University Press, 1986.

———. "History of Music in Boston," chap. 7 in vol. 4 of *The Memorial History of Boston, including Suffolk County Massachusetts, 1630–1880,* edited by Justin Winsor. Boston: J. R. Osgood and Co., 1880–1881.

Endsley, Gerald R. *Herbert L. Clarke, Cornet Soloist of the Sousa Band.* See Recordings.

European Music and Musicians in New York City, 1840–1900, edited by John Graziano. Rochester, NY: University of Rochester Press, 2006. This collection includes essays by Camus, Cipolla, and Graziano.

Fennell, Frederick. *The Civil War: Its Music and Its Sounds*, with extensive notes by Fennell. See Recordings.

———. *Fennell Favorites!* (with brief notes by Fennell). See Recordings.

Foreman, George C. "The Remarkable Monsieur Jullien and His Grand American Tour." See *The Wind Band in and around New York ca. 1830–1950.*

Frizane, Daniel E. *Arthur Pryor: Trombone Soloist of the Sousa Band.* See Recordings.

Glackens, Ira Dimock. *Yankee Diva, Lillian Nordica and the Golden Days of Opera.* New York: Coleridge Press, 1963; reprinted in 1972.

Goldman, Edwin Franko. *Band Betterment, Suggestions and Advice to Bands, Bandmasters, and Band-players.* New York: Carl Fischer, 1934.

Goldman, Richard Franko. *The Band's Music.* New York: Pitman, 1938.

———. *The Concert Band.* New York: Rinehart, 1946.

———. "John Philip Sousa." In *Selected Essays and Reviews, 1948–1968,* edited by Dorothy Klotzman. Brooklyn: Institute for Studies in American Music, Dept. of Music, Brooklyn College, City University of New York, 1980.

———. *The Wind Band: Its Literature and Technique.* Boston: Allyn and Bacon, 1961.

Grant, Mark N. *Maestros of the Pen: A History of Classical Music Criticism in America.* Boston: Northeastern University Press, 1998.

Graziano, John. "An Opera for Every Taste: The New York Scene, 1862–1869." See *European Music and Musicians in New York City, 1840–1900.*

———. "New York Bands in the Nineteenth Century." See *The Wind Band in and around New York ca. 1830–1950.*

Hamm, Charles. *Yesterdays: Popular Song in America.* New York: W.W. Norton, 1979.

Herndon, Booton. *The Sweetest Music This Side of Heaven: The Guy Lombardo Story.* New York: McGraw-Hill, 1964.

Hitchcock, H. Wiley. *Music in the United States: A Historical Introduction.* Englewood Cliffs, NJ: Prentice-Hall, 1969 (often reprinted).

Hoover, Cynthia Adams. Notes to *19th Century American Ballroom Music.* See Recordings under Allen Dodworth.

Horowitz, Joseph. *Moral Fire: Musical Portraits from America's Fin de Siècle.* Berkeley: University of California, 2012.

———. *The Post-Classical Predicament: Essays on Music and Society.* Boston: Northeastern University Press, 1995.

———. *Wagner Nights: An American History.* Berkeley: University of California Press, 1994.

Ingalls, David M. *Francis Scala: Leader of the Marine Band from 1855 to 1871.* Master's thesis, Catholic University of America, 1957.

Johnson, Ellen S. "The Paul E. Bierley Band Record Collection Featuring John Philip Sousa." See *The Wind Band and Its Repertoire.*

Kirk, Elise K. *Music at the White House: A History of the American Spirit.* Urbana: University of Illinois Press, 1985.

Krehbiel, Henry Edward. *Chapters of Opera: Being Historical and Critical Observations and Records concerning the Lyric Drama in New York from Its Earliest Days down to the Present Time.* New York: Henry Holt, 1908.

———. *More Chapters of Opera: Being Historical and Critical Observations and Records concerning the Lyric Drama in New York from 1908 to 1918.* New York: Henry Holt: 1919.

Lawrence, Vera Brodsky. *Strong on Music,* vol. 2: *Reverberations, 1850–1856: The New York Music Scene in the Days of George Templeton Strong.* Chicago: University of Chicago Press, 1995.

———. *Strong on Music*, vol. 3: *Repercussions, 1857–1862.* Chicago: University of Chicago Press, 1999.

Levine, Lawrence. *Highbrow/Lowbrow: The Emergence of Cultural Hierarchy in America.* Cambridge, MA: Harvard University Press, 1988.

Madeja, James Thomas. "Herbert L. Clarke and the Long Beach Municipal Band, 1923–1943," see *The Wind Band and Its Repertoire.*

———. "The Life and Works of Herbert L. Clarke, 1867–1945." PhD diss., University of Illinois, 1988. UMI Dissertation # 8823188.

Mattfeld, Julius. *A Handbook of American Operatic Premieres, 1731–1962.* Detroit, MI: Information Service, Inc.; Detroit Studies in Music Bibliography, no. 5, 1963.

Mead, Leon. "The Military Bands of the United States." *Harper's Weekly,* 28 September 1899.

Mencken, H. L. *H. L. Mencken on Music,* selected by Louis Cheslock. New York: Schirmer Books, 1975.

Nathan, Hans. *Walt Whitman and the Marine Band.* Boston: Boston Public Library, 1943. Pages 47–56 appeared as an article in the library's bulletin, *More Books*; February 1943.

New Grove Dictionary of Music and Musicians. London: Macmillan, 1983.

New Grove Dictionary of Opera. London: Macmillan, 1992.

Newsom, Jon. "The American Brass Band Movement in the Mid-Nineteenth Century." See *The Wind Ensemble and Its Repertoire: Essays on the Fortieth Anniversary.*

Old York Road Historical Society. *Willow Grove Park,* Images of America series. Charleston, SC: Arcadia Publishing, 2005.

Preston, Katherine K. "Art Music from 1800 to 1860." In *Cambridge History of American Music.*

———. "Between the Cracks: The Performance of English-Language Opera in Late Nineteenth-Century America." *American Music* 21, no. 3 (Fall 2003).

———. *Opera on the Road: Traveling Opera Troupes in the United States, 1825–60.* Urbana: University of Illinois Press, 1993.

Rayno, Don. *Paul Whiteman: Pioneer in American Music*, vol. 1: *1890–1930.* Lanham, MD: Scarecrow Press, 2003.

Ritter, Frédéric Louis. *Music in America*, 2nd ed. New York: Scribner's, 1890.

Sablosky, Irving. *What They Heard: Music in America, 1843–1881, from the Pages of* Dwight's Journal of Music. Baton Rouge: Louisiana State University Press, 1986.

Schabas, Ezra. *Theodore Thomas: America's Conductor and Builder of Orchestras, 1835–1905.* Urbana: University of Illinois Press, 1989.

Schwartz, H. W. *Bands of America: A Nostalgic, Illustrated History of the Golden Age of Band Music.* Garden City, NY: Doubleday, 1957.

Shanet, Howard. *Philharmonic: A History of New York's Orchestra.* Garden City, NY: Doubleday, 1975.

Sousa, John Philip. *Marching Along, Recollections of Men, Women, and Music.* Boston: Hale Cushman & Flint, 1941 (repr. of orig. 1928 ed.). Reprinted with footnotes, foreword, afterword, and revised list of works by Paul E. Bierley. Westerville, OH: Integrity Press, 1994.

Southern, Eileen. *The Music of Black Americans: A History*, 2nd ed. New York: W.W. Norton, 1983.

Teran, Jay Robert. *New York Opera Audiences, 1825–1974.* PhD diss., New York University, 1974. UMI Dissertation # 75-9708.

Upton, George P. *Musical Memories: My Recollections of Celebrities of the Half Century 1850–1900.* Chicago: McClurg, 1908.

Warfield, Patrick Robert. "John Philip Sousa and 'The Menace of Mechanical Music.'" *Journal of the Society for American Music* 3, no. 4 (Winter 2009).

———. "Making the Band: The Formation of John Philip Sousa's Ensemble." *American Music*. 24, no. 1 (Spring 2006).

———.The March as Musical Drama and the Spectacle of John Philip Sousa." *Journal of the American Musicological Society* 64, no. 2 (Summer 2011).

———. Review of the recording *Sousa Marches Played by the Sousa Band: The Complete Commercial Recordings* (see Recordings). *American Music* 21, no. 3 (Fall 2003).

———. "'Salesman of Americanism, Globetrotter, and Musician': The Nineteenth-Century John Philip Sousa, 1854–1893." PhD diss., Indiana University, 2003. UMI Dissertation # 3094154.

Weber, William. *The Great Transformation of Musical Taste, Concert Programming from Haydn to Brahms.* Cambridge: Cambridge University Press, 2009.

Wilder, Alec. *American Popular Song: The Great Innovators, 1900–1950.* New York: Oxford University Press, 1972.

Willow Grove Park. See Old York Road Historical Society.

The Wind Band and Its Repertoire: Two Decades of Research as Published in The College Band Directors National Association Journal, edited by Michael Votta Jr. Miami: Warner Bros. Publications, 2003. With essays by James T. Madeja and Terry Austin.

The Wind Band in and around New York ca. 1830–1950: Essays Presented at the 26th Biennial Conference of The College Band Directors National Association,

New York, NY, February 2005, edited by Frank J. Cipolla and Donald Hunsberger. Donald Hunsberger Wind Library [n.p.]: Alfred, 2007. With essays by George C. Foreman, John Graziano, and Tim Brooks.

The Wind Ensemble and Its Repertoire: Essays on the Fortieth Anniversary of the Eastman Wind Ensemble, edited by Frank J. Cipolla and Donald Hunsberger. Rochester, NY: University of Rochester Press, 1994. In addition to appendixes on repertoire, the book has essays by Jon Newsom and Frank Byrne.

RECORDINGS

(Including reference to the essays that accompany the recordings.)

Allentown Band, cond. Ronald Demkee. *Kaleidoscope: A Collage of Cailliet Classics.* Our Band Heritage, vol. 22, including Cailliet's arrangements of the overture to *Nabucco,* the waltzes from *Der Rosenkavalier,* Musetta's waltz from *La Bohème,* "One Fine Day" from *Madame Butterfly,* and his "Pop Goes the Weasel."

American Bandmasters Association. *Journal of Band Research,* CD-ROM, 1964–2005. Contains 81 issues in full-text format with an index of 465 research articles in the database.

Arthur Pryor: Trombone Soloist of the Sousa Band. Crystal Records, CD 451. See Daniel E. Frizane, "Biographical Notes."

Detroit Concert Band, cond. Leonard B. Smith. *Gems of the Concert Band.* Walking Frog Records, WRF 306, a five-disc set: vol. 1, "Great Performances"; vol. 2, "Magnificent Marches"; vol. 3, "Music of the Masters"; vol. 4, "Virtuoso Soloists"; vol. 5, "Legendary Overtures."

Dodworth, Allen. Arrangements for all-brass band of "The Star-Spangled Banner," "Home, Sweet Home," and his own "Gift Polka." In *19th Century American Ballroom Music, Waltzes, Marches, Polkas & Other Dances,* played by the Smithsonian Social Orchestra & Quadrille Band, James Weaver, director, and using "historical instruments." Nonesuch Records: H-71313; with an instructive essay and description of the instruments and dances by Cynthia Adams Hoover.

Fennell, Frederick, conducting the Eastman Wind Ensemble. *The Civil War: Its Music and Its Sounds.* Mercury Recording 432 591-2, with detailed, descriptive notes by Fennell.

———, conducting the Eastman Wind Ensemble. *Hands Across the Sea, Marches from Around the World.* Mercury Recording 434 334-2, including six marches of Sousa, Kenneth J. Alford's "Colonel Bogey," and Edwin Franko Goldman's "On the Mall"; with explanatory notes by Fennell.

———, conducting the Dallas Wind Symphony. *Fennell Favorites!.* Reference Recordings, RR-43, with Fennell's brief notes on the music: Bach, Brahms, Halvorsen; arr. Fennell, MacDowell, Goldmark, and Prokofieff.

Gems of the Concert Band. See Detroit Concert Band.

Herbert L. Clarke, Cornet Soloist of the Sousa Band. Crystal Records, CD 450. Gerald R Endsley, "Program Notes."

The Original All-American Sousa. New Sousa Band, cond. Keith Brion (Delos, DE 3102), featuring thirteen Sousa marches and the only recordings of the band conducted by Sousa.

Smith, Leonard B. See Detroit Concert Band.

Sousa, John Philip. *Music for Wind Band.* Royal Artillery Band, cond. Keith Brion, vol. 2 (Naxos, 8.559059), featuring "Suite: At the Movies," "King Cotton," and "Songs of Grace and Songs of Glory."

———. *Music for Wind Band.* vol. 4 (Naxos, 8.559093), featuring "Stars and Stripes," "Glory of the Yankee Navy," "The Aviators," "Tales of a Traveler," and "Riders for the Flag."

———. *Music for Wind Band.* vol. 7 (Naxos, 8, 559247), featuring "Naval Reserve March," "Sheridan's Ride," "Rifle Regiment March," "Sounds from the Revivals," and "El Capitan March."

———. *Sousa "At the Symphony."* Razumovsky Symphony Orchestra, cond. Keith Brion (Naxos, 8.559013), including the suite "Dwellers of the Western World," "Songs from Grace and Songs from Glory," and two humoresques, on Gershwin's "Swanee," and Kern's "Look for the Silver Lining."

———. *Sousa "On Stage."* Razumovsky Symphony Orchestra, cond. Keith Brion (Naxos, 8.559008), selections from *The Bride Elect, El Capitan,* and *Our Flirtations.*

Sousa Marches, Played by the Sousa Band, the Complete Commercial Recordings. Crystal Records, CD 461-3. The recordings include all seven marches conducted by Sousa, as well as many by Herbert L. Clarke, Arthur Pryor, and others; as well as a forty-six-page pamphlet of essays, including "The Uneasy Silence of History" by Keith Brion, and "Recorded Sousa Marches—Story and Sound" by Frank Byrne.

U.S. Marine Band. *Grand Scenes.* Cond. Col. Timothy Foley (Boston Records (BR1051CD), featuring "Grand Fantasie from *Die Walküre*," Overture to *William Tell,* and "Le ballet de la Reine" from *Don Carlos.*

———. Wind Band Classics series. Cond. Michael J. Colburn (Naxos, 8.570727), featuring José Serebrier's *Carmen Symphony*, and Sousa's "The Stars and Stripes Forever."

General Index

Works Index

About the Author

George W. Martin has published books on a variety of topics and has been often praised for his attention to the social and cultural contexts of his subjects. Formerly a lawyer, he has written not only about Italian opera—he is accounted a Verdi expert—but also about American law and government. His biographies include that of the great composer in *Verdi: His Music, Life and Times*; the mother of social security in *Madam Secretary: Frances Perkins*; and the story of a family of German immigrant musicians who came to influence music in the United States in *The Damrosch Dynasty*. In *CCB: The Life and Century of Charles C. Burlingham*, Martin examines the life of the New York City admiralty lawyer and power broker of the early twentieth century who famously defended the White Star Line against claims for loss of life and property in the sinking of the *Titanic.*

Other books by George W. Martin:

Verdi in America, Oberto *through* Rigoletto (2011)
CCB, the Life and Century of Charles C. Burlingham, 1858–1959, New York's First Citizen (2005)
Twentieth Century Opera: A Guide (1979, 1999)
Verdi at the Golden Gate: Opera and San Francisco in the Gold Rush Years (1993)
Aspects of Verdi (1988, 1993)
The Damrosch Dynasty: America's First Family of Music (1983)
Madam Secretary: Frances Perkins (1976)

Causes and Conflicts: The Centennial History of the Association of the Bar of the City of New York, 1870–1970 (1970, 1997)
The Red Shirt and the Cross of Savoy: The Story of Italy's Risorgimento, 1748–1870 (1969)
Verdi: His Music, Life, and Times (1963, 2001)
The Battle of the Frogs and the Mice: A Homeric Fable (1962, 2013)
The Opera Companion (1961, 2008)